SAINT JOHN'S ABBEY CHURCH

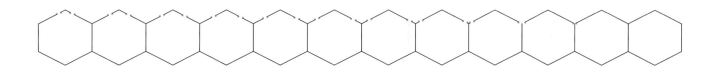

SAINT JOHN'S ABBEY CHURCH

MARCEL BREUER AND THE CREATION OF A MODERN SACRED SPACE

VICTORIA M. YOUNG

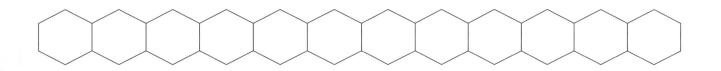

UNIVERSITY OF MINNESOTA PRESS
Minneapolis • London

Published by the University of Minnesota Press
111 Third Avenue South, Suite 290
Minneapolis, MN 55401–2520
http://www.upress.umn.edu

LIBRARY OF CONGRESS CATALOGING-IN-PUBLICATION DATA
Young, Victoria M.
Saint John's Abbey Church : Marcel Breuer and the creation
of a modern sacred space / Victoria M. Young.
Includes bibliographical references and index.
ISBN 978-0-8166-7616-3 (hc)
1. Saint John's Abbey Church (Collegeville, Minn.)
2. Benedictine architecture—Minnesota—Collegeville.
3. Liturgy and architecture—Minnesota—Collegeville.
4. Breuer, Marcel, 1902–1981. 5. Collegeville (Minn.)—
Buildings, structures. I. Title.
NA5235.C65Y68   2014
726.509776'47—dc23   2014024952

Printed in Canada on acid-free paper

The University of Minnesota is an equal-opportunity
educator and employer.

20 19 18 17 16 15 14   10 9 8 7 6 5 4 3 2 1

The University of Minnesota Press gratefully acknowledges financial assistance for the publication of this book from Saint John's Abbey, Saint John's University, McGough Companies, and the College of Arts and Sciences at the University of St. Thomas.

SAINT JOHN'S
ABBEY

Saint John's
UNIVERSITY

McGough

UNIVERSITY *of* ST.THOMAS
MINNESOTA

College of Arts and Sciences

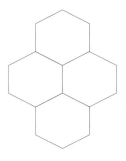

CONTENTS

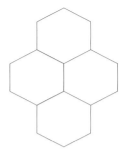

ACKNOWLEDGMENTS

This book is dedicated to the Benedictines of Saint John's Abbey. Their support, interest, and encouragement sustained me as I traveled down a long and winding road to its completion. I am most grateful to Saint John's archivist Brother David Klingeman for years of finding things for me and for his wisdom and kindness. I also owe a great debt of gratitude to Father Hilary Thimmesh, the youngest member of the church building committee, for many fruitful discussions about the building. His memoir *Marcel Breuer and a Committee of Twelve Plan a Church* (2011) is a gift to all who want a firsthand account of this project. Brother Alan Reed helps me to see the church in a new way every time we walk through it together, and he has graciously aided in finding many of the illustrations included here. Thanks to the many abbots, subpriors, university presidents, faculty, and staff who expressed interest in my work over the years. I am also greatly indebted to the abbey for generously providing many of the illustrations in this book.

Many colleagues and friends gave me expert advice, and I am deeply appreciative to them for their insight and wisdom. I particularly acknowledge Paul Ivey's detailed and careful reading and support of this manuscript. Gretchen Buggeln contributed comments essential to the final formulation of this work. Isabelle Hyman, whose work on Breuer's career is the gold standard, revealed Breuer to me during my days at New York University and commented on early chapter drafts, as did Kathleen James-Chakraborty.

I am fortunate to have such supportive colleagues at the University of St. Thomas, and I thank them all for their encouragement over the years. I am particularly grateful to Craig Eliason and Mark Stansbury-O'Donnell for their meticulous reading of the manuscript, and to Craig and Andy Barnes for our summer writing club. I am surrounded by a wonderful community of architectural historians in the Twin Cities, including Kate Solomonson at the University of Minnesota, and I thank her for years of talks about our work while seated on her lovely porch sipping lemonade. Great appreciation goes to my students who read and shared their ideas about the building, and to those who commented on versions of the text: Kristine Elias, Brady King, Marria Thompson, and Maria Wiering Pedersen. I thank the helpful staff in the Breuer Archives at Syracuse University, as well as the many institutions that provided archival or photographic aid. The University of Minnesota Press staff, most notably my editor, Pieter Martin, receives my utmost gratitude for their unfailing enthusiasm over the many years it took to complete this book.

My family and friends, especially my husband, Erich, and son, Max, have been steadfast in their support, and for that I am grateful. My mother, Carol Krinke, often took care of Max during my retreats to write on-site in Collegeville, and my sister and photographer, Wendy Zippwald, helped me see the building in yet another manner during our photo shoot on a very cold day in November 2013.

Finally, the financial support of many, including Saint John's Abbey, Saint John's University, the College of Arts and Sciences at the University of St. Thomas, and the builders of the church, McGough Companies, has made this beautiful book possible. Thank you all for believing in this great story, this fascinating building, and me.

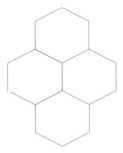

On a warm day in late August 1961, eighteen hundred friends, donors, and professed religious men and women descended on Collegeville, Minnesota, for the dedication ceremony of the Abbey and University Church of Saint John the Baptist (Figure I.1).[1] With Abbot Baldwin Dworschak in a choir stall and architect Marcel Breuer seated in the front row of the balcony, Bishop Peter William Bartholome of St. Cloud, Minnesota, consecrated the building, officially recognizing eight years of collaboration between the Benedictines and Breuer and his architectural firm. The five-hour ritual transformed the building into a "House of God." In the first portion of the ceremony the Seven Penitential Psalms were recited, the Litany of the Saints sung, water and salt blessed, and the exterior walls of the church sprinkled with holy water before the congregants solemnly entered the building. Then the "Veni Creator Spiritus" was sung and a second litany recited. The celebrant traced the Greek and Latin alphabets in ashes on the floor of the church, before mixing salt, ashes, and wine with water and blessing the resulting Gregorian Water. In the second section of the service the bishop consecrated the altar with song, water, and oil, placed relics in the altar dedicated to Saint Peregrine, and sprinkled the inside walls and floor of the church with holy water before anointing the twelve stone crosses on the walls with Sacred Chrism.[2] The celebration of the Mass completed the process.

This powerful ritual deeply moved Breuer, who later remarked to Abbot Dworschak, "All I can say, Father Abbot, is that this is the first building I have designed and the first object I have designed which has been made so sacred, or, as you would say, consecrated to God."[3] These rites of dedication, ceremonially assigning the building to the sacred purpose of worship, date back to the

FIGURE I.1. Bishop Peter William Bartholome of St. Cloud, Minnesota, presides over the consecration of Saint John's Abbey Church, August 24, 1961.

early days of the church, providing an inherent contradiction to the modern nature of the Collegeville building's form and theological underpinnings. Yet this very paradox, the modern and innovative versus traditional and historical, underlies the story of the church's creation.

Responses to the building after its completion were bifurcated, revealing a tension in avant-garde design for a Catholic church. Admirers of the building placed it in a lineage of the most important churches of the past. Wilfrid R. Ussner of Port Moody, British Columbia, called the church "the most exciting thing in church architecture since Michelangelo's great dome."[4] The British scholar Peter F. Anson, whose *Churches: Their Plan and Furnishings* was an important resource for the monks throughout the design process, related the building's success to its functionality, a modern quality in design:

> Your plan is epoch-making because it is the first instance, so far as I am aware, that a monastic church has been designed so scientifically, and with the deliberate intention of making it convenient for the monks and lay congregation.[5]

Dominican friar Illtud Evans, editor of the English journal *Blackfriars*, was pleased with Breuer's creation of a sacred place:

> And here it can be said without hesitation that the church is a triumph of intelligence and humility. Of humility most of all, because the imaginative genius of Marcel Breuer, which has so often, in such buildings as the Paris UNESCO, moulded the concrete forms with masterful authority, has here submitted itself with fidelity to the sacred purpose of the place.[6]

He was also pleased that this building had been erected in the United States, a nation that "has known the traditions of the West chiefly through academic copies . . . of work that never was indigenous in American soil."[7] Evans concluded his thoughts by calling the Saint John's church "one of the great sacred buildings of our time." Maurice Lavanoux, a founding member of the U.S.-based Liturgical Arts Society, called the church "a milestone in the evolution of the architecture of the Catholic church in this country" (Figure I.2).[8]

Yet not all were ready for such a brazen statement within religious architecture. For many, modernism was not an appropriate building style for the Catholic faith. A parish priest from California commented on the machine-like quality of the church, referring to a comparison made in *Architectural Forum* between the medieval church of Maria Laach Abbey in Germany and Saint John's: "Maria Laach has the character of an organism, St. John's Abbey looks like a tool; Maria Laach is the house of God; St. John's is a machine to pray in."[9] Another clergy member from England said the building was "absolutely stark and naked . . . devoid of beauty and seems merely utilitarian, a sort of 'Mass-and-psalm' factory."[10] A layperson from New Mexico, Beatrice Jenkins, was appalled at the use of modernism for sacred space, asking, "Is there any valid excuse of modernism to surrender the cruciform plan of the Christian Church?"[11] Mrs. Jenkins went on to tell the abbot that her two sisters had been Benedictine oblates and she was glad that they had gone on to their final resting place "before this Bauhaus project was perpetrated." Mrs. Jenkins and others wanted the building to look like

FIGURE I.2. Saint John's Abbey Church, eastern façade and bell banner.

a church, with traditional and figural decoration and a Latin cross plan symbolizing the crucifix. Instead, what Breuer and the Benedictines gave the world was an "ecclesiastical garage," as the local Catholic hierarchy was known to call it.[12]

Calling for a return to traditional materials, forms, and plan was unrealistic, however, as a Catholic church of the midcentury based on a redefined liturgical philosophy could not be built in the historical manner that some demanded. The unity of worship promoted by the Benedictines and the broader liturgical reform movement commanded a new space. This book recognizes the significance of architectural experimentation and collaboration between a skillful architect and an engaged client in support of new liturgical reforms at Saint John's Abbey Church, and adds to a growing field of studies on mid-twentieth-century sacred space.[13]

Whitney Stoddard's 1958 *Adventure in Architecture: Building the New Saint John's* is an important predecessor to this work. It focused on the early stages of the design (1953–58) but stopped short of the three-year construction period, a time during which many modifications were made because of input from the Benedictine patrons. Shaping space around the new liturgy was, for the Benedictines, central to their role in the Catholic world, and their church needed to uphold this mission. The Benedictines taught Breuer about the ritual of the Catholic Mass, and he in turn instructed the monks on the potential value of engineered, sculptural midcentury architecture where the form that supported the building became its direct expression. Father Hilary Thimmesh, the youngest member of the building committee, was intimately involved in this process. His book *Marcel Breuer and a Committee of Twelve Plan a Church: A Monastic Memoir* reveals his keen intellect and sharp memory as he outlines aspects of the church design and building process that are impossible to understand unless you were present at meetings or walking around the construction site. It is an essential counterpart to this work.

By examining Breuer's commission, we also better understand the complexities of building a twentieth-century monastic space. Most works on monastic architecture focus on medieval structures; Wolfgang Braunfels's *Monasteries of Western Europe: The Architecture of the Orders*, for example, discusses just one modern building, Le Corbusier's 1960 design for La Tourette, a Dominican monastery near Lyon, France. The importance of Saint John's Abbey Church has been insufficiently appreciated. This project seeks to add to Howard Niebling's work on modern Benedictine churches and Benedictine Father Kevin R. Seasoltz's essay "Contemporary Monastic Architecture and Life in America," in which he called Saint John's church a "major accomplishment in the history of monastic architecture."[14] The American Institute of Architects embraced the building with one of its eight honor awards in 1962, thereby placing a work of monastic architecture at center stage in the discourse of American architecture.[15] As one of Breuer's students, the well-known architect I. M. Pei, has pointed out, Saint John's Abbey Church would be Breuer's best-known building, and one of the greatest examples of twentieth-century architecture, if it were located closer to architecture's critical establishment on the East Coast of the United States.[16]

CREATING THE SPIRITUAL AXIS: COLLABORATION AND INNOVATION

The Collegeville Benedictines never underestimated the power of tradition, always placing themselves in the long line of prominent Benedictines such as Lanfranc of Le Bec-Hellouin and William of Volpiano. They not only appreciated the religious character of these predecessors but also admired their determination and strength as they founded new monasteries and built churches that were innovative for their time. As Bavarian monks from the abbey in Metten moved first to Saint Vincent's Abbey in Latrobe, Pennsylvania, and then to central Minnesota, they brought with them the traditions of Benedictine architecture like that of their medieval predecessors. The first monastery on the Collegeville site, designed and built by monks in a German-inspired brick idiom, was a strong visual link to the German homeland for Catholic immigrants, as we shall see in the next chapter.

As the abbey and university of Saint John's grew in size, its leadership was determined to play a larger role on the international stage. Zealous abbots insisted on expanding the brethren's knowledge through education, encouraging monks to attend undergraduate and graduate schools, including the University of Minnesota, the Catholic University in Washington, D.C., and Saint Anselm's, the international Benedictine college in Rome. Many brethren of Saint John's became involved with the reforms of the liturgical movement, which had started in nineteenth-century Europe but which, after World War I, spread to such outposts of Catholicism as Collegeville.

Under the leadership of Father Virgil Michel, in the 1920s Saint John's became the American center of the liturgical movement and a major player internationally. The liturgical movement challenged established ritual traditions and emphasized the participation of the laity in the worship service through the use of vernacular languages, as well as the repositioning of the altar and the celebrant. Among the faithful, it also sought to renew an appreciation of the sacraments.[17] These changes mandated alterations in the layout of Catholic churches and revitalized an interest in liturgical arts for the new settings. The principles of the liturgical reform movement

became a primary focus for the Benedictines when the time came to rebuild and redesign the abbey church in the middle of the twentieth century. They wanted the new building not only to reflect these reform ideas but also to be an exemplar of a new and modern liturgical architecture.

A walk along the "spiritual axis" at Saint John's reveals the Benedictines' vision of the reformed ritual (Figure I.3).[18] Outside the building, one transitions from the profane world to the sacred realm by passing under the concrete bell banner inset with a cross, Breuer's version of an architectural portal. A preparatory piazza or atrium leads worshippers to the baptistery entrance. Inside the baptistery, light is dim and height is compressed, forcing one to focus on the baptismal font and statue of the abbey's patron saint, John the Baptist, completed by Doris Caesar in 1961. The baptistery's placement near the beginning of the spiritual path recalls one's entry into the church through baptism. Next, one moves through a second tripartite doorway separating the baptistery from the sanctuary, emerging under the balcony and into the open expanse of the nave with the high altar situated prominently on the spiritual and visual path, surmounted by a cross and baldachin. Unlike the traditional Latin cross plan church with aisles, all worshippers have a clear view to the altar with no seat more than eighty-five feet away. The abbot's throne, flanked by the monastic choir stalls, terminates this visual pathway. The choir and abbot face to the north with a clear view of the altar framed by the northern window wall, with its 430 concrete hexagons filled with colored glass abstractly representing the liturgical seasons. The axis of the church maintains but reorganizes the hierarchical components of this building. The reinforced concrete shell over the path provides a minimalistic backdrop for modern art, all of which makes tangible the reformed liturgical ideals of the twentieth-century Catholic Church.

This building project announced the Benedictines as leaders of liturgical reform within monasticism and confirmed Marcel Breuer's position as one of the most innovative architects of the mid-century (Figure I.4). Their relationship was an architectural collaboration of the highest level. Knowledgeable clients carefully delivered a plan for reinvigorated worship and liturgy to a skillful architect, who sensitively shaped a space to support it. The case of Saint John's is no different from Cass Gilbert's Woolworth Building in New York City (1913) or Frank Gehry's Guggenheim Museum in Bilbao, Spain (1997), where the success of the project is the direct result of a marriage between a talented architect and a client with a clear and focused vision.[19] As Breuer associate Hamilton Smith would later state, "The Saint John's abbey church is a building fully realized, and I regard it as Marcel Breuer's finest achievement."[20] The story of the Collegeville church fulfills architectural historian Judith Hull's request to understand "not only how congregations

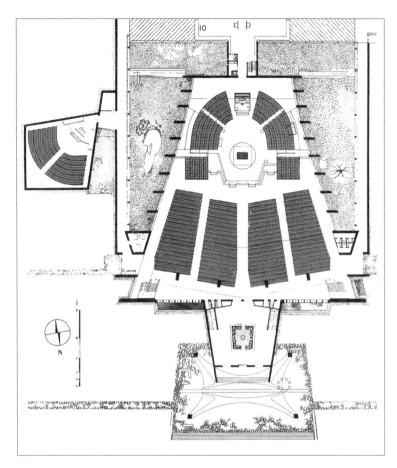

FIGURE I.3. The spiritual axis organizes the worshipping experience along the center of the church's main floor.

FIGURE I.4. Architect Marcel Breuer at Saint John's Abbey.

and the vernacular. They also participated in the appropriate placement of liturgical furniture and art within the building.

What was it about Breuer, a man without an ecclesiastical project on his architectural résumé, that encouraged the Saint John's brethren to hire him? Seeking a designer to direct a one-hundred-year master building plan anchored by the new abbey church, the Benedictines originally contacted twelve architects. The international list of twelve included five European architects: Hermann Baur of Basel, Switzerland; Albert Bosslet of Würzburg, Germany; Robert Kramreiter of Vienna, Austria; Rudolf Schwarz of Cologne, Germany; and Thomas W. Sharp of Oxford, England. There were seven American-based designers: Pietro Belluschi, Marcel Breuer, Barry Byrne, Walter Gropius, Joseph D. Murphy, Richard Neutra, and Eero Saarinen. Four of the five Europeans were already known as great church designers; the other was a planner. Only three of the seven Americans had any experience designing ecclesiastical spaces.

As we shall see in chapter 2, examining the process of choosing an architect from the twelve candidates is crucial to understanding the Benedictines' modern architectural and artistic mindset. The selection process was broad and international in scope, thanks to the nature of the order and the commitment of Saint John's to liturgical reforms. The Benedictines, however, were interested in more than hiring an exceptional archi-

reconcile their ideals with social and economic realities in general, but in particular how they behave as clients in their negotiations with architects and builders" in order to guarantee the success of a building campaign.[21] The Benedictines worked with Breuer to give form to the church, ensuring that its shape was responsive to liturgical and monastic needs of unity, the sacraments,

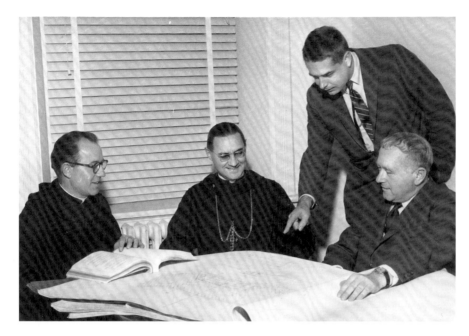

FIGURE I.5. Marcel Breuer (far right) and his associate architect, Hamilton Smith, confer with subprior Father John Eidenschink (far left) and Abbot Baldwin Dworschak at the abbey.

tect. They wanted to engage a designer of great character, someone who would listen as well as inform, a designer with whom they could collaborate to create significant monastic and liturgical space that would serve their order for the coming centuries (Figure I.5).

MIDCENTURY MODERNISM AND SACRED SPACE

In the post–World War II era, churches hired designers to build numerous sacred spaces, spending $1 billion in 1960, or 13.2 percent of funds for all public buildings erected in the United States.[22] Liturgical scholar Peter Hammond has called this period one of the most active and experimental in ecclesiastical architecture since the sixteenth-century Reformation, yet scholarship is just now beginning to evaluate the period's religious buildings for their contributions to the history of modernism in art and architecture.[23] When sacred architecture is considered in the broader history of modernism, the focus has often been on formal stylistic qualities, the exploitation of new materials, or the redefinition of space and structure. The importance of a building's function and whether it fulfills a client's needs and responds appropriately to a ritualistic function have not received the same emphasis.[24]

Church builders since the early twentieth century had experimented with modern design, eschewing traditional decoration and plans in favor of sparse, cleverly lighted, simple rectilinear forms that encouraged an openness in interior space required by liturgical reforms. Midcentury architects experimented with engineering and materials such as concrete to create expressive, free-flowing shapes. Enlightened patrons like the Benedictines were ready to embrace engineered, modern forms and materials in order to create churches that responded to their new conception of the liturgy as well as the demands of a modern world. Of all the architectural styles available to the Collegeville Benedictines, modernism was an obvious choice for a new liturgical architecture. This study, therefore, does not focus on the entrance of architectural modernism into religious design. Architects and clergy already had been receptive to modernism in the design and building of many post–World War I churches.[25] By the mid-twentieth century, architects were beginning to move beyond the established tradition of the International Style just as the Benedictines were ready to move beyond the customary liturgical traditions.[26]

The inclusion of modern art, including decorative art, is an important part of this study, as we shall explore in chapter 4.[27] Otto Spaeth, founder and president of the Liturgical Arts Society, a major force in the promotion of appropriate and well-designed art for worship, implored readers in a 1955 *Architectural Record* article not to "destroy the architectural beauty of a good church by embellishing it with cheap artifacts."[28] Architects and their clients needed to work together and bring in artistic and liturgical advisers to ensure success, as a church's artistic program, according to liturgical leader Josef Jungmann, must be in "service to the Christian community" and be "a reflection of the liturgy and somehow itself liturgy."[29]

A full-scale application of modern art and Christian thought, with forms moving toward abstraction, began in Europe after World War II.[30] In France, the Dominican Father Pierre Marie-Alain Couturier commissioned fifteen well-known modern artists, including Henri Matisse, Pierre Bonnard, Georges Rouault, and Georges Braque, to decorate the interior of the church of Notre-Dame de Toute Grâce at Assy in 1950. In that same year, Matisse completed all the artistic furnishings and vestments for a Dominican nuns' chapel at Vence, France. The design of interior furnishings for Saint John's Abbey Church was a response to ideas put forth by church documents, liturgical reform, and groups like the Liturgical Arts Society. These entities encouraged the use of novel, modern forms understandable by the contemporary worshipper. Saint John's commissioned or purchased more than fifty pieces of art to fill the church and its many chapels, and the majority of them were modern in style and concept.

In the United States, liturgical consultants and *Liturgical Arts*, the monthly publication of the Liturgical Arts Society, were the major proponents of the use of modern art in religious space. Members of the Liturgical Arts Society demanded that art be liturgically significant, rather than just aesthetically pleasing and decorative.[31] Although the Benedictines were aware to some degree of trends in liturgical art, Breuer and his office were not as informed. Saint John's hired a liturgical and artistic consultant, Frank Kacmarcik, to work with them and ensure the proper furnishing of their building with objects that upheld the tenets of the liturgical reform movement, the Benedictine Order, and the Catholic faith.

Even though Breuer and the Benedictines understood, listened to, and respected one another, there were moments of tension in their lengthy collaboration. The greatest of these came during the design of the building's most commanding artistic element, the northern stained glass wall. At the heart of this controversy were the rights of an architect and those of a patron. Breuer hoped that his former Bauhaus colleague, Josef Albers, would fashion the stained glass window. Instead, the monks selected a local artist and faculty member, Bronislaw Bak, without Breuer's approval. The ramifications of Bak's selection go beyond the rights of an architect to choose associated artists to decorate his building. The conflict over the window's designer prevented the completion of the second-largest iconographic component in the church, the apse screen.

The collaboration between the Benedictines and Marcel Breuer and his architectural team reveals important themes in midcentury religious architecture. Central to the subject is how the building operates as a vessel for the reformed liturgy, reconciling the visions of a modern architect and the traditions of his monastic patrons. Today, the concrete buildings designed by Breuer remain in partnership with the nineteenth-century brick, German Romanesque Revival quadrangle. Each set of structures affirms the historical identity and importance of the Collegeville Benedictines. As Julian Luxford noted in his research on the English Benedictines, for the monastics an act of patronage had a "symbolic importance" in that all projects are an oblation to God and to a patron saint. But perhaps most important is that they provide "an opportunity to enhance the reputation of a given monastery, and the Benedictine order as a whole."[32] As the following chapters illustrate, the Abbey and University Church of Saint John the Baptist did just that. It not only secured a position as a significant building in the tradition of monastic structures dating back to the Middle Ages, it also provided inspiration for the architecture, art, and theology of the modern church, ideas that would be codified a year after its completion by participants at the Second Vatican Council (1962–65).

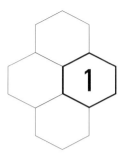

BRICKS AND BROTHERS

Establishing the Benedictines in Collegeville

During the Middle Ages, Western monasticism helped shape social, political, and artistic events, and the influence of a monastery was directly linked to the strength of its abbot, many of whom were confidants to kings and local lords. An abbot could craft his legacy not only through his pious works but also through the architectural projects he commissioned. Although monastic buildings served necessary functions of everyday life, their tall church steeples, medieval style, and fortress-like walls functioned as power statements, visual reminders of institutional importance. Abbot Baldwin Dworschak of Saint John's, like other builders of the twentieth century, understood this desire for symbolic architecture when he and the brethren decided to build a new abbey in Collegeville. Marcel Breuer's buildings were not the first on the site, however, so the Benedictines had to consider the relationship of their new abbey to the mon-

astery's and college's original nineteenth-century brick structures. Built in a German-Romanesque style and funded with money from the Bavarian king, these buildings provided Catholic immigrants settling in the region with a visual link to their German homeland. They also set the stage for Saint John's ambitions of international leadership in monasticism and liturgy at the middle of the twentieth century.

BENEDICTINE MONASTICISM PRIOR TO THE FOUNDING OF SAINT JOHN'S

Although the Benedictines were not the founders of Christian monasticism, they became one of its foremost proponents with the order's establishment at Monte Cassino, Italy, in 529 CE (Figure 1.1).[1] At Monte Cassino Saint Benedict of Nursia (ca. 480–ca. 547) wrote the Rule of Saint Benedict, outlining his expectations for the order.[2]

FIGURE 1.1. The Abbey of Monte Cassino in Italy, ca. 1058–87.

A prologue and seventy-three chapters described the basic monastic virtues of humility, silence, and obedience, and provided directives for daily living with regulated times for prayer, work, sleep, and meals.[3] A monk's duty was *opus dei*, or "work of the Lord," and members lived balanced lives of work and prayer, drawing support from each other as they overcame their human shortcomings and focused on their service to God.

The Benedictines, like other religious orders, understood that architecture upheld and facilitated their work and life. The master plan for the Abbey of Saint Gall in Switzerland (830) was an unsuccessful attempt to provide a paradigmatic layout for future monasteries.[4] Strong abbots like Lanfranc of Le Bec-Helloüin, France, built complexes at Bec (1042–63) and Caen, France, where the Abbaye aux Hommes (1063–70) and its church of Saint-Étienne (1064–77) supported William the Conqueror's spiritual goals. With the arrival of Abbot Suger at the Abbey of Saint-Denis outside Paris, the building blocks of Norman Romanesque architecture gave way to a fresh approach in religious design, the Gothic style in the construction in 1144 of the church's new choir.[5] Suger's architect brought together for the first time elements that infused the building with light and color. The double-aisled ambulatory with radiating chapels was integrated into the choir fabric rather than separated from it as was common in Romanesque churches (Figure 1.2).

FIGURE 1.2. The twelfth-century Gothic choir at the Abbey Church of Saint-Denis, completed under the leadership of Abbot Suger.

From interior columns sprang ribs leading to groin vaults with large expanses of stained glass filling the windows. Abbot Dworschak and the brethren at Saint John's were well aware of the importance of leaders like Lanfranc and Suger; in their search for an architectural expression for the ages, they drew inspiration from them to employ novel, modern forms in their twentieth-century building campaign. Father Cloud Meinberg told the community on September 29, 1953:

> We are Benedictines and Benedictines historically have a tradition of inventive architecture. William of Volpiano, Lanfranc, and

Suger of St. Denis at one time led Europe in architectural development. They were great builders precisely because they looked to the future, refusing to be bound by the accomplishments of the past. Nothing could be more uncharacteristic of our Order than to fall back upon limitations of the past, no matter how successful.[6]

Religious orders thrived into the sixteenth century, when the Protestant Reformation nearly halted their growth. In the late eighteenth century, the orders witnessed further decline because of upheavals in the secular and political realm, for not only did monasteries wield religious power, they also owned land and goods that many worldly rulers wanted to possess. When Emperor Joseph II came to the Austrian throne in 1780, there were 500 monastic houses in Austria, and by the time of his death ten years later, only 233 remained.[7] Following the French Revolution in 1789, the new National Assembly banished monastic activity in France.[8] By the early 1800s only fifty active Benedictine monasteries existed worldwide.[9]

In the early decades of the nineteenth century, as Catholicism regained a foothold in society, certain political leaders renewed their support of monastic life. The Benedictines found a safe haven in Germany, where the pious King Ludwig I of Bavaria spearheaded the reinstatement of the medieval and Renaissance abbeys of Metten (1830), Ottobeuren (1834), Scheyern (1838), and Andechs (1850), while founding eighty new monasteries, including those at Augsburg (1834), Munich (1835), Weltenburg (1842), and Schäftlarn (1866).[10] The resurgence in Germany had important consequences for monasticism in central Minnesota, as monks from Metten immigrated to America, settling first in Pennsylvania before moving on to Minnesota.[11]

THE FOUNDATION OF THE ABBEY OF SAINT JOHN THE BAPTIST, COLLEGEVILLE, MINNESOTA

At the Abbey of Saint Michael in Metten, Germany, Father Boniface Wimmer formulated a model for his "New World" monasticism.[12] Missionary work by monks would bring the faith to the German immigrants, providing a link to their homeland through language, education, and architecture. Supported by King Ludwig I and other important religious leaders, Wimmer arrived in New York City in September 1846 with five students and fifteen brother candidates. Finding no suitable place to settle in New York, Wimmer and his group made their way to Beatty, Pennsylvania, where they established the first Benedictine monastery in the United States, Saint Vincent's, on land donated by Bishop Michael O'Connor of Pittsburgh. By 1855 Pope Pius IX raised the monastery to abbey status and appointed Wimmer its first abbot.

Wimmer understood that monastic expansion should follow the westward path taken by German immigrants and provide the settlers social, religious, and academic support. After 1850, Germans settled in Minnesota along the Mississippi and Minnesota Rivers, spreading north along the Mississippi from Minneapolis toward St. Cloud in Stearns County, the site of the first permanent German Catholic settlement in 1854.[13] Bishop Joseph Cretin of St. Paul encouraged Wimmer to send the Benedictines into this region, not only to aid his priests with their missionary work, but also to assist with the settlers' education.[14]

In the spring of 1856, Abbot Wimmer sent the prior of Saint Vincent's, Demetrius de Marogna, to Minnesota to establish a monastery and teaching institution. Two clerics (monks studying for ordination) and two brothers went with him, along with a supply of the articles needed for worship, including missals, a ciborium, chalices, furniture, and money.[15] The group stayed briefly with Bishop Cretin in St. Paul before departing for the new mission site outside St. Cloud, where they established living quarters and a chapel dedicated to Saint John the Baptist (Figure 1.3). Settlement at this location was short lived,

FIGURE 1.3. The first settlement of the Benedictines near St. Cloud, Minnesota, ca. 1862.

FIGURE 1.4. Saint John's Abbey, ca. 1869, with the Old Stone House at the center with cupola. The wooden chapel at left was brought from the St. Cloud site.

however, as the group needed more land with better natural resources for homesteading and cultivating food. In 1863 they discovered their present-day site, two thousand acres northwest of St. Cloud, complete with a lake, woods, and meadows. Here the group assembled and established the monastic schedule, rising at 3:45 a.m. and ending the day in silence at 7:30 p.m., living and praying in temporary structures.[16] These buildings sheltered community members until work began on the monastery's first permanent home.

BUILDING THE FIRST ABBEY OF SAINT JOHN THE BAPTIST

In 1866 the monks erected the first monastic building on the site, a simple, two-story stone structure measuring forty-six by fifty feet. Commonly known as the Old Stone House, this building contained a kitchen and dining room in the basement; monks' rooms, a study, and classrooms on the first and second floors; and dormitory space for students in the attic (Figure 1.4).[17] The space was small but livable, since eleven of the nineteen brothers were continuously away on

missions around the region. The monks brought
the wooden frame house with them from their
previous location and placed it to the southwest
of the Old Stone House, using it for the brothers' quarters, carpenter and tailor shops, and a
chapel. The monks furnished the fifty-by-twenty-
by-twelve-foot-tall chapel with simple handmade
pews separated by a three-foot-wide aisle that
led from the door to a wooden altar. The abbot's
chair was placed to the right side of the altar as
seen from the nave.

In the same year as the completion of the Old
Stone House, Pope Pius IX raised Saint John's
priory to abbey status, an upgrade that required
additional buildings. Subsequently, the brethren elected Father Rupert Seidenbusch abbot on
December 12, 1866. Abbot Seidenbusch quickly
took on the task of expanding the abbey to provide more services for the continuously growing
number of German Catholics in the region.[18] To
facilitate construction, they built a sawmill and
brickyard on-site. The need for more classrooms
and living space for students increased after the
first year of instruction in 1867, when more than
fifty-one students began their studies at Saint
John's.[19] Students of the seminary and college
moved into a new 140-foot-long, two-story brick
building in the fall of 1868, and the monastery
annexed all the space in the old stone building.
Using local materials and providing as much of
the labor as possible, the community began work
in the summer of 1870 on a second brick addi-

FIGURE 1.5. The second brick addition of 1871 seen at center with cupola.

tion, this time a four-story structure one hundred
by fifty feet, placed perpendicular to the north
end of the first brick building (Figure 1.5). Completed in the fall of 1871, this building had dining rooms and a kitchen in the basement, parlors
and classrooms on the first floor, and the abbot's
apartment on the second floor. The forty-foot-tall
third floor was intended for use as a chapel, but
instead served as much-needed student dormitory
space. Brother Vincent Schiffrer designed the
brick buildings with help from carpenter Wenzel
Wolke and brick burner Charles Creven of St.
Cloud, painter August Leivermann of Chaska,

and teamster Peter Eich of Collegeville, as well as the other resident monks.[20]

When new buildings could not be erected, the Benedictines reallocated space in existing structures. Once the second brick building was finished, the monks adjusted the interiors to support the needs of the monastery, erecting a thirty-by-fifteen-foot choir chapel on the first floor of the middle building (the first brick building), complete with an altar on the southern end and kneelers and benches operating as choir stalls facing the altar. The abbot kept himself warm at the back of the church by placing his chair next to a wood stove. Four oil lamps hung above the choir to light the room. The monastic space of the brethren was now divided, with the monks chanting their offices in the choir chapel and saying Mass in the wooden chapel they had brought with them to the site. It would remain this way until 1882, when the first abbey church at Saint John's was completed.

BUILDING COLLEGEVILLE'S FIRST MONASTIC CHURCH: BRICKS AND BROTHERS

After spending years in a makeshift chapel space, the growing community, as well as the rising prestige of Saint John's, demanded a new and proper church for worship. The work on the abbey's first purpose-built church began under a new abbot, Alexius Edelbrock, who had been appointed by Abbot Seidenbusch in 1875, when

he decided to leave Saint John's to become the bishop of the newly formed diocese of northern Minnesota. Abbot Edelbrock believed the abbey needed a new and noteworthy church, and in December 1878, he made a visit to the new Cathedral of Saint Francis Xavier (1876–81) under construction in Green Bay, Wisconsin, for patron Bishop Francis Xavier Krautbauer (Figure 1.6). Abbot Edelbrock found the cathedral to be a suitable model for his new abbey church, likely because of the strong political and architectural associations it had with the Ludwig-Missionsverein (Ludwig Mission Society) and King Ludwig I's own church, the Ludwigskirche (1829–44) on the Ludwigstrasse in Munich, Germany.

King Ludwig I was a great patron of the arts, hiring notable artists and architects to create a new Athens in Munich. For Ludwig, architect Leo von Klenze turned the city into a monumental souvenir of the Grand Tour, completing a new version of the Athenian Propylaia as the gateway to the Königsplatz and a modern Roman Arch of Constantine at the entrance to the Ludwigstrasse, a street lined with Klenze-designed public buildings inspired by the Florentine Renaissance. Klenze also theorized the manner in which churches should be built with his 1822 *Directions on the Architecture of Christian Worship*, a booklet distributed free to the public as its printing was likely paid for by the king.[21]

In addition to his love of the classical past, Ludwig was also a strong supporter of medievalism and Catholicism. In 1826 he founded the church and Benedictine monastery of Saint Boniface, the patron saint of the German and Bavarian peoples, adjacent to the Königsplatz in Munich. The religious space most strongly associated with Ludwig I, however, was his church, the Ludwigskirche (Figure 1.7). This building became the symbol of Ludwig and his Catholic mission, both at home and abroad. Architect Friedrich von Gärtner designed the building in the popular *Rundbogenstil* or rounded arch style over a Latin cross basilica plan taken from early Christian sources. Its twin towers and rounded arches came from the German Romanesque.[22] Frescoes by Bavaria's leading muralist, Peter Cornelius, decorated the space.

Ludwig took care of his citizens who immigrated to America, as he was "interested in the growth of the Church in pagan lands. . . . He wanted them to preserve the German spirit, even if they had forsaken their fatherland, since he deemed this necessary for the preservation of their faith."[23] Over the years King Ludwig donated more than twenty million marks to various foundations and groups to fund building projects, including a town plan, twenty-three Benedictine monasteries, two seminaries, eight colleges and universities, eight preparatory schools, and numerous churches.[24] On December 12, 1838, the king gave control of the funds to his court chaplain, Father Josef Mueller, the director of the Ludwig Mission Society, a group established for

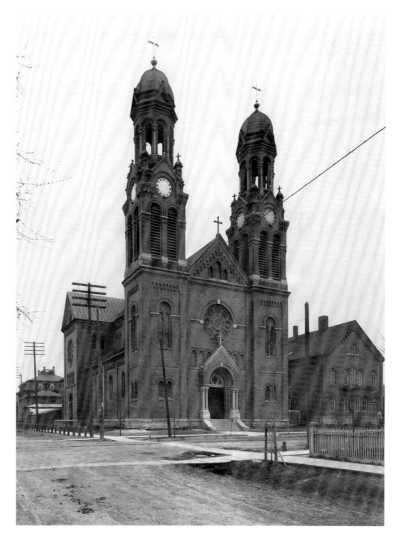

FIGURE 1.6. The Cathedral of Saint Francis Xavier, Green Bay, Wisconsin, completed in 1881. This building was a direct source for the first abbey church at Saint John's.

FIGURE 1.7. The Ludwigskirche in Munich, Germany, was an inspiration for many German Catholic churches in the Upper Midwest.

the purpose of supporting German Catholic immigrants in North America and Asia.[25] The society provided funding not only for the new cathedral in Green Bay but also for its newly founded diocese, contributing 10,500 gulden and 45,250 marks from 1868 until 1909.[26] In order to establish a visual religious and political link to Munich, the Ludwig Mission Society encouraged American Catholic patrons to use Ludwig's church in Munich as their architectural model. Green Bay complied, as would Saint John's.[27]

Clients and architects worked together to create buildings that spoke to the German settlers. Roy Hampton credits the design of Green Bay's cathedral to the German émigré architect Adolphus Druiding.[28] Druiding provided the first bishop of the Green Bay diocese, Joseph Melcher, with sketches for a new building in 1873 (Figure 1.8). Krautbauer, who had trained as an architect, became bishop in 1875; he used Druiding's sketch as the basis for his proposal to the Ludwig Mission Society for financial support. Keeping in mind the importance of a physical resemblance to the Ludwigskirche in Munich, Krautbauer replaced Druiding's towers with those from another Catholic church in St. Paul, Minnesota, the recently completed Church of Saints Peter and Paul, more commonly known as Assumption Church (1869–73) (Figure 1.9). A strong connection to King Ludwig was found in this church, too, as his court architect, Eduard Riedel, designed it.[29] After seeing the image, the Ludwig

FIGURE 1.8 (*left*). An 1873 drawing by Adolphus Druiding for the Cathedral of Saint Francis Xavier in Green Bay, Wisconsin.

FIGURE 1.9 (*above*). Assumption Church in St. Paul, Minnesota, completed in 1873, was inspired by the Ludwigskirche in design.

FIGURE 1.10. The first church of Saint John the Baptist in Collegeville, Minnesota.

Mission Society granted funds to the bishop, and by the building's 1881 dedication, work was completed through to the base of the spires.[30]

Although Krautbauer made revisions to Druiding's original 1873 drawing, Abbot Edelbrock took Druiding's version back to Collegeville after his 1878 visit. Father Gregory Steil, a monk trained in architectural drawing, revised the design according to the abbot's wishes, although a comparison between the completed façade of Saint John's first abbey church and Druiding's drawing reveals many similarities between the two Romanesque Revival buildings. The design of Saint John's Abbey Church incorporates nearly every element found in the Green Bay façade, except for its elevation of the belfry with the inclusion of an additional story with circular openings on each side (Figures 1.8 and 1.10).

With their round arches, corbel tables, and twin towers, both façades show key characteristics of the Romanesque style. Saint John's central portal contains a round arch inset within a gable with a cross at its apex. A cornice line springs from the ends of the entry portal gable, supplanted by a brick corbel table and surmounted in the nave section by a round arched blind arcade. Directly above the entrance door is a rose window with tracery configured of eight stone circles around a central quatrefoil. Another corbel table runs from the center of the rose window out to the end of each tower. Flanking the rose window in each tower section is a round-headed arched opening infilled with two elongated rounded arch windows, each topped by a circular window. The uppermost portion of the building above the roofline displays a center gable with brackets under its roofline, and a tripartite arch grouping similar to those found in the interior elevations of Romanesque churches. Each of the two 150-foot-tall towers has an inset of a circular window and above, just prior to the base of the steeple, a belfry with round arches.

Monks and local builders erected the abbey church (Figure 1.11). Excavations began in early

FIGURE 1.11. The nineteenth-century church under construction, ca. 1880.

April 1879, under Brother Andrew Unterburger, who had some previous experience as a building contractor. Brothers and clerics acted as carpenters and masons, felling trees and transporting them to the site; they also dug local clay they baked into bricks on-site in kilns that produced an average of fifteen thousand bricks a day. Although the brethren provided the bulk of the labor, sixty workmen were hired to assist them.[31] The workers used granite boulders from the surrounding fields for the foundation walls and local St. Cloud granite for the watertable that would divert water away from the building. Abbot Edelbrock often could be found on-site encouraging his crew, as Father Alexius Hoffman described:

> Everyone worked, and many of us did work
> we were not fitted for. For instance not
> everybody can stand on a scaffolding fifty feet
> high above the ground, nor can everybody
> sit on the roof of a five-story building and lay
> shingles near the cornice. I could not and
> was not asked for that matter as I was a priest.
> But the clerics and scholastics did go up there
> to work, and the Abbot clad in a long linen
> duster would clamber out on the roof as if he
> had been used to that sort of thing from his
> cradle days and "speed them up." Some of
> them were too slow for him and he ordered
> them down.[32]

Providing labor upheld the Benedictine tradition of *laborare est orare* or "to work is to pray." The crew completed the roof in October 1880, and Bishop Seidenbusch, the abbey's first abbot, consecrated the structure on October 24, 1882. The monks held only special ceremonies and feast day Masses in the building for six years, before completing the interior in 1888 and being able to use the space fully.

The interior provided a new setting for worship on campus (Figure 1.12). The church held four hundred people, a far cry from the twelve-hundred-seat structure envisioned by Abbot Edelbrock, but still an appropriate size for the community.[33] The monastic choir, elevated four feet above the nave floor, filled the transepts of a Latin cross plan. Three white marble altars on wooden platforms lined the west walls of the apse and transept. Interior decoration, like the architecture, kept the congregation's German heritage alive.[34] Over the altar hung German émigré artist Wilhelm Lamprecht's painting depicting Saint Benedict in glory surrounded by eminent saints of the order.[35] The Mayer Studios in Munich, founded in 1847 as the Mayer Institute of Christian Art, provided statues for the church, including one representing the death of Saint Benedict. Windows came from the George A. Misch Studios in Chicago.[36] The eastern rose contained symbols of the Benedictine order while the transept windows represented themes from

FIGURE 1.12. Interior, Saint John's Abbey Church, October 1888.

FIGURE 1.13. Saint John's Abbey and University, ca. 1930.

the Old and New Testaments. Aisle windows featured Benedictine and other important Catholic saints.

During the construction of the church, Abbot Edelbrock also oversaw the construction of new brick wings that formed a traditional monastic quadrangle. Architect-monk Steil designed a set of buildings that rose five stories in height, had a depth of 55 feet, and ran 125 feet in length per side. The church enclosed the quadrangle on the north, and the second brick addition of 1868 completed the south (Figure 1.13). The east and west wings were new additions, along with an extension to the existing southern building. Once complete, the quadrangle provided space for six hundred students—the school's enrollment was only three hundred—as well as guest accommodations, dormitory space for the monks, a new dining room, kitchen, classrooms, gymnasium, and auditorium. The first Abbey of Saint John the Baptist was a dominating presence on the central Minnesota plain.

Drawing inspiration from the Ludwigskirche, the Ludwig-funded Green Bay cathedral, and medieval churches in the German homeland, the Collegeville buildings assumed a place in an architectural lineage that aided and supported immigrant Catholics in a strange land, as noted by former *Commonweal* editor George N. Shuster in 1953:

> For the Assumption came right out of the heart of the German Rhineland, and is as close as the builders could come to the score of small minsters in which the glory of Mainz or Maria Laach was scaled down to meet the needs and desires of lesser towns like Andernach. It belongs where it was put up, because at the time it was the Catholic Rhineland which moved into Minnesota.[37]

Although Shuster was referring to Assumption Church in St. Paul, he could just as easily have been talking about the buildings in Green Bay or Collegeville. For the viewers of Saint John's the architecture provided a dual meaning, as it spoke to German nationalistic notions in its form and style, while at the same time carrying an international meaning communicated through Benedictine mission work and identity.

The Benedictines and monasticism were now established in central Minnesota and the institutional seeds planted for the creation of a midcentury architectural aesthetic that moved beyond ethnic and national associations to make an international statement, with sculptural modernism setting the stage. There was just one more piece of the puzzle to complete prior to the midcentury, however. The Benedictines would become a part of the international leadership in liturgical reform and have a hand in reinventing the ritual that would be integral for the design of the second abbey church.

THE LITURGICAL MOVEMENT AND SAINT JOHN'S ABBEY

At the dawn of the twentieth century, the Benedictines continued their version of missionary monasticism, ministering to and educating immigrants and American Indians in Minnesota.[38] The language of instruction was German, as was the architectural identity. The growth of the abbey and its associated schools created the need for more space, as 102 priests, nineteen clerics, six novices, thirty lay brothers, and numerous students called Collegeville home.[39] During Abbot Peter Engel's tenure (1894–1921), the Benedictines upgraded Saint John's facilities in an architectural mélange of styles and types, completing in succession a nonextant observatory (1894); a library/music department/photography studio, now Wimmer Hall (1901); a gymnasium, now Guild Hall (1901); a residence for the Franciscan sisters who staffed the kitchen, now Saint Francis House (1904); and an infirmary, now Greg House

(1907). The 1910 science building, now Simons Hall, included reinforced concrete stairs, the first use of the constructional material at Saint John's. Engel turned on the first electric lights at Saint John's on October 10, 1898, using electricity generated by the new dynamo in the powerhouse. By the end of Abbot Engel's administration the numbers of students in the high school, college, seminary, and commercial departments had doubled and the number of brethren had also grown. Abbot Engel not only modernized the campus but also encouraged his brethren to stay current with developments in theology and other disciplines by pursuing graduate degrees at important schools across the world, from the Catholic University in Washington, D.C., to Saint Anselm's, the international Benedictine college in Rome, Italy.

A change in the abbey's leadership in the early twenties did not slow the pace of building or learning. Upon Abbot Engel's death in 1921, Alcuin Deutsch became the fifth abbot of Saint John's, a position he held until 1950, when Baldwin Dworschak succeeded him. He, too, added to the physical facilities. Benet Hall, the first college residence separate from the quadrangle, was completed in 1921.[40] Seven years later an auditorium was completed, followed by a powerhouse (1945) and diocesan seminary (1950). Also a supporter of education, Abbot Deutsch, a holder of a doctorate in philosophy, reorganized the schools to include a preparatory school, college of the arts and sciences, and seminary. By emphasizing the scholarly study of liturgy and ritual, he set in motion an involvement in promoting liturgical reforms that would help make Saint John's a world leader in the movement.

THE TWENTIETH-CENTURY REFORM OF THE LITURGY

The word *liturgy*, derived from the Greek words *leitos* (the public or people) and *ergos* (work), proclaims an emphasis on the participation of individual believers in the worship service. With roots in the nineteenth century, the reforms of the twentieth century, culminating at the Second Vatican Council (1962–65), challenged established liturgical practices and advocated the development of a traditional liturgy inclusive of chant and responsorial elements, the use of vernacular with Latin, an emphasis on the sacraments, and a focus on devotion to the Eucharist with active participation by the faithful.[41] This new liturgy would be quite different from the scene that predated the change, whereby the worshipper gathered more personal benefits than communal ones, praying silently, kneeling, and sitting at will while the celebrant had his back to the laity or was even hidden behind a screen of some sort.

Dom Prosper Louis Pascal Guéranger (1805–75) laid the foundation for liturgical reconsiderations when he restored the Benedictine order at

Solesmes, France, in 1833.[42] Abbot Guéranger noticed that French Catholics observed many different liturgical practices because the Catholic Church in France had never promulgated the decrees of the Council of Trent (1545–63).[43] Guéranger used the monastery to showcase his desire for a single communal observance of the liturgy (based on the Roman rite), which united worshippers and eliminated the popular personal devotions to Mary and the Blessed Sacrament that dominated contemporary practice.

The Abbey of Saint Peter in Solesmes became the center of Guéranger's reforms. It was here that Guéranger published his most famous work in 1841, *L'année liturgique*, a widely read tract that documented and commented on the church's annual liturgical celebrations.[44] The monks at Solesmes took up an intense study of the liturgy, focusing on the Mass and Divine Office (the Liturgy of the Hours). Guéranger used Gregorian chant to reform liturgical practice, providing a direct link to traditional monastic worship. For Guéranger, the liturgy was the key to the spiritual life of the laity.

Although Guéranger's efforts were more theoretical than practical, his nineteenth-century reform of the liturgy encouraged an early twentieth-century practical focus on ecumenism, pastoral care, and the involvement of the worshipper in the service. Pope Pius X supported and encouraged Guéranger's efforts at promoting monastic chant with the November 22, 1903, publication of his *Motu proprio Tra le sollecitudini* or "The Restoration of Church Music."[45] Pope Pius X's document called for the active participation of the laity in the Mass through song, such as Gregorian chant, in hopes of reviving faith and piety in an increasingly secular world:

> It being our ardent desire to see the true Christian spirit restored in every respect and be preserved by all the faithful, we deem it necessary to provide before everything else for the sanctity and dignity of the temple, in which the faithful assemble for the object of acquiring this spirit from its foremost and indispensable fount, which is the active participation in the holy mysteries and in the public and solemn prayer of the Church.[46]

Music encouraged the active participation of the faithful, a notion that would become the cornerstone of reform.

Abbot Lambert Beauduin of the Abbey of Mont César at Louvain, Belgium, transformed Pope Pius X's ideas into reality.[47] A young monk who had the support of established leaders, including Désiré-Joseph Cardinal Mercier and the historian Godefroid Kurth, Beauduin addressed the 1909 National Congress of Catholic Works at Malines, Belgium, effectively launching the liturgical movement. During a conference session on Christian art and archaeology, Beauduin delivered "La vraie prière de l'Eglisé" (The true prayer of the Church), a paper that emphasized the full and active participation of all in the liturgy. He published his ideas in several articles and texts, including *Liturgy, the Life of the Church* (1926), a work that stated the goals for the movement:

1. Active participation of all Christian people in the Mass by understanding and following the rites and texts
2. Emphasis on the importance of the High Mass, Sunday services, and liturgical singing by the faithful
3. Preservation and the reestablishment of Sunday Vespers and Compline as parish celebrations
4. Acquaintance and active association with the rites of the sacraments received and assisted, and the spread of this knowledge to others[48]

He also went on to discuss the role of the arts in the new liturgy, asking for artists working on church commissions to have the proper education in and to be inspired by the "spirit and rules of the Church's liturgy."[49] While Beauduin kept Belgium at the center of the practical side of the movement with a focus on laity participation at the parish level, Germany set in place the theological underpinnings.

In 1913 the monks at the Benedictine Abbey of Maria Laach, on the southwest bank of Lake Laach near Andernach in the German Rhineland, selected a new abbot, Ildefons Herwegen (Figure 1.14).[50] Abbot Herwegen invited learned men from universities and the religious professions to spend time at the abbey, indoctrinating them in their understanding of the liturgy. With the aid of periodicals and letters published by the abbey, these scholars spread the word on liturgical changes throughout Europe. These ideas were acknowledged more formally in 1931, when Abbot Herwegen founded the Institute of Liturgical and Monastic Studies at Maria Laach.[51] He also encouraged celebration of the Mass in the Romanesque church *versus populum*, with the priest facing the assembly.[52]

From Maria Laach came three of the liturgical movement's leaders: Odo Casel, Romano Guardini, and Pius Parsch. Casel's contribution to the movement included many scholarly publications and his concept of the *Mysteriengegenwart* or "mystery in the present." In this belief, Christ was made manifest again both historically and mystically in the liturgy. The passion, death, and resurrection of Christ were the events through which Christians knew him, and they became the heart of the liturgy performed by the entire church, not just the clergy.[53] Casel's tripartite idea was crucial to the Saint John's Benedictines, who used art, along with architecture, to provide a setting for all to understand the historical and mystical power of God.

FIGURE 1.14. The Abbey Church of Maria Laach, Germany.

In *The Spirit of the Liturgy* (1935), the Italian-born and German-bred priest Romano Guardini called for a greater understanding of the mysteries of the Mass and a stronger participation by the laity for, as Guardini explained, it was during the Mass that one was closest to Christ: "It is only when we participate in liturgical action with the earnestness begotten of deep personal interest that we become aware why, and in what perfection, this vital essence [the beauty of the liturgy] is revealed."[54] Guardini's influence moved reform from the monastery to the parish laity and specifically its youth, most notably when he made contact in 1922 with the Jungbrunnen or Quickborn movement.[55] Working with architect Rudolf Schwarz, Guardini turned the castle on the Main River in Rothenfels, Germany, into a home for Catholic youth, a place Guardini hoped would "infuse the whole of life, literature, and art with the Catholic spirit."[56] At Burg Rothenfels, Guardini's young followers could live, learn, and develop a renewed sense of society based on merging the life of the church with their own personal activities. Mass was said in the vernacular, and Guardini eventually included German hymns.[57]

The Augustinian canon Pius Parsch, working from the Abbey of Klosterneuburg outside Vienna, espoused the same pastoral ideals as Guardini but with an added emphasis on the knowledge of the Bible.[58] Through the Volksliturgisches Apostolat or Popular Liturgical Apostolate, he published pamphlets, journals (including *Bible and Liturgy*), and books such as *The Church's Year of Grace* (1929), which, according to liturgical scholar Clifford Howell, "won more adherents to the liturgical movement than any book ever written."[59] The *Church's Year of Grace*, with its meditations on saints of the day, resonated with parishioners, and Parsch focused on change at this level while he was responsible for the Church of Saint Gertrude outside the monastery's walls. With architect Robert Kramreiter's help, in 1935 Parsch transformed the church into a liturgically appropriate worship vessel, placing the altar closer to the laity to facilitate their participation in the Eucharist with the celebrant saying the Mass *versus populum*.[60]

THE LITURGICAL MOVEMENT AND THE IMPORTANCE OF FATHER VIRGIL MICHEL

While Europe remained essential in the development of a liturgy responsive to twentieth-century society, the center of the liturgical movement shifted from Europe to the United States with the onset of World War I. The Saint John's Benedictines took up the cause, led by Abbot Alcuin Deutsch and Father Virgil Michel (1890–1938).[61] The abbot wanted to reform the liturgy of the monastery, so he reinstated the custom of praying the Divine Office in the church rather than in a separate choir chapel, and he renewed an appreciation of music in the liturgy, sending his monks to liturgical music schools and bringing in experts on Gregorian chant to speak at the abbey.[62]

The abbot's most important contribution to the American liturgical revival occurred in 1924, when he sent Michel to Saint Anselm's in Rome, where Michel met and studied with Abbot Lambert Beauduin.[63] Beauduin recalled that Michel was never satisfied with his knowledge of the liturgy, and the two spent time outside the classroom discussing it. Michel even asked Beauduin to arrange for him "to spend the holidays in our monastery in Louvain, in order to become familiar with all the details of the organization of liturgical work."[64] Michel left Saint Anselm's after one semester and traveled to better understand the work being done at other leading liturgical institutions in Europe, including Mont César, Maria Laach, and Solesmes.

Michel's journey encouraged him to write Abbot Deutsch and implore him to have Saint John's become a center for liturgical writings in America. Their work would be threefold: they would translate European ideas into English, pen new ideas for a Popular Liturgical Library, and publish a monthly journal, *Orate Fratres* (later called *Worship*).[65] Michel returned to Collegeville in the fall of 1925 and went to work, establishing the Liturgical Press by the following fall and becoming editor in chief of *Orate Fratres*. In addition to writing much of its first issue of November 28, 1926, Michel also published the first three volumes of the Popular Liturgical Library, including a translation of Beauduin's *Liturgy: The Life of the Church*.[66] The liturgical movement was finding a home in the United States.

Michel required that the American movement be popular and broadly based. In his "Liturgy in the Vernacular" (1938) he was the first to promote the use of English in the American Mass. He also sought to allow celebration of the Mass in the evening, making worship more convenient for working people. Michel believed participation in the liturgy at a pastoral level could resolve perceived social ills, including capitalistic individualism and Marxist collectivism.[67] In his view, all Catholics were family members with Christ, whether during the Mass or in the profane realm. Movements like Catholic Action and the Catho-

lic Worker carried Michel's social and religious vision to the faithful. National and international liturgical conferences, such as the first American Liturgical Week, held in Chicago in 1940 with 1,260 people in attendance, provided settings for clergy and monastics to discuss and refine ideas regarding reform.[68] With theological ideas well in place, Michel also played a role in the discussion of how architecture could support liturgical change in the United States.

LITURGY AND ARCHITECTURE AT SAINT JOHN'S: IDEALS AND THE FIRST ABBEY CHURCH

Michel deemed it essential that clerical leaders craft worship space in ways that would support the goals of liturgical reform. During his European travels, Michel evaluated the setting of the liturgy, understanding its critical influence on the broader revival movement as a whole. In 1924, while at the Abbey of Maria Laach, he wrote to Abbot Deutsch lamenting the lack of a liturgical spirit in the architecture at Saint John's: "The project [liturgical projects and pamphlets] itself is developing in the realm of ideas, at least; it would be aided greatly later if our life were an open living example of the liturgical life. But there our church is a great handicap."[69] He presented more developed ideas on the appropriate setting for the ritual of the Mass in his 1936 article, "Architecture and the Liturgy," published in

Liturgical Arts.[70] Originally a lecture delivered to architects in St. Paul, Minnesota, Michel's article established a clear understanding for designers of sacred space:

> The spirit of man demands something more than the purely practical, and it is precisely architecture, as an art, that must, in supplying the practical, also give that which is more, which points beyond. . . . Architecture therefore, as artistic construction, must embody an ideal. And it is precisely this character that gives enduring value to architecture, as to all art.[71]

Michel's ideal for enduring architecture? The reformed liturgy. Architecture and its associated decorative arts were necessary to support the liturgy's key elements. The most important notions at Saint John's were the active participation of all in the Mass, the significance of the High Mass and its focus on the altar as the table at which worshippers and the clergy gathered with God, and the dynamic involvement of the faithful with the sacraments.

Michel's ideas on liturgical reform reorganized the arrangement of participants and their actions, and changed architectural space, requiring either the adaptation of existing spaces to the new actions or a new building form. Designers and their theological advisers eschewed the Latin cross plan in favor of an open plan with unencumbered views of the altar as the focal point of participation. Since the Mass is a ritual that focuses on the altar as it represents the sacrifice of Christ, Michel believed the altar's positioning must be central and prominent in the church. As he explained, "The altar should not only be so placed that the faithful are within better earshot of it, but it should by its elevation above all else indicate the eminent part it plays in Catholic worship."[72] This change also enabled members of the congregation to see each other, facilitating the engagement of all worshippers. Responsorial elements in the Mass also encouraged participation, as did readings delivered from the ambo by members of the laity rather than clergy. Further engagement of all worshippers was promoted through the use of the vernacular rather than Latin. Michel and other theologians also supported the deepening understanding of the sacraments in the life of the Catholic congregant. He called for the baptistery to be positioned at the entrance to the church, as it is the "initiatory sacrament of the Catholic faith."

Liturgical change and worship informed two efforts to redecorate the first abbey church during Michel's lifetime. In 1909, Abbot Engel had architect Anton Dohmen of Milwaukee, Wisconsin, remove the wooden reredos and replace it with a low marble version. He also took down the wooden communion rail (Figure 1.15).[73] The

FIGURE 1.15. Saint John's Abbey Church after the interior renovation in 1909.

FIGURE 1.16. The interior of Saint John's Abbey Church was redone in 1933 with Beuronese art by Brother Clement Frischauf seen in *Christ the Way, the Truth, and the Life.*

altar's significance was highlighted by raising it on a podium, pulling it forward from the apse wall, and surmounting it with a ciborium. By 1929 the arrival of additional clerics to study at the abbey dictated a need for seating in the back of the transepts where additional altars had been located. Because of the position of these additional choir stalls, the altar was pulled forward eighteen and a half feet from the wall for visibility. On May 19, 1939, when Brother Clement Frischauf's Beuronese-style altar painting of Christ Pantocrator was completed above the altar, an iconographic element upheld its role as the most important decoration in the church (Figure 1.16).[74]

But it was more than just a church building that created the appropriate atmosphere for worship and work, as Michel wrote Abbot Deutsch in September 1924 while traveling in Europe: "How nice it will be to see the square at home beautified! How often I thought of that this summer and of the beautiful cloister we could have had there. We surely ought to get a unified plan of buildings and get it at once, even if we do not build now, and cannot complete it for a hundred years."[75] He also called for an "architectural kick" in the buildings, wanting the architecture to be interesting and make a bold statement for the Benedictines. As Michel's biographer, Paul Marx, pointed out, this call for stimulating and fitting architecture predates by thirty years the 1950s start of the one-hundred-year plan. Michel is laying the groundwork for art and architecture to support and beautify the liturgy and monasticism, an ideal that will become the cornerstone of Breuer and the Benedictines' midcentury work at Saint John's.

Michel made it clear to architects that they were not to impose their style or philosophy on the church building but instead must allow the building to respond to "religious perfection as expressed in Catholic ideals or worship."[76] Although Michel did not refer directly to a modernist style of architecture, he believed that functionalism was the key element in the design of the building, a core focus for architects in the early twentieth century. The liturgical reforms and church forms he witnessed firsthand in Europe and was now promoting in America would play crucial roles in the new Saint John's Abbey Church. Now the Benedictines just had to find the right architect to execute their vision.

THE TWELVE APOSTLES
Selecting the Architect

Saint John's abbey, university, and prep schools grew rapidly in the first half of the twentieth century. By midcentury, 306 brethren and 1,177 students were crowded into the cramped quarters of the nineteenth-century monastery at Saint John's, including the Romanesque Revival church, which held only four hundred people (Figures 2.1 and 2.2).[1] Even before the brethren elected him abbot on December 28, 1950, Baldwin Dworschak had recognized that the largest Benedictine house in the world required a more suitable setting for worship and work. Within a year of his appointment, he created a building committee to look into improving the physical character of the abbey.[2] The abbot tasked the committee with creating a prioritized wish list of structures. After a year and a half of meetings and discussion, the building committee reported its findings to the senior council on March 3, 1953. Saint John's was in desperate need of space to house aged and infirm fathers and brothers; guest rooms for visitors; a library, administrative offices, and classrooms for the associated university; and a larger church for the worshipping community.

At first, committee members intended to solve the problem by working in the manner of their predecessors as monk-architects and monk-laborers. They prepared sketches of their ideas, under the leadership of Father Cloud Meinberg, head of the art department, who had a degree in architecture from the University of Illinois and three years of experience with an architectural firm and statuary company in St. Paul, Minnesota.[3] Their vision included a proposal by Father Joachim Watrin for a new church (Figure 2.3). They located a new church on an east–west line in front of the nineteenth-century buildings, structures they would convert into space for administration, guests, and a monastic dormitory.

FIGURE 2.1 (*above*). Saint John's Abbey and University, 1948.

FIGURE 2.2 (*right*). Abbot Baldwin Dworschak presides over Mass in the first abbey church, ca. 1950.

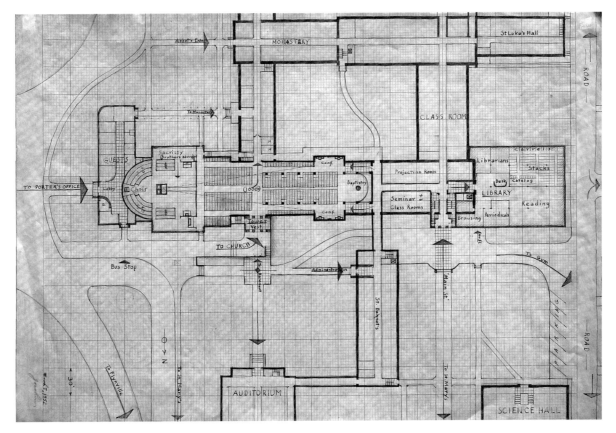

FIGURE 2.3. Father Watrin's plan (created in 1952) to enlarge the church would have reversed its orientation and positioned the altar in a prominent location.

The senior council soon understood, however, that this project was greater than they could manage, so they decided to seek the advice of an architect through an invited competition.[4]

Abbot Dworschak charged Father Meinberg with composing a letter of invitation. He sought the aid of his colleague, Frank Kacmarcik, as both had excellent knowledge of design at the midcentury.[5] Other members of the brethren, including the youngest member of the yet-to-be-formed church committee, Father Hilary Thimmesh, assisted in writing the letter in "language designed to interest major architects in doing a comprehensive plan with a bold new church at the heart of it."[6] The Benedictines believed in the power of their liturgical vision to create architecture of international and lasting importance, and the letter and the list of architects selected to receive it would clearly communicate their intent.[7]

This winner of the competition would design a hundred-year master plan for the abbey and its associated schools. The Benedictines called for architects to consider carefully a plan in which the "buildings would form a completed and unified whole," unlike the piecemeal quality of the nineteenth-century complex. They also explained the needs of the community, outlining the requirements of the three-hundred-member group and providing information on the university and the Benedictine order. Notable in these paragraphs is the Benedictines' understanding of their role in the Catholic world: "The Abbey is one of the largest Benedictine communities in the world at the present time, and has become rather widely known as the center of the liturgical movement; principally through its publications." Implicit in this mention of the liturgical movement is the importance of a church building in the project, even though the selected architect was not promised the job of designing any of the buildings within the plan. Intent on changing the face of Catholic architecture, the Benedictines were interested in "building a church which will be truly an architectural monument in the service of God." This meant going beyond the functional requirements of a church, as clearly expressed in the letter of invitation's last paragraph:

The Benedictine tradition at its best challenges us to think boldly and to cast our ideals in forms which will be valid for centuries to come, shaping them with all the genius of present-day materials and techniques. We feel that the modern architect with his orientation toward functionalism and honest use of materials is uniquely qualified to produce a Catholic work. In our position it would, we think, be deplorable to build anything less, particularly since our age and our country have thus far produced so little truly significant religious architecture.

This meant that modern architecture would be the means by which religious architecture could again be made significant in the United States, an ideological stance supported by many, including the Catholic bishops of Germany, the Holy See, and the Liturgical Arts Society of America. For the Benedictines, modernism was not a stylistic issue but rather a tectonic one, for they were interested in materials that could shape appropriate forms for a newly refined worship.

A building should be first and foremost functional and pragmatic. Function had become the linchpin of a new architectural philosophy with architect Walter Gropius's founding in 1919 of the Bauhaus in Weimar, Germany. Designers of early twentieth-century modern architecture went beyond tradition and historical elements with techniques and materials employed in industrial fabrication and manufacture.[8] In 1932 Henry-Russell Hitchcock and Philip Johnson codified the Bauhaus's architectural ideas with their Museum of Modern Art exhibition, *Modern Architecture: International Exhibition*, and book, *The International Style*. Architecture should highlight volume rather than mass and be organized by a regularity informed by the underlying structure of a building, rather than by a strict symmetry inspired by the classical tradition. Ornament should be avoided. Kathleen James-Chakraborty has pointed out that Hitchcock and Johnson's definition should have included an emphasis on dramatic light, both colored and artificial, as seen in the work, for example, of European expressionistic architects like Bruno Taut, Hans Poelzig, and Erich Mendelsohn.[9] Her point applies particularly well to religious architecture, in which light can emphasize the most sacred portions of a building, providing an almost decorative quality and a contemplative focus.

Modernism evolved as an architectural style throughout the first half of the twentieth century. As architects grew tired of creating steel-and-glass boxes, they embraced organic, playful forms that went beyond the rectilinear and entered the realm of expressionism. They used materials such as stone, tile, wood, and concrete as they shaped functional space of any type. Experiments in reinforced concrete by designers such as Félix Candela and Pier Luigi Nervi showed that space could be shaped with forms like the para-

bolic arch, a feat impossible for steel and glass.[10] As Adrian Forty notes, "Indeed, some of its most spectacular and creative applications have been for religious architecture."[11]

Concrete could be used to create a range of forms as it provided the integrity needed for a successful worship space. As Donald Bruggink and Carl Droppers discuss in *When Faith Takes Form: Contemporary Churches of Architectural Integrity in America*, "Integrity in a church must include the church in its wholeness, i.e. the relationship of all its parts to each other and to the whole."[12] Breuer understood concrete's architectural utility in creating a great whole, stating several years after the completion of the Saint John's project, "At the present point in architectural history, when reinforced concrete flamboyance seems fashionable, one might say that no other material has the potential for such a complete and convincing fusion between structure, enclosure and surface; between architecture and detail; between the minute great form and the great small particle."[13] With the many items necessary for a Catholic Mass, this unity of elements was crucial for architectural and liturgical integrity in a church building. Concrete's plasticity could even be seen as a metaphor for the vision the Benedictines had for Saint John's as it highlighted an engineered aspect in architecture they deemed necessary to shape liturgical reform.

As leaders of liturgical reform the Benedictines sought to create a vision of architectural space to support their ideals. Church layout was reevaluated. An open plan featuring the central placement of the altar and unobstructed sight lines to it and the priest was preferred. Sacramental accoutrements like baptismal fonts should be prominent in their placement within a building, and creative in their design. Reformers also encouraged simplicity in decoration in order to maintain the laity's focus on their relationship with the clergy and ultimately with God. Together, these items should unify the experience of worship in a Catholic church.

The first step toward making a new vision of liturgical architecture a reality was to select an architect. Who were the possible candidates? Could the Benedictines find someone with whom they could collaborate? Should it be someone experienced in designing churches? Did the designer have to be Catholic? Would modernism be an appropriate stylistic choice? And would reinforced concrete prove a viable option for an architect designing this building?

CONCRETE MOLDS THE LITURGY IN THE EARLY TWENTIETH-CENTURY CHURCH

Reinforced concrete played a significant role in the development of a liturgically reformed Catholic church building in the first half of the twentieth century, moving building forms from traditional into the realm of original and innovative.[14] It also was economical and could be fash-

ioned more easily by workmen. In 1933 architect Barry Byrne championed its virtues in *Liturgical Arts:* "Concrete offers again the possibility of this unity of material for a monumental architecture, no longer restricted by the narrow limits of the Gothic plan, but adaptable to modern space arrangements and to great vaulted spans."[15] Although architects discussed the virtues of concrete in their writings, churchmen and -women generally did not proclaim, as Forty notes, a sacramentality for the material. It had no particular advantage over other materials.[16]

The use of reinforced concrete to replicate earlier styles was considered a *retardataire* approach to church form, like Anatole de Baudot's 1894 Church of Saint John the Evangelist in Montmartre, France, and its Gothic-inspired forms.[17] Fellow French architect Auguste Perret's design for the Church of Notre-Dame du Raincy near Paris (1922–24) might have replicated traditional forms with concrete, but it aided the cause of liturgical reform by increasing the visibility of the altar (Figure 2.4).[18] Like his mentors Viollet-le-Duc and Baudot, Perret regarded the structure of the building as its most expressive element, and at Raincy reinforced concrete provided the meaning with exterior walls filled with expanses of stained glass.[19] Critics proclaimed Perret's work as a unification of the past and present in its "solidity and rational geometry of Classicism with Gothic daring and spirituality," and they praised him for making reinforced concrete "the most immate-

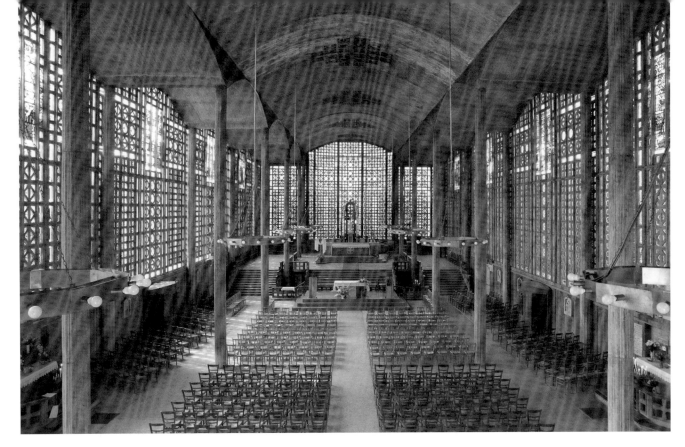

FIGURE 2.4. Interior of Auguste Perret's Church of Notre-Dame du Raincy, France, 1924. Concrete enables an openness and a focus on the altar.

rial of materials."[20] Concrete tracery comprised all four walls of the building and lightened the visual and physical load of the structure. Francis Onderdonk championed the versatility of concrete tracery as part of the eternal traditions of architecture, dating back to Gothic tracery, yet it was able to move beyond tradition to bend, twist, and turn in previously unimaginable ways.[21] For Onderdonk, this was a contribution modern architecture had been waiting for.

Perret used concrete at Raincy in response to costs and new liturgical notions fostered by the building's patron, Abbé Nègre.[22] Indeed, the openness enabled by the use of concrete placed a palpable focus on the altar, which was further emphasized by its position on a platform that spans the entire eastern end of the building. Keith Pecklers notes that the church directly connected to the beginning of pastoral reforms of the liturgy in Europe, specifically Lambert Beauduin's presentation at the Malines Conference of 1909.[23] For many scholars, the unification and consolidation of the interior space served as the starting point of a new modern spirit in religious design. Peter Hammond called Notre-Dame du Raincy

> a landmark in the development of the modern church not only on account of the way in which it reflects the dawn of a new understanding of the liturgy, but even more in its uncompromising honesty and the stark purity of its structural geometry.[24]

Yet even though Raincy's structural honesty, spatial redefinition, and bold exposure of material would encourage other architects to explore the use of reinforced concrete in religious design, it lacked an original form for the new liturgy.

There was one European architect who was making inroads into planning with innovative concrete forms for liturgical space, the German designer Dominikus Böhm. Martin Weber, an oblate of the Abbey of Maria Laach and an architectural student of Böhm's at the School of Architecture and Applied Arts in Offenbach am Main, connected Böhm with the Catholic chaplain Johannes van Acken.[25] Van Acken's 1922 booklet, *Christocentric Church Art: Towards the Total Work of Liturgical Art,* directly addressed issues of architecture, from the "unmediated view of the altar" to the demand for less spatial division in the church, finding it "impossible when these

piers, lining the side aisles, block [congregants'] view of the Altar."[26] Van Acken's influential booklet was reprinted and expanded within one year of its original publication, with the second edition of 1923 containing Böhm's illustrations. Their collaboration was important for the liturgical reform movement in Europe.

Böhm's opportunity to realize unity in worship centered on the importance of the altar as promoted by van Acken came in the early 1930s. He was commissioned to design the Church of Saint Engelbert in Riehl, Germany, near Cologne, a strongly Catholic city that was important in the liturgical revival. Böhm used eight parabolic arches of reinforced concrete faced with brick on the exterior, six in the nave and two in the choir, to span the centrally planned building in a single volume. This shape was one of concrete's contributions to architectural form. According to Onderdonk, "The parabolic arch is characteristic of Ferro-Concrete which in its absolute freedom to accept any form is well adapted to the ever changing curvature of the parabola. The parabola in turn expresses the monolithic quality of reinforced concrete by merging sides and top in one unbroken curve."[27]

Lighting the liturgy inside the church concerned Böhm, so into the stucco-covered nave vaults he inserted small circular windows of stained glass. He drew attention to the apse and altar from the dimly lighted nave with larger, clear windows (Figure 2.5). This provided a focus

FIGURE 2.5. The interior of Dominikus Böhm's Church of Saint Engelbert uses light to emphasize the altar.

on the altar and God, for as Böhm put it, "Light is the most noble, the chastest building material, presented to us by God."[28] Acting as a decorative element in its own right, light created an atmosphere that architects could exploit in religious buildings, and whether colored or clear, light and the way it was applied directed the attention of worshippers, focusing their thoughts and prayers.

Böhm's skillful work at Saint Engelbert's

prompted German art historian Anton Henze to classify it as one of four churches that formed "the cradle of modern ecclesiastical architecture."[29] The remaining churches Henze included were Perret's Notre-Dame du Raincy, Karl Moser's Saint Antonius in Basel (1927–31), and the German architect Rudolf Schwarz's Corpus Christi Church in Aachen (1928–30). All these buildings set a new standard for religious design, using an industrial material like concrete to create vast open spaces with clear vantage points to the altar and a focus on key liturgical elements in the buildings with light and finely crafted artistic elements. Modern church architecture proponent Frédéric Debuyst called Schwarz's design for Corpus Christi "the first clearly and totally *modern* church" for its unification of the altar and laity in a single space, although the connection between the two was largely visual due to the fixed pews.[30] Debuyst appreciated the "functional simplicity of the church" and noted that every designed element came together with the architectural form to create a kind of "incorruptibility."

Romano Guardini provided theological support for Schwarz's architectural ideas. Schwarz designed portions of the Quickborn movement's home base at the sixteenth-century Castle Rothenfels, as discussed in chapter 1.[31] Not only did he complete the chapel for the complex in 1928, he also fashioned the liturgical space in the castle's Knight's Hall, where large groups could celebrate the Mass. This multifunctional room was a spartan, flat-ceiling room similar to Schwarz's design for Corpus Christi Church. In the Knight's Hall, Guardini and Schwarz moved the altar away from the end wall into the center of the space, allowing the priest to face the congregation with the youth seated on sleek, black, cuboid stools arranged around the altar in various configurations depending on the nature of the assembly.[32] This flexible arrangement, unifying the laity and priest, rested well within the

simple, white, unornamented container created by Schwarz.

Schwarz secured a prominent place as a religious architect and theorist in 1938 with the publication of his treatise on modern church architecture, *Vom Bau der Kirche*, a work that architect Mies van der Rohe believed threw "light for the first time on the question of church building."[33] Schwarz divided the church plan into seven archetypes centered on a deep understanding of new liturgical requirements, particularly the need to bring worshippers into close contact with the chancel and altar. For example, his 1949 design for the Roman Catholic Church of Saint Michael's in Frankfurt used an elliptical plan with projecting side chapels to unify the entire room in his theoretical archetype of the Sacred Parting: the Open Ring, with an altar surrounded on three sides by the congregation (Figure 2.6).

Schwarz's buildings were forward thinking and modern. Even though he appreciated the validity and truth of the Gothic cathedral, with its steeple and its "procession of pillars and arches, the crowds of pinnacles and responders," he upheld the need for an architecture fashioned of modern materials, such as concrete, steel, and glass, that could emphasize the simplified volume rather than a complicated mass of a building.[34] Schwarz believed in the building as sculpture, where "walls and construction may be regarded as a plastic theme and we may then allow space and walls to orchestrate the structure contrapuntally."[35] This notion of flexible volumes of space well suited the transformed liturgy as architects across the world, including designers in America, began building modern worship spaces for the Catholic Church.

CONCRETE LITURGICAL FORMS IN AMERICA

Architects, church leaders, and artists sustained the rise of modern architecture, specifically the use of concrete, in American church building. The leaders of the Liturgical Arts Society, including its secretary and founding member Maurice Lavanoux, insisted that religious art and architecture supported by the society be modern, for "a modern church must find its religious expression in contemporary art forms."[36] In 1933 an issue of the society's journal *Liturgical Arts* focused on one topic, the design of ecclesiastical space in concrete, in an attempt to inform and educate clergy who were worried about using concrete as a building material for their churches.[37] Lavanoux's editorial laid out the issue's goals and dealt with the topic of style in modern church architecture:

> To discuss the use of concrete in monumental architecture inevitably leads to the whole question of the "modern" style of design. The engineering of concrete is so fundamentally different from that of brick and stone that one is almost forced into novelties of design if one is to use concrete with honesty. For the tradi-

FIGURE 2.6. St. Michael's Church in Frankfurt, Germany, by Rudolf Schwarz, is a built example of his theoretical archetype of the Open Ring.

tional styles of church building . . . all grew out of systems of engineering imposed by the older masonry of stone-upon-stone or brick-upon-brick. . . . Concrete vaulting for the first time makes possible the fireproof spanning of large areas without the necessity of counter-balancing outward thrusts. And in this very fact lies the reason why honest concrete construction almost makes necessary the development of a new style of architecture. . . . Indeed all of the writers who discuss concrete in the present issue are agreed that its use implies profound modifications of traditional design, and it is probably indisputable that for those who desire a purely traditional building, concrete would not be given consideration as a material suitable for major use.[38]

However, contributors to the issue did not present the goals of a new, expressive concrete architecture in a strong visual fashion, and Lavanoux notes that the illustrations—a parish school and chapel of Saint Madeleine Sophie in Germantown, Pennsylvania, and the Church of the Precious Blood in Los Angeles—showcased Gothic and early Christian forms fashioned out of concrete and faced with stone. Lavanoux lamented the uninspired design of these buildings:

Indeed we are left after re-reading the discussions in this issue, with the feeling that perhaps American concrete construction

has been a little too traditional. Many of the modern European structures in this medium seem to us ugly and unchurchlike, but the finest of them perhaps have a certain sincerity and dignity which would seem to be the proper goals of all church architecture.[39]

Unfortunately, Lavanoux does not name any of the European buildings, but one can be certain that he is thinking of work by Schwarz, Böhm, and Perret.

European architects' determination to provide a new liturgical space was matched in the United States by the work of the Chicago architect Barry Byrne (1883–1967), an innovator of Catholic architectural space from the 1920s through the 1960s. Not only was Byrne familiar with European architectural and religious trends, he also took an active role in the liturgical movement, particularly through the publication of design philosophies and plans for liturgical space in journals such as *America*, *Commonweal*, and *Liturgical Arts*.[40]

Byrne was interested in shaping new liturgical space in a pragmatic and efficient way. He created an open setting for the liturgy, including a 90-by-139-foot nave, with steel frame construction in his 1921 design for the Church of Saint Thomas the Apostle in Chicago. Scholars labeled Saint Thomas "the first modern Catholic church in America," and although the brick exterior spoke to a Prairie School version of the Gothic,

FIGURE 2.7. Church of Saint Patrick in Racine, Wisconsin. Architect Barry Byrne opens up worship space and expands the architectural style of the American Catholic church.

the building was too modern for some, including Chicago's George Cardinal Mundelein, who forbade Byrne to work again in his archdiocese.[41] Byrne then explored modern design beyond Chicago, traveling to Europe and visiting important architectural sites from the cathedral at Chartres, which he called tremendous and "greater than I imagined a building could be," to the Dessau Bauhaus.[42] Expressionistic buildings such as those by Mendelsohn, Poelzig, and Böhm influenced Byrne more than the Bauhaus ideals he encountered in Dessau.[43]

Byrne's subsequent church designs reflect the influence of his travels and connections, as well as his figurative exile by Cardinal Mundelein. The Church of Saint Patrick in Racine, Wisconsin (1923–24) and the Church of Christ the King in Tulsa, Oklahoma (1926), showcase his desire to provide unencumbered worship space shaped by new materials (Figure 2.7). Lavanoux's description of the Racine building in *Liturgical Arts* addressed the change in sacred design from architecture inspired by the past to original forms of a modern society. Finding joy that the "romantic fog" of traditional church building was starting to lift, he complimented the lack of columnar obstruction and the close proximity of the altar

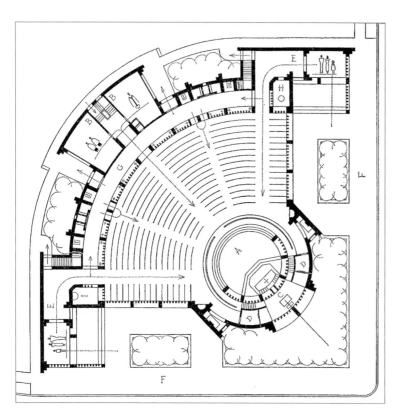

FIGURE 2.8. Barry Byrne's 1942 prototype plan for a Catholic church as featured in *Liturgical Arts*. A, sanctuary with high altar; B, sacristies; C, choir; D, working sacristy and storerooms; E, entrances; F, sidewalks; G, arcaded aisle; H, baptistery; I, shrines.

to the congregation.[44] Lavanoux noted that Byrne had not gone far enough in the transition from traditional to modern methods, however, observing that the plaster ceiling suspended from steel trusses could have been a stronger architectural element if reinforced concrete had been used: "Today, fortunately, with modern developments in concrete construction, another type of ceiling could well be used: a saucer dome, for example. Such a dome would afford an opportunity to achieve an added elevation of some fifteen feet, and would most probably result in a more pleasing outline than the present arrangement."[45]

In 1927 Byrne completed his first church in reinforced concrete and steel, the Cathedral of Christ the King in Cork, Ireland. Byrne believed that concrete was the masonry building material "most closely identified with modern developments in engineering science" and that therefore it was the "most challenging to an architectural mind which is preoccupied with the age-old problem of the form which shall reveal the underlying structure of a building."[46] Byrne likened this material to Gothic cathedrals, in which stone revealed the buildings' engineered forms. He believed the cathedral in Cork was his best religious work whose "basis was practical functionalism, imaginatively treated."[47]

In his "Plan for a Church" published in the May 1942 issue of *Liturgical Arts*, Byrne outlined the requirements of a new liturgical worship space (Figure 2.8). First, it would use contemporary structural systems and have a contemporary identity, for Byrne saw the church "as a living organism" that should not employ historical styles or "dead architectures, the envelopments of musty, discarded clothing."[48] The plan would shape the structure, but he encouraged a solution that gave each functional part of the building a clear emphasis yet was one in which all parts were synthesized within an overall whole. Byrne's plan integrated the nave with the sanctuary space not only by its shape but also in the manner in which the space was used. With the main sacristy located at the entry, the celebrant and procession moved forward through the people to the altar. This process encouraged a unification of the laity and clergy from the earliest moments of the worship service. But note that the baptistery was off to the side of the worship space, something the Benedictines would change in their design for Saint John's Abbey Church.

The forms for the new church would be modern, as Byrne stated:

What I saw . . . was a better identity of church architecture with its religious purpose, with its contemporary use, and with modern structural systems. If this identity were achieved, the road would be opened toward a living, contemporary architecture.[49]

Byrne's idealized church plan counteracts a traditionalism favored in American church design in the first decades of the early twentieth century. Ralph Adams Cram was a leader in Gothic Revival–based church design, and he published numerous essays and gave many public talks on the subject.[50] Cram fought against modernism and its impact on architecture, comparing, as Denis McNamara has noted, its glorification of the new and idiosyncratic with the individualistic interpretation of standards of faith and beauty legitimated by the Reformation.[51]

The Benedictines, even though steeped in an awareness of history, needed to find an architect who could create innovative forms to express their building's intended liturgical function. They were not interested in an architecture that replicated the past but rather in one that supported contemporary rituals based on a strong connection between celebrant and laity. In addition to the reformed liturgical function of the building, the brethren wanted a church that would hold up to the best buildings ever constructed by and for adherents to the Catholic faith. Specifically they looked to the Middle Ages and the development of the Gothic style in architecture, now not for its iconic, traditional form for a church but for its engineering and clearly expressive structure. The materials of the Gothic were not new. Stone, brick, wood, and mortar had been used previously, but the manner in which they were used in the Gothic style, with flying buttresses and vaults, changed the understanding of structure. The Collegeville monks wanted to create this same sensibility with their mid-twentieth-century church. Although they did not specifically call for the use of concrete in their buildings, they certainly understood that reinforced concrete had an unlimited means of expression that could successfully articulate their ritual requirements. Furthermore, the use of modern forms had received the sanction of the Holy See.

ARTISTIC DECREES FOR THE NEW LITURGY

Nearly five decades of work on reforming liturgical practices gained papal approval on November 20, 1947 with the publication of Pope Pius XII's (1876–1958) encyclical, *Mediator Dei* or "On the Sacred Liturgy," the first encyclical devoted to the liturgy. It stressed the involvement of the community, focusing on the priesthood of the laity.[52] Pope Pius hoped that

> the clergy and people become one in mind and heart, and that the Christian people take such an active part in the liturgy that it becomes a truly sacred action of due worship to the eternal Lord, in which the priest, chiefly responsible for the souls of his parish, and the ordinary faithful are united together.[53]

A unity in spirit required an appropriate physical setting and space; therefore the pope also included artistic guidelines in the encyclical, encouraging modern artists to join ranks with the centuries of designers who had fashioned art of their own time and style for the church.

Mediator Dei was liturgically sensitive in its call for architects of church buildings to "draw their inspiration from religion to express what is suitable and more in keeping with the requirements of worship."[54] But Pius XII cautioned that modern art and architecture should tend "neither to extreme realism nor to excessive symbolism and that the needs of the Christian community are taken into consideration rather than the particular taste or talent of the individual artist."[55] He wanted art and architecture that kept the sanctity of the place as its central focus. Although the encyclical encouraged a new approach to design, it did not eliminate tradition from art and architecture.

Pius XII's thoughts were general, allowing for the use of modernism in art and architecture, but at the same time urging that new forms of expression not become too conceptual or abstract. In 1947 the Holy See encouraged the German Catholic bishops to form a liturgical commission to fashion specific architectural guidelines for church design.[56] Composed by Father Theodor Klauser, "Directives for the Building of a Church" addressed the communal element of worship, but instead of surrounding the laity with traditional architectural or artistic forms, the bishops supported the use of art and architecture "for the people of our times. Hence it must be fashioned in such a way that the people of our times may recognize and feel that it is addressed to them."[57] The monks of Saint John's published the directives in the December 1949 issue of *Orate Fratres*. With these proclamations, the clerics codified what was already happening in the field: modern architecture was appropriate for the new liturgical structure. The use of modern architectural forms would be a welcome advancement in religious art and architecture, and it encouraged the Benedictines of Saint John's to employ a modern vocabulary in their designs for the monastery as well as for the church and its associated art. But these modern forms did not appear for the first time at the abbey. For decades, as we have seen, architects had brought architectural modernism to church building, setting the stage for a free-flowing, midcentury modernism that the Saint John's Benedictines would use to answer the German bishops' call.

ARCHITECTS BY INVITATION ONLY: THE INTERNATIONAL GROUP

The Benedictines' letter stated that this was to be "an outright and direct contract" and that this job would not be won in an architectural competition. Abbot Dworschak turned again to Meinberg and Kacmarcik for assistance in compiling the list of architects to contact. From their frequent travels overseas for education, conferences, and meetings, Meinberg and others were well versed in the

European architectural scene, with particular interest in the designers shaping the space of a reformed liturgy. It was not essential, however, that a finalist selected had designed a sacred space. In the December 1949 issue of *Architectural Forum* the writer of "Churches: Must the Church Build in Gothic?" stated that a recent survey revealed that more than half the leading contemporary architects had done no recent church work.[58] Although some monks wanted to select an alumnus of the university's architecture department, in the end the group pursued designers beyond Collegeville, posting letters on March 7, 1953, to Germany, Austria, England, and various cities in the United States.[59] The recipients were a who's who of design, including five European architects—Hermann Baur of Switzerland, Albert Bosslet and Rudolf Schwarz of Germany, Robert Kramreiter of Austria, and Thomas W. Sharp of England—and seven American-based designers—Pietro Belluschi, Marcel Breuer, Barry Byrne, Walter Gropius, Joseph D. Murphy, Richard Neutra, and Eero Saarinen. Why were these individuals invited? One essential requirement for the Benedictines was a strong reputation in comprehensive planning or religious design. The architect's faith and character were also important, and in order to assess the character of an individual, the Benedictines encouraged the world's most reputable designers to visit Collegeville.[60]

Since liturgical reform's architectural inception was in Europe, it was natural for the brethren to look across the Atlantic for designers of great reputation and skill. It is no surprise, then, that four of the five Europeans approached by the Benedictines had a solid reputation in church design. The first considered was Rudolf Schwarz (1897–1961) of Cologne, Germany. The Benedictines appreciated his idea that "what begets sacred works is not the life of the world but the life of faith—the faith, however, of our own time."[61] Schwarz replied to the abbot's letter with great interest in the project, stating that he was pleased he was considered and that the task corresponded to what he cherished most in his professional life, namely, building successful churches.[62] He went on to remind the abbot that a number of his buildings had received acclaim and that he would do his best work for the Saint John's brethren.

Modern materials and liturgical notions also inspired the work of Hermann Baur (1894–1980) of Basel, Switzerland.[63] During the rise of the Nazi Party in the early 1920s, Swiss architects took the lead in promoting church design based on modern liturgical and aesthetic principles, and Baur's oeuvre impressed the Collegeville Benedictines. His thirty church designs included the Church of All Saints in Basel (1951). At All Saints, Baur employed reinforced concrete—in the historical manner of Auguste Perret's influential Church of Notre Dame in Raincy, France—leaving it exposed on the interior but facing it with brick on the exterior. Transverse barrel vaults of concrete supported by thin concrete columns provided a

less obstructed view of the altar. Baur added color and symbolism to the building through furnishings made by well-known contemporary artists, something the Benedictines would also find important for the church at Saint John's. The Swiss sculptor Albert Schilling fashioned the altar, French sacred artist Alfred Manessier completed the primary-colored stained glass side chapel window, and the Swiss surrealist/Dadaist Hans (Jean) Arp designed the baptismal font in simple forms not reminiscent of the past. Baur replied to the abbot that he was "honoured" by his letter and he would gladly accept the task.[64] He went on to say that he was not aware of "a monastery which shows at the same time its fundamentally religious character with the features of our time, as an expression of contemporary religious life." He was also pleased that Saint John's was "a center of the liturgical movement, for the 'renovation liturgiae' is indeed the starting-point for our new churches."

In addition to the modern liturgical forms advocated in church design by Baur and Schwarz, the brethren were also naturally interested in speaking with architects who had already worked on monastic commissions. Thus, they added the seventy-one-year-old Albert Bosslet (1880–1957) of Würzburg, Germany, to the list.[65] During his career Bosslet completed more than one hundred churches. Most relevant to the Benedictines was the 1938 extension and restoration of the Benedictine abbey church at Münsterschwarzach,

Germany, a project the building committee discussed in its early deliberations.[66] Bosslet favored a romantic, nationalist approach in his religious design, drawing upon the historical Gothic and classical styles for inspiration while using local stone and brick. Bosslet was not afraid of using concrete and steel under these traditional materials, however, as it opened up interior space for the communal nature sought in liturgical reforms. Bosslet's health prevented him from replying until April 9, 1953, and by this time most of the other invited architects had visited the abbey.

The Austrian representative in the European group was Robert Kramreiter (1905–65) of Vienna, a former assistant to Dominikus Böhm.[67] Kramreiter's book *New Church Art in the Spirit of the Liturgy* (1939), coauthored with the Augustinian canon and liturgical pioneer, Dr. Pius Parsch, impressed the monks. Kramreiter and Parsch both worked in the popular liturgy movement, and Kramreiter also served as president of the Austrian Society for Christian Art. Parsch espoused the same ideal as Guardini, that of preaching directly to laypeople regarding the importance of their participation in the liturgy, a change he sought to make on the parish level. Together with Kramreiter in 1936, Parsch transformed the Church of Saint Gertrude outside the walls of Klosterneuburg, Austria, into an appropriate worship vessel for this need by placing the altar closer to the laity to better facilitate their participation in the Mass. When the monks

sought out Kramreiter, the abbot wrote to Parsch in search of his address, telling Parsch that they were impressed by *New Church Art in the Spirit of the Liturgy* and that they understood the two had worked together.[68] Kramreiter replied to the abbot with great interest, reminding him that he had been working on the Catholic church problem for nearly thirty years, much of that time with Parsch, and he went on to list several of his buildings that had been recently featured in exhibitions and magazine articles, including Queen of Peace Church in Vienna (1935).[69]

The monks of Saint John's considered the final European architect not for his skill as a religious architect but as an urban planner. Thomas W. Sharp (1901–78) of Oxford penned a number of books on urban design, including the influential *Town Planning* (1940), and created master plans for Durham, Salisbury, and Exeter after World War II.[70] In discussing his efforts to rebuild Exeter, Sharp talked about the character of a city, the need to integrate the old and the new, and the importance of good architecture within a good plan.[71] He also realized that monumental religious buildings were at the heart of these great cities. Sharp's understanding of planning fit the brethren's stipulation that the designer of the comprehensive plan did not have to be the architect of its individual buildings. Unlike the other European architects who were first and foremost church builders with some experience in large-scale planning, Sharp understood the concept of centering an environment on a significant church building, a skill set particularly important for the Collegeville commission. He was intensely interested in the project, calling it "an important kind which gives one great satisfaction to work on."[72]

THE AMERICAN-BASED ARCHITECTS

Unfortunately, none of the Europeans ever really had a chance to secure the Saint John's contract. The building committee had worried about a lack of American interest in the project, but this never materialized, as all but two of the seven American-based designers responded favorably to the call.[73] Furthermore, the cost and timing of bringing the European designers to Collegeville concerned the brethren. The building committee wanted to move quickly with the project, specifying that "our selection be made not on the basis of competency in which all are quite equal, but rather on the basis of their ability to make a preliminary investigation without delay."[74] Given their desire to create architecture of international importance, the Benedictines needed to engage designers across the globe, and with the European benchmark covered, they could now focus on the Americans.

The Benedictines' one-hundred-year plan included numerous building types needed for a college, seminary, monastery, and prep school. The project's cornerstone was a church structure

centered on reformed liturgical principles and built in a way that would be "valid for centuries to come." These criteria not only provided a practical framework for the commission, they also dictated that the leading architects in America be considered for the position of architect of Saint John's. So, how would the monks decide on a designer? Because of the complexity of the program, architectural skill mattered. The potential for an architect's long-term connection to the site was just as important, so a candidate's age and relative youth were also factors. Of the seven American-based designers who received the abbot's letter, Belluschi, Byrne, and Murphy had experience designing churches. Breuer, Gropius, Neutra, and Saarinen were well-known designers on an international scale, focusing on domestic space and large-scale planning. All embraced modernism as the cornerstone of their design philosophy.

Pietro Belluschi's (1889–1994) letter of regret arrived in Collegeville on March 17, 1953; in it he explained that his commitments both as a practicing architect and as dean of the School of Architecture and Planning at the Massachusetts Institute of Technology were too great to take on the project (Figure 2.9).[75] He found the challenge of designing a new abbey very exciting and said that "it is not possible for a modern architect not to be impressed and keenly interested" in the offer.[76] In 1938 Belluschi already indicated the importance of giving the church building a new style:

Rather than blindly copying the anachronistic forms of the past, the architect should try to recapture the essence of the type, with a simple, straightforward solution in tune with life as it is, in sympathy with local materials, the people, and the existing landscape.[77]

He agreed with the abbot's desire for significant religious architecture: "I will confess a great fondness for designing religious structures—a creative field in which, as you remarked, so much has to be done yet, and where the modern architect's philosophy is still confused." He offered his services as a consultant to the abbey, provided "they find a capable architect in the vicinity who could furnish the working drawings and supervision." In an article in *Liturgical Arts* three years earlier, Belluschi stated:

> The danger to contemporary religious architecture does not come so much from our right to express ourselves in a modern idiom, but from the fact that so few designers have the gift, the integrity, and the discipline to make such an idiom of convincing significance.[78]

Belluschi would have been a first-rate consultant, for he had already built churches for several different faiths, mostly in the Pacific Northwest. These commissions included the First Presbyterian Church in Cottage Grove, Oregon (1948–51),

FIGURE 2.9. Pietro Belluschi, 1954.

which used local, natural materials and showcased an exceptional handling of light. The Saint John's building committee may also have been aware of Belluschi's ability to work closely with his clients. For example, prior to designing First Presbyterian, Belluschi questioned church representatives intently about the parish's traditions, values, and liturgical needs.[79] At the time of the Collegeville commission, Belluschi was also at work on a Benedictine priory in Portsmouth, Rhode Island (1953–61), including its chapel with geometric forms of wood highlighted by an astute play of light to provide focus on the altar. Materials, forms, and light had become decoration in modern churches.

FIGURE 2.10. Eero Saarinen and Kevin Roche in their Bloomfield Hills, Michigan, office sometime between 1953 and 1961.

Eero Saarinen (1910–61) of Ann Arbor, Michigan, also declined the abbey's invitation (Figure 2.10).[80] The younger Saarinen was near the peak of his career when Saint John's contacted him, owing to his skillful handling of many building types and large-scale planning, including projects such as the Jefferson National Expansion Memorial in St. Louis (1947–48) and the General Motors Technical Center in Warren, Michigan (1948–56). Also under way were a small nondenominational chapel and auditorium (1950–55) at the Massachusetts Institute of Technology. In the two buildings at MIT, Saarinen used the boldness of an engineered modernism to create an otherworldly sense of space, a facet of mod-

ern architecture that he felt was more important than a sense of mass.[81] Several brethren had seen the church he finished with his father, Eliel, in Minneapolis in 1949, Christ Church Lutheran, where the Saarinens used a light buff-colored brick to shape a rectangular building with tower in the manner of Karl Moser's work in Basel.[82] The building's scale and humble use of materials also responded to its context, a working-class neighborhood of bungalows. The exterior clearly reveals the interior of the building, a tour de force of simplicity in its use of exposed brick in very slight variations of color. Lighting plays an important role in the church. Although the only illumination source for the nave is the bank of windows in the side aisle, the light-colored brick reflects light rather than absorbs it. Saarinen saved the strongest light source for the altar, bathing it in a strong white light that draws the participant's focus to the important point in the building. Christ Church is one of the Saarinens' greatest designs. In 2002 the American Institute of Architects designated it as one of the thirty-one structures that "changed modern life."[83] The younger Saarinen's reputation made him attractive to many clients, and his reply to Abbot Dworschak stated that his firm's current commitments would tax them for the next ten to fifteen months, but he did find the abbey's planning problem "complex but an exceedingly interesting challenge."[84] Like Belluschi, Saarinen undoubtedly regretted not being able to tackle a commission that would showcase his skill at creating exceptional buildings of many different types.

The remaining five Americans on the list—Breuer, Byrne, Gropius, Murphy, and Neutra—visited the abbey. The architect site visits provided a chance for the Benedictines to study their potential designer, to understand his human qualities as well as his architectural abilities. The Benedictines took each guest around campus, showed him the church, the dormitories, the stairwell congestion, the land, and took him to the distant high ground to view the campus.[85]

At midcentury the California-based architect Richard Neutra (1892–1970) was second only to Frank Lloyd Wright in popularity, and *Time* magazine had put him on its August 15, 1949, cover (Figure 2.11).[86] Early twentieth-century European modernism, with a Wrightian interlude, shaped the Austrian-born Neutra's architectural aesthetic. He studied under Adolf Loos in Vienna and Erich Mendelsohn in Berlin before leaving for the United States in 1923. He made his way to Southern California after a nearly two-year stay in Chicago, working as a draftsman in the offices of Frank Lloyd Wright and William Holabird and Martin Roche. Once in California he opened his own practice out of the studio of fellow Austrian architect Rudolf M. Schindler. Neutra fashioned a modern International Style for Southern California in works such as the Philip Lovell Health House in Los Angeles (1928–29), a project Esther McCoy claimed put American modernism

on an international stage, as it was "through this house that Los Angeles architecture first became widely known in Europe."[87] Neutra integrated a machine aesthetic with nature, as seen in his design for the Kaufmann House in Palm Springs, California (1946), where the glass, stucco, and natural stone building was set carefully into the desert landscape. He worked easily with large-scale construction, too, having spent time building skyscrapers in Chicago with Holabird and Roche before moving on to design the California Military Academy (1936) and the competition entry for the new Goucher College in Towson, Maryland (1938).

Neutra's acceptance of the Collegeville invitation revealed an interest in creating architecture that was conceptually pure and a sincere

FIGURE 2.11. Richard J. Neutra, 1959.

expression of its day. He recalled the monasteries he had visited during his childhood in Austria, finding them impressive in "the minds of today with convictions and convincing power that has never turned obsolete. It should be a blessing to produce such genuine value today."[88] The monks picked up Neutra at the airport in Minneapolis on the evening of March 23, 1953. On doctor's orders because of a heart condition, he brought along his architect son, Dion. He spent his visit looking over the site and crawling through the extant buildings with Mr. Blattner, a local building contractor.[89] He talked extensively with the brethren, and according to Kacmarcik, Neutra put on a spectacular show, memorizing long passages from the Rule of Saint Benedict and quoting them in Latin, as well as making sure his *Time* magazine cover was on the table at most meetings.[90] He also asked questions about the nature of the Benedictine Order, stating that he found the tradition of the order to be "characterized by mildness, discretion and moderation and these characteristics were to be found in its architecture." He discussed the local historical component with the brethren and asked if they wanted to use a regional idiom for the design, even though Neutra did not think that this would be the best way to proceed. He did not promote any one architectural style, but instead made it known that he was interested in staying true to the spirit of architecture in the temperate zones. "The forms of Italy, Greece, and

the southern U.S. are moderate," he said, "not the harsh emphatic forms of Nordic Islands." Neutra went on to tell the brethren that these forms were now possible in the north because of advances in climatic and temperature control. One of the brothers immediately interpreted this to mean International Style architecture and stated that Saint John's might not want this approach. To this Neutra calmly replied, "I certainly am not a representative of the International Style—Mr. Gropius is that."

Walter Gropius (1883–1969) arrived at the abbey the day before Neutra left, and the two shared breakfast together that morning (Figure 2.12).[91] Neutra was right: Gropius was a representative of the International Style, seen most clearly in his designs for the Bauhaus in Dessau, Germany (1925–26) with its sense of volume, lack of applied ornament, free plan, and asymmetricality driven by industry, technology, and the machine. Gropius, among others, brought the International Style to the United States in the post–World War I years, when he emigrated from England (having moved there to escape Nazi persecution in Germany) and began teaching at the Graduate School of Design at Harvard University. His pedagogical style was a powerful counterpoint to the classical- and traditional-based Beaux-Arts methods well established at American schools of architecture, including the Massachusetts Institute of Technology and the University of Pennsylvania.[92]

As an architectural educator from 1937 until 1952, Gropius taught many young American architects the characteristics of the new, modern architecture. He also built in the style, completing several houses in the region, including his own home in Lincoln, Massachusetts (1937), with the help of his friend and former Bauhaus colleague Marcel Breuer.

Gropius arrived as a representative of the Architects Collaborative in Cambridge. In his mid-March reply to the invitation, he shared examples of previous campus planning with the monks, including the Graduate Center at Harvard University and Hua Tung University in Shanghai.[93] During his Collegeville visit, Gropius pored over all aspects of the site and its buildings.[94] He talked to the brethren about good planning and about the proper use of materials. He called the extant church's design quality "middling" and recommended that the monks remove the top floor of the quadrangle to give the buildings more pleasing proportions, which for him meant more horizontal proportions like that favored by the International Style. Gropius listened to the monks carefully, and in discussions with the brethren he rarely mentioned religion or theology. The monks liked his practical, problem-solving approach to design. Unlike Neutra, who pushed his own architecture at every turn, the monks appreciated Gropius's humility. Gropius brought out examples of his own architecture, a skyscraper

FIGURE 2.12. Walter Gropius, Le Corbusier, Marcel Breuer, and Sven Markelius discussing plans for the new UNESCO complex, Paris, 1952.

project for the McCormicks in Chicago, at the very end of his visit, sharing it with just a few of the brethren.[95]

Gropius and Neutra were notable architects, and the building committee wanted to hire someone prominent in the field, regardless of religious background. A small group of the breth-

FIGURE 2.13. Joseph D. Murphy.

ren wanted a Catholic architect, so Joseph Denis Murphy (1908–95) of St. Louis, Missouri, was on the list (Figure 2.13). At the April 20, 1953, building committee meeting Father Stanley stated that Murphy was a good, versatile, Catholic architect—but not a great one—who should be considered for the commission.[96] Murphy attended architecture school at MIT and in 1923 won a nationwide competition to attend the École des Beaux-Arts in Paris for three years.[97] In addition to building four churches in the St. Louis area, Murphy and his partner, Eugene J. Mackey, had also planned hospitals, schools, office buildings, and an urban redevelopment scheme for old St. Louis. Murphy also served as the dean of the Col-

lege of Architecture at Washington University in St. Louis from 1948 to 1952.

After his arrival on the afternoon of April 7, Murphy looked over the site and recommended that the Benedictines take greater advantage of the lake in their new plan, feeling that they had neglected it thus far.[98] He recommended building modern new structures of glass and brick as the glass would foster an open feeling and the brick would harmonize with the extant redbrick buildings of the first abbey. When asked to talk about his own work, Murphy impressed the brethren with construction photographs of his 1950 design of Saint Ann Catholic Church in Normandy, Missouri, a building indicative of the engineered, brick architecture he proposed for Saint John's. But when he showed the group slides of the church's completed interior, the brethren were not impressed, feeling that the possibilities suggested by the engineering were not present in the finished product; as Father Meinberg stated, "The structure becomes the framework of the beauty of the architecture—as it was in Gothic times. This is absolutely essential to good modern architecture."[99] The brethren, knowing that a modern engineered architecture would influence the design of their buildings, worried that Murphy and Mackey—who contracted out all their engineering rather than doing it in-house like the offices of Gropius and Neutra—might not be up to the task. Although Murphy lacked the talent and status of the others, his Catholic faith and the strong recommendation by the well-respected stained glass artist Emil Frei enabled him to be part of this prestigious list. This type of personal, networked connection also brought Marcel Breuer to Saint John's.

Marcel Breuer's (1902–81) work prior to Saint John's focused on domestic architecture, and for this reason, according to Frank Kacmarcik, he made the list of selected architects (Figure 2.14). On a trip to New York City in the summer of 1949, Kacmarcik visited Breuer's exhibition house at the Museum of Modern Art and was greatly impressed by his handling of the domestic challenge (Figure 2.15).[100] The brethren liked Breuer's work in the May 1952 issue of *House and Home*, which devoted several pages to domestic designs.[101] Kacmarcik put Breuer on the list because his domestic architecture could positively inform the monastic and student dorms, and because Breuer had a reputation for being adept with innovative, modern forms.

Breuer was born in Pécs, Hungary, and studied art on a scholarship in Vienna at the Akademie der bildenden Kunst, imagining then, according to biographer Isabelle Hyman, that his future career would likely be as a sculptor (Figure 2.16).[102] His stay in Vienna was brief, somewhere between six and eight weeks. The conservatism and limitations of traditional classical instruction frustrated Breuer, but fortunately one of his friends told him about a new kind of art school in Weimar, Germany.[103] Breuer entered the Bauhaus in the fall of 1920 in its second class, studying under Swiss designer Johannes Itten in his preliminary course before entering the carpentry workshop. He remained at the Bauhaus until 1924, when he left for a year to work with architect Pierre Chareau in Paris before returning to head the furniture workshop at the Dessau Bauhaus until 1928, when he left for good.

The Bauhaus method gave Breuer a broad view of design and an understanding of many artistic elements that would later shape his buildings,

FIGURE 2.14. Marcel Breuer, ca. 1950s.

FIGURE 2.15. Marcel Breuer's exhibition house in the courtyard of the Museum of Modern Art, summer 1949.

from furniture to door handles to art. The Bauhaus also eliminated the differences between artist and artisan, pushing Breuer to focus attention and clarity of purpose on every part of his buildings. His knowledge of architecture grew as well during his stay, not from any formal training provided by the school but through time spent with Walter Gropius.[104]

After leaving Dessau, Breuer headed to Berlin, where he practiced architecture in a small flat a few doors down from Gropius until 1935, when Gropius convinced him to follow him to London. Upon his arrival he joined the firm of Francis Reginald Stevens (F. R. S.) Yorke, one of the few English architects interested in the modern movement. In England Breuer continued designing domestic architecture, the mainstay of his career until the years after World War II. In 1937 Gropius again persuaded Breuer to change his location, inviting him to come to the United States and teach with him in the architectural school at Harvard. Breuer not only taught at Harvard with Gropius, they also went into practice together until a falling-out in 1941. The war intervened, and finally in 1946 Breuer set up shop in New York City, eventually forming Marcel Breuer and Associates. It was on the firm's behalf that he would visit Saint John's.

Breuer arrived at the abbey on April 17, 1953. He prefaced this visit with a written reply to the abbot's call for architects, in which he stated that he was enthusiastic about the possibilities of the

FIGURE 2.16. Marcel Breuer, *The Athlete*. His only public sculpture is located outside the Warner Palaestra Athletic Complex on the Saint John's campus.

project and moved by the abbot's reference to "modern" architecture, believing that "the potentialities of this architecture have not been sufficiently recognized up to now, and that, generally speaking, our religious buildings have not taken full advantage of them."[105] He spent time studying the existing structures, asking and answering questions, and listening to the brethren.[106] Father Meinberg recalled his visit: "The most tight-lipped of all was Breuer. It was almost two hours before Breuer uttered a full sentence. . . . If he did not know the answer, he said so. By the time he talked to the community that night he made very good sense."[107] At the evening meeting Breuer would have discussed his views of contemporary modern architecture with the brethren, indicating a dislike of what he called "Hollywood modern" and mere fashionableness in design. He desired more depth in architecture, part of which would come from the use of engineering as a key element of the design process, echoing Father Meinberg's notion that structure was essential in good modern architecture. For Breuer this architecture was demonstrative, providing a Gothic analogy: "The way the weight of the building was supported (or the engineering) was actually the form of the church as it demonstrated the engineering." Although Breuer was trained in the modernist idiom at the Bauhaus, he had an excellent understanding of and respect for historical design, penning the preface to the Egyptian volume of the Living Architecture series in 1964.[108] For Breuer, Egyptian and modern architecture shared simplicity, an architectural underpinning that the Benedictines also sought in their liturgically reformed worship space.

During his visit, the monks questioned Breuer about his ability to design religious architecture. When asked if he had ever built a church, Breuer said, "No . . . actually none of the leading architects ever had." The brethren also asked if he thought it necessary that the architect be a practicing Catholic. Breuer replied that "he was a Lutheran and that he certainly would understand if the brethren chose a Catholic, in that there were many details that a Catholic would know because he was a Catholic." Breuer went on to say that it was more important to speak of the expressive nature of design in executing a church commission and he wanted the Saint John's building to exhibit something more than pure Catholic functionalism. He compared this aspiration to his design for the UNESCO (United Nations Educational, Scientific and Cultural Organization) complex in Paris (1952–58), which exemplified a new tradition using modern forms in shaping modern space (Figure 2.17). He later described this concept:

The rhythm of space is that of its structure, despite important differences of technology and form; in the old days, stone on stone,

FIGURE 2.17. The conference building at UNESCO, Paris (shown here in the foreground under construction), was the design precursor for the abbey church.

held in place by the weight of the parts—now, one flowing line of concrete held in place by the continuity of integral steel bars.[109]

Breuer made it clear that his building would be without a great deal of the traditional elements often present in church design. Yet, even though he was an architect of great skill, Breuer lacked the familiarity of practice in Catholic sacred space. One architect who had expertise in this area was Barry Byrne (1883–1967), and in the three-day period between Breuer's departure and the final meeting to select the architect, Byrne made the trip to central Minnesota (Figure 2.18).

As noted earlier, the Catholic Byrne had

the right experience for the job, including the completion of several important churches in the United States and Ireland and, more important, a specific involvement with the Liturgical Reform movement in America.[110] In addition to the new, modern plan published in *Liturgical Arts*, Byrne also addressed the distinction of modern versus traditional decorative forms in church design. He minimized decoration and used motifs influenced by art deco's streamlined and stylized forms. From project to project, these forms became even more modern and reductive and eventually were subsumed by the building in the series of "fish churches" Byrne completed from 1947 to 1950. Labeled "fish" because of their oval

FIGURE 2.18. Barry Byrne, ca. 1950.

shape, these highly symbolic buildings solidified the aims of liturgical reformers. The churches of Saint Francis Xavier in Kansas City, Missouri (1947), and Saint Columba in St. Paul, Minnesota (1950), integrated the nave and altar space in the same way as Byrne's earlier churches (Figure 2.19). To shape this sacred space, Byrne used malleable concrete—a building material whose engineering virtues he had been espousing since his 1933 *Liturgical Arts* article "A Philosophy of Design for Concrete."[111]

Byrne was also a good candidate because of his familiarity with monastic design and his many previous visits to Collegeville.[112] In 1945 he finished the master plan for the Abbey of Saint Benedict in Atchinson, Kansas, and in 1953 he designed Saint Columbanus's Seminary in Milton, Massachusetts. Yet even with his extensive background, Byrne's trip to Collegeville lacked the formal sanction granted to the four architects who preceded him. Byrne did receive an official letter of invitation from the abbot in March, but on April 2, 1953, he got notice that it was not necessary for him to travel to Minnesota. The building committee recommended only Murphy and Breuer be asked to come for preliminary discussions, given the success of Neutra's and Gropius's visits.[113] They believed that one of these four men would be a suitable candidate for the position, and Abbot Dworschak did not want to give Byrne false hopes of obtaining the commission.

Byrne came anyway, postponing his trip by five days to accommodate Breuer's visit. Byrne could sense that the commission would not be his, as he told the abbot, "I am glad that you are to meet Marcel Breuer. All architects who profess, or exploit, modernism are not necessarily talented. Mr. Breuer is one of the few exceptions and, for what it is worth, he has my respect."[114] Byrne's visit to the abbey also encouraged the monks to follow through on this extraordinary project, as Abbot Dworschak noted in a letter to Byrne shortly after he left:

I know that the members of the Building Committee and other members of the community appreciated your visit and your graciously giving of your time and experience

FIGURE 2.19. Barry Byrne's midcentury concrete Church of Saint Columba, St. Paul, Minnesota.

to answer their questions and to explain the wisdom of a comprehensive plan for an institution such as this. I feel, that as a result of your visit, the members of the community are now quite enthusiastic about our comprehensive plan, for I know some had doubts.[115]

THE BENEDICTINES SELECT AN ARCHITECT

Byrne's convincing the monastic community of the value of a planned, well-constructed expansion was easy in comparison to the brethren's task of selecting their architect. On April 20, 1953, the monks began their deliberations. Three key concerns emerge from the minutes of their discussions. Their focus on designers' architectural ability is no surprise. They were also extremely interested in each architect's religious preference, his age, and his health. The Benedictines were not hiring just a great architect; they were looking for an exceptional person filled with character, vigor, and real concern for their project. They also wanted someone whose youth would keep him around to see the design through to its completion, years, even decades, down the road.

When it came to architectural skill, the only person with a perceived deficit was Murphy, who was not viewed on the same level with Breuer, Byrne, Gropius, or Neutra. As Father Paschal had pointed out at a building committee meeting on April 21, 1953, it would be "better to choose an artist who is not a Catholic than a Catholic who is not an artist."[116] Paschal's statement leads us into the second consideration, the religious affiliation of each man. Several members of the community wanted a Catholic architect at all costs, even if that decision resulted in a design of lesser quality. Although they liked the Catholic Murphy, his talent did not match that of the others. With regards to Neutra the brethren noted that he "never gave any indication of practising any religion," and when Neutra was told there was a split in the community between hiring a good architect and hiring a Catholic architect, he replied that "he did not feel he had to be a Catholic, but that he must be a believer."[117] It was not clear what Gropius's religious status was, but the minutes note that he did not talk much when religious notions were brought up.[118] This reticence made the monks hesitant about his ability to understand their project. Breuer was born a Jew, but he denounced the faith at a young age, filing papers with the Official Provincial Rabbinate in Dessau in 1926.[119] At the time of the Saint John's interview, Breuer was Lutheran.[120] The final consideration was age: relative youth was important since the many buildings of this plan would take years to build. Gropius was seventy years old, yet the monks found him to be very nimble and apparently in good health. Byrne was also seventy. Neutra was sixty-one and had a heart condition that required him to rest often. Breuer and Murphy were in their early fifties and mid-forties, respectively, and full of energy. According to Frank Kacmarcik, Gropius told the Benedictines during his visit that a young guy like Breuer would be right for the job.[121]

In the end, religion, youth, character, and architectural expertise came together best in one man, and on April 23, 1953, four days after they had started deliberating, the monastic community in Collegeville selected Marcel Breuer as the architect of their comprehensive plan. His various comments and suggestions demonstrated a grasp of their entire project that neither Neutra, Gropius, Murphy, nor Byrne could rival.[122] As Isabelle Hyman has noted, the monks liked Breuer because he would listen to them, an important factor given his lack of knowledge about church design, Catholicism, new liturgical notions, or monasticism.[123] They appreciated Breuer's inclination to rely on engineering principles in design, as well as his preference for employing basic materials in their undisguised and natural state. Most important, however, was his unassuming, attentive style and his youth—his readiness to discuss and follow up on his designs. As Abbot Dworschak stated in his letter to the community:

He struck us as being not only an outstanding architect, but also a simple, straightforward, sincere and rather humble person. This combined with his zeal for achieving the best possible results, recommended him in every way to the monastic community of Saint John's.[124]

Abbot Dworschak called Breuer at home on Saturday, April 25, to inform him of the decision. Breuer's written response three days later indicated his pleasure with the outcome: "I am looking forward with the greatest enthusiasm to this task." He closed the letter: "Again my deepest appreciation for your, and your community's confidence."[125] Meanwhile, the abbot asked his community to support the choice: "I do not hesitate to ask you all to accept him and to cooperate with him in whatever manner you are asked to do so. Since such a plan is certain to have a vital effect on our community spirit, I beg of you to continue praying that in all this God may be glorified."[126]

RECONSIDERING THE TWELVE MIDCENTURY ARCHITECTURAL APOSTLES

The monks were fortunate to find Breuer, who, according to many, including Byrne and Gropius, was the only true artist in the group. In retrospect, however, had the brethren included the most qualified designers on their original list of twelve? In addition to the final candidates, other names came up during their deliberations and consultations with notable artists and religious persons. At the March 4, 1953, senior council meeting, the monks discussed nine men as potential architects for the project.[127] Several of those made the final list, including the Europeans Baur, Bosslet, Schwarz, and Sharp, and the Americans Belluschi, Neutra, and Saarinen. Three additional architects—Edward J. Schulte and the brothers Edo J. Belli and Anthony J. Belli—did not. The Roman Catholic, Cincinnati-based Schulte built dozens of churches for the faith from 1921 to 1967, "more churches by a single man than . . . any other architect in the history of Cincinnati."[128] Schulte had learned architecture as an apprentice in Cincinnati and was not formally educated beyond high school. His interest in building churches was entirely self-motivated, and his knowledge of church design was self-taught. Ralph Adams Cram, with his love of the Gothic and his honest use of materials, made a great impression on Schulte at a candlelight lecture Cram delivered in Pittsburgh in late 1912. Sir Banister Fletcher's *A History of Architecture on the Comparative Method* (1896) provided him with models to copy and ornamental details on which to focus.[129] Schulte's churches were built mainly in the lower Midwest states, but included his Gothic-inspired chapel at Mount Marty College in Yankton, South Dakota of 1946. The Benedictines at Saint John's would have been familiar with his work from their missionary travels and from periodicals such as *Liturgical Arts*, which published a good number of Schulte's ecclesiastical designs.

Edo J. Belli and Anthony J. Belli started their firm in 1941 and almost instantly became favorites of Samuel Cardinal Stritch, archbishop of the Archdiocese of Chicago.[130] Through their numerous commissions for Stritch they met many Benedictine abbots, leading to the commission for Marmion Abbey in Aurora, Illinois, in the early 1950s. In order to understand the Benedictine way of life, the brothers lived in the monastery as monks for three days. *Liturgical Arts* also published a number of Belli and Belli's designs.

In addition to the Belli brothers and Schulte, Abbot Dworschak and the building committee also considered architects recommended by others, including two Mexican architects, Carlos Lazo and Juan O'Gorman, whose work at the University of Mexico City impressed the brethren. Maurice Lavanoux, editor of *Liturgical Arts* magazine, suggested the additions of Town Planning Associates, headed by Josep Lluís Sert, the town-planning firm Pal Lest Weiner, and William Lescaze.[131] American stained glass master Emil Frei of St. Louis, Missouri, noted that Mies van der Rohe was absent from the list as was Bruce Goff, a man he called "one of the most imaginative architects."[132] Mies van der Rohe had built only one religious space in his career, the Robert F. Carr Memorial Chapel of Saint Savior (1952) on the campus of the Illinois Institute of Technology. Saint Savior's exhibited the rational side of modernism as its brick, steel, and glass box bore no exterior resemblance to a traditional church. Goff's reputation rested on his Boston

Avenue Methodist Episcopal Church (1929) in Tulsa, Oklahoma. Frei also mentioned Frank Lloyd Wright but stated that Wright was a "bit too old to be considered for a continuing project."[133]

Of these men, Schulte and the Bellis were similar to Murphy in their regional leadership in church design and their Catholic background. Lescaze, Mies, and Wright were, like Gropius, men with prolific careers but getting on in years. Mies's architecture was cold, calculated, and very rational, an unlikely match with the Benedictines. Sert came from Breuer's generation of modernism, and his emblematic works, such as the concrete apartment towers on the Charles River in Boston, shared Breuer's love of the same building material.

Given their interest in concrete, the work of Oscar Niemeyer should have struck a chord with the committee. His Church of Saint Francis of Assisi in Pampulha, Brazil (1943), used concrete curving parabolas over a T-shaped plan, in a building called the most daring exploration in concrete since Perret's work at Raincy.[134] This was a new version of modernism that went beyond the rectilinear nature of the early twentieth century, as Niemeyer noted: "Rationalism, limited as it was, did not express the new world of shapes made possible by reinforced concrete," explaining why he "covered the chapel at Pampulha with curves."[135] The local bishop did not like the building upon its completion and would not consecrate it until 1959.

Niemeyer's architectural mentor, Le Corbusier, had it easier in France. Given the familiarity of his 1950 design for Notre Dame du Haut in Ronchamp, France, Le Corbusier is perhaps the most notable omission from the Benedictine's list. His chapel dedicated to the Virgin Mary quickly became one of the icons of modern architecture and is included in every survey book on modern architecture ever published. It dramatically changed the path of the modern movement in architecture, moving away from the rectilinear nature of Bauhaus-inspired modernism to a more plastic version in which materials such as concrete created curvilinear and flowing forms.[136] The chapel at Ronchamp was extremely influential, even affecting the design at Saint John's, as we shall see in the next chapter.

The Benedictines sought something more than an admired architect, however. Even above the aforementioned determining criteria—architectural reputation, experience, religious identity, and health—they placed collaboration. They were looking for a designer who would have his own vision and style, but who would listen to what they wanted to achieve. Deciding on Breuer showed that a man of character was essential to the success of this commission and that a good artist did not need to be a Catholic. The time for cooperation had come as the Benedictines and Breuer and his associates sought the architectural solution most supportive to liturgical reform.

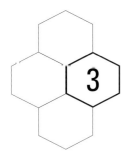

3   BUILDING THE SPIRITUAL AXIS

Marcel Breuer and the Benedictines
Design a Modern Catholic Church

When the invited architects visited Collegeville in the spring of 1953, they toured the campus, talked with the brethren, and spent time in meeting rooms in the nineteenth-century complex. The Benedictine community made it clear during the interview process that the selected architect's primary focus was the comprehensive plan for the monastery and university, and not necessarily the design of buildings within it, as architects for those commissions would be selected later.[1] But with the hiring of Marcel Breuer and Associates to plan a new, modern campus, they knew that with this gifted design team they no longer had to worry about additional competitions to find architects for each individual structure, including the abbey church (Figure 3.1).[2]

The church was an instant focal point for Breuer and his team. They recognized its significance within the overall plan and worked intently on its design from the start. The complexity of the church's program, a combination of monastic space and regular parish space reflecting new liturgical reforms, would be a challenge even for an architect familiar with the workings of the Catholic faith. Its function centered on the "spiritual axis," a term I have coined for worshippers' processional way based on monasticism, liturgical reform, and modern design. The building highlights a unity of these elements through its form, its emphasis on the holy sacraments and their accessories, and the use of the vernacular language and customs. Clarity and simplicity were key to the church's integrity, as supported by the German bishops and the Holy See:

Sacred architecture, even when it takes new forms, cannot in any way resemble profane edifices, but must always perform its own

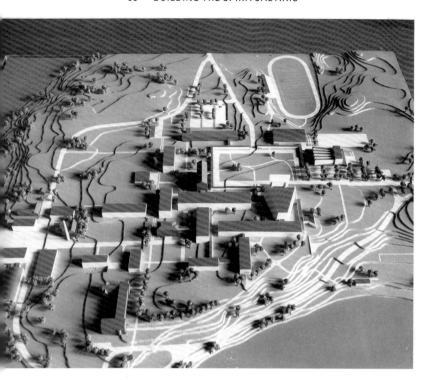

FIGURE 3.1. Marcel Breuer's 1953 campus plan for Saint John's would have eliminated most of the original buildings on the site.

task, which is to build the house of God and a house of prayer. In the construction of churches, the comfort of the faithful should be satisfied so that they can participate of the divine offices with clearer sight and better disposition of spirit. Also a new church should shine in the simplicity of its lines, eschewing indecorous ornamentation; anything that speaks of negligence in its conception and execution should be avoided.[3]

The Benedictines played a crucial role in guiding their architect through the complexities of the project, and this chapter details their collaboration.

ASSEMBLING THE DESIGN TEAM

Hamilton Smith served as the Breuer office lead for the project. Smith had a degree in architecture from Yale and experience in the office of Eero Saarinen before joining Breuer's team in New York City in 1953. Robert Gatje, a Cornell graduate who worked for Percival Goodman before joining Breuer in 1953, was also vital to the project. Breuer sent architect Valerius L. Michelson to manage the site.[4] Like Gatje, Michelson came to Breuer in 1953 from the office of Goodman. Michelson was Russian born and trained, having studied architecture at the National Academy of Fine Arts in Leningrad from 1935 to 1941. After surviving World War II (he escaped from a German prison camp in Russia), he attended the Technische Hochschule in Karlsruhe, Germany, before immigrating to the United States with his wife in 1949. In 1952 he completed an architecture degree at Columbia University while working in Goodman's office.

Michelson was the liaison between Breuer's office and the site team. He worked closely with the local associated architect from St. Cloud, Minnesota, Ray T. Hermanson, and the construction crew from McGough and Associates of St. Paul,

Minnesota.[5] As it was with the selection of the architect, the religious affiliation of the builder also came under scrutiny, not by the monks but by Hamilton Smith, who noted on a letter of February 28, 1959, "I bet there is some feeling that Church should be built by Catholic builders to offset the 'heathen' architect."[6] Even though the religious affiliation of a builder or architect was still foremost in the minds of some, in reality, McGough had presented the lowest bid for the job.[7]

Ted Hoffmeyer was the field superintendent for McGough Construction (Figure 3.2).[8] He obtained degrees in mechanical and structural engineering before moving to Siberia in 1929 to work for Albert Kahn, building cities for the Soviets until 1932. During World War II, Hoffmeyer built airports for the U.S. military. Upon seeing the 1957 model of the abbey's church in a Universal Atlas Cement advertisement, he convinced Pete McGough to hire him as the field superintendent.[9] Hoffmeyer's ingenuity and perseverance helped create the structure Breuer and the Benedictines wanted.

The Benedictines approved construction of the abbey church on April 22, 1958. They had not been able to begin work in 1957 as they had hoped because of a lack of funds. But now, in addition to raising $245,000 in donations, the monks noted that construction bids for St. Thomas Aquinas Hall, the student dormitory under way, had come in $250,000 less than the government budget for the building. This in turn affected the loan and

interest figures. The monks remarked that "the work of Mr. Breuer and his engineers is careful and substantial, not wasteful or extravagant."[10] McGough Construction was also standing by its original bid on the church, and the costs of steel and concrete had dropped. On-site work began on May 19, 1958.

Building the church was not an easy feat.[11] Creation of the concrete shell alone required

FIGURE 3.2. McGough Construction field superintendent Ted Hoffmeyer was essential in crafting the abbey church.

more than 250 pages of shop drawings, more than sixty-three boxcarloads of lumber from the western United States for the formwork, and 2,500 tons of concrete.[12] Twenty-seven different trades worked on the project; most dominant in numbers and importance were the carpenters who put up the formwork for the large-scale concrete pours. The brethren aided the construction crew, and from the onset of construction there was at least one brother on the job. Brothers Julius Terfehr and Stephen Thell put in over 6,500 hours of work on the church, inserting the steel reinforcing rod and bush hammering the concrete. The clerics also joined in, working over 3,200 hours, mostly during the first summer of construction, digging the foundations of the church and unloading the lumber needed for the formwork from the railroad boxcars.[13] But none of this work could start until Breuer and his team crafted the architectural solution appropriate for their client, and to do so, they first needed an education.

A BENEDICTINE EDUCATION OF ARCHITECTS AND BUILDERS

On April 27, 1953, Breuer wrote to Saint John's asking for:

1. The Building Committee Report to the Community of March 3, 1953
2. Site plans of all the existing buildings, including the function of each space within
3. 1/16" scale plans and sections of existing buildings for an understanding of the structural parts and dimensions
4. Notes, comments, and ideas—even contradictory ones—from the community
5. Father Cloud's report on churches of the Benedictine order
6. A list of informative books or articles
7. A program of expansion for the next 5–10–50 years in terms of function[14]

Just over a month later, on June 4, 1953, Breuer and Smith visited Collegeville for three days.[15] They studied the existing nineteenth-century structures at Collegeville, compiling a thick binder of notes that included a history of the many parishes run by the Benedictines in the Upper Midwest and gathering maps of the site, aerial photographs, plans, and descriptions of the abbey buildings. They also completed space and occupancy study drawings of the nineteenth-century church and quadrangle.[16] The team spent a great deal of time talking with the brethren, and most important, they observed how the monks used their space. They wanted to see how the Benedictines moved to work and worship from various locations on-site, and how these patterns changed through the course of a day. The Benedictines had sent ahead a "Daily Schedule of Priest Members of St. John's Abbey, Collegeville, Minnesota," so the team had an idea of the times and locations of the Divine Office, Masses, meetings, and meals.[17]

In addition to understanding the layout and workings of the site, Breuer and his team had to learn about the history of monasticism and liturgical reform.[18] Naturally they read the Rule of St. Benedict, a copy of which remains in the Breuer office files at Syracuse.[19] The Benedictines recommended other works, including E.C. Butler's *Benedictine Monachism*. Hamilton Smith's notes from his reading of Butler's work highlight the importance of the community, rather than the individual, and emphasize the high level of liturgical observance or "work of God" that the group observed throughout the day.[20] Smith also noted that the "importance of the liturgy makes [the] church itself important" and "the focus of the community." The office also read "The Monastic Ideal" by Dom Aelred Silliem. In this work Silliem emphasized the Benedictine family life, a strong connection to one's locale, and the use of manual labor to provide economic rewards for the common good, all traits that manifest themselves later in the design and construction of the church.[21]

The Benedictines passed along liturgical ideas to Breuer's office via reviews of books such as Peter F. Anson's *Churches: Their Plan and Furnishing* and Hans Ansgar Reinhold's *Speaking of Liturgical Architecture*.[22] The former Benedictine monk Anson provided sensible knowledge of liturgical matters for patrons commissioning Catholic art and architecture. His text situated church plans, fonts, sacred vestments, and bells into their historical contexts before providing the legislative rules for their placement and use in the current day. Reverend Reinhold's work focused on the liturgical setting, particularly the placement of items such as altars, lecterns, and baptismal fonts. During construction of the abbey's church, liturgist John O'Connell provided useful information for the Benedictines and Breuer in his *Church Building and Furnishing: The Church's Way*. His work, like Anson's, was a detailed look at the historical, theological, and practical aspects of church design. Breuer and his team also received essays by Father Meinberg that united art, liturgy, and monasticism, including "The Orientation of Church" and "The Monastic Church."[23] Meinberg told Breuer that he sent these essays not to criticize but with the thought of "perfecting what I hope will be the best religious building in America. I want to assure you also that the Art Department will be very happy and proud to cooperate with you in the design of any works you may wish."[24]

In addition to books and articles, Breuer, Smith, and Gatje explored the history of monastic architecture for design inspiration. The Benedictines in Collegeville had a strong connection with their colleagues at Maria Laach in Germany, primarily because of the liturgical reform movement, and Breuer was encouraged to visit Maria Laach on one of his many trips to Europe. He did so in the fall of 1953, with a letter of introduction from Abbot Dworschak.[25] Breuer's office archives at Syracuse University contain not only site and floor plans of Maria Laach but also two copies of its guidebook, one in German and one in French.[26] Hamilton Smith made a careful study of Maria Laach's plan, noting room functions on it in yellow pencil. With this research complete, Breuer and his associates could begin the design work and start an architectural workshop with the Benedictines.

FINDING LITURGICALLY APPROPRIATE ARCHITECTURAL FORM

Breuer's general approach to design was, according to former partner Robert Gatje, rather mysterious. He began by studying the needs of the client and through basic instinct sought to form a shape appropriate to them. Breuer conveyed his ideas to his clients by explaining how the function of the building created the form. He was not a great draftsman and drew his architectural studies more as an artist, with a wavy black line in ballpoint pen or with a 2B pencil. The draftsmen and associates would make refinements to these ideas, with Breuer's continual guidance and insights.[27] Breuer recalls making "various sketches of the church and the bell tower. I usually give sketches of parts of the buildings to the office, and they develop them. Hamilton Smith, one of my associates, worked closely with me."[28]

Breuer and his team formulated a shape for the church through an analysis of the building's requirements. The Benedictines asked for space to house 1,110 collegians, high school students, and seminarians, as well as 180 monastic brethren. Breuer and his associates worked through the problem in word and image on an analysis sheet called the "Story of a Church and Connected Problems" in July 1953 (Figure 3.3).[29] They came up with five different solutions. The first idea was to build in the manner of the old church, a Latin cross plan with the choir in the transept arms. Breuer vetoed this version because the two parts of the choir created a large void between them. Next, the associates offered a traditional English layout with a screen separating the laity from the choir, the monks' stalls arranged perpendicularly to the screen in three parallel rows, and the altar positioned at the easternmost end. This layout obscured the altar from the nave and therefore was not practical for a church that needed to include the laity in the worship service. The third solution called for the placement of a square choir below grade with low screens separating it from the rest of the church, which proved impractical because it did not help to define the overall form of the church. The fourth option organized the space in a triangular shape, with a progression of congregation, choir, and altar, but this created problems with circulation and again the altar was located, as Breuer noted, "too far away from the congregation."

Finally, the office discovered the answer that would best serve their clients' needs. They decided to place the altar between the congregation and choir in a form that combined a trapezoid (for the congregation) and square (for the choir). This combination of shapes quickly transformed into a single trapezoid, a form familiar to Breuer from his 1936 Garden City of the Future (also known as the Concrete City) and the 1953 conference building at UNESCO, Paris (Figure 3.4; see also Figure 2.17).[30] In Breuer's architectural oeuvre, the trapezoid was a gathering place for large numbers of people, whether it was a gymnasium, assembly hall, or theater. But within the Catholic faith, the trapezoid's use and symbolism was untapped. With a new emphasis on the unity of worshippers and clergy, a trapezoid was not only practical but also inclusive. It had the ability to shelter and unite the large number of clergy and laity the commission required. And it retained an important historical association, as noted by Father Joachim Watrin, who upon completion of the floor plan informed the architects that it nearly represented the golden section, one of the most harmonious and pleasing architectural forms dating back to the Greeks.[31] Breuer moved the trapezoid to several different positions in the plan of the new monastery before securing its place on the eastern side of the overall plan, on a north–south line in front of the old monastic church, the only large open space available.[32]

FIGURE 3.3. "Story of a Church and Connected Problems," created by Hamilton Smith and Robert Gatje with handwritten comments by Marcel Breuer, shows the process of creating the church's form.

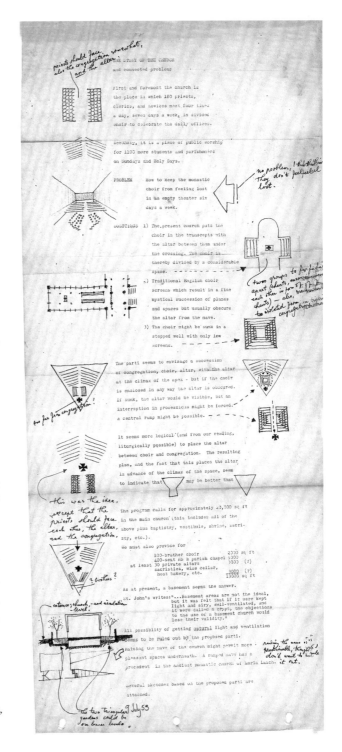

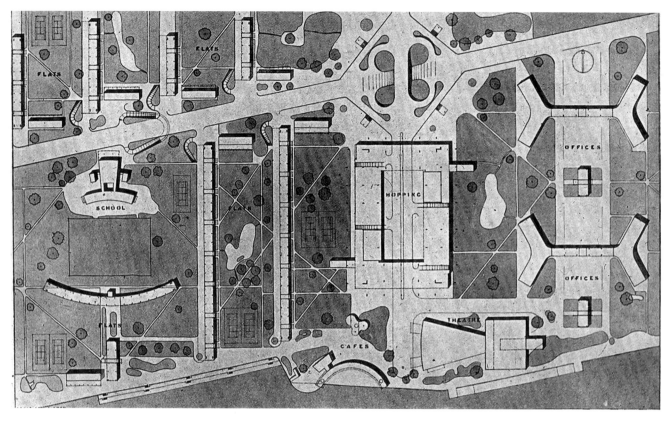

FIGURE 3.4. Breuer's 1936 plan for a Garden City of the Future. The theater is the trapezoidal building at lower center.

In general, when it came to designing sacred space, Breuer likened the spirituality of a work to its size and form:

I have the feeling, and this is not a very clear-cut program or idea, that any space which is larger than necessary and higher than necessary, and in which the structure and the whole building of the space is visible as it is in all churches . . . that this space created is

simply automatically religious. . . . I think that any large space which is built so that the process of construction is visible on the inside, is a religious space.[33]

The design of a large shell for Saint John's that revealed its constructed form on the interior was made possible by the use of engineered concrete. For Breuer, "The shape of such a structure is so close to the engineering that you don't know

PLATE 1. The first model of the abbey church and monastic dormitory designed
in December 1953 and presented to the brethren in January 1954.

PLATE 2 (*above*).
The church's interior
provides a new setting
for the Catholic liturgy.

PLATE 3 (*right*).
Marcel Breuer's
original concept for the
church's interior (1953).

PLATE 4. The crypt chapel dedicated to Saint Thomas Aquinas.

PLATE 5. The lay brothers' chapel dedicated to Saint Benedict.

PLATE 6. The Lady Chapel, featuring a twelfth-century Burgundian wooden sculpture of the Madonna and Child, shows how materials can become decoration.

PLATE 7. The crypt chapel dedicated to Saint Francis of Assisi.

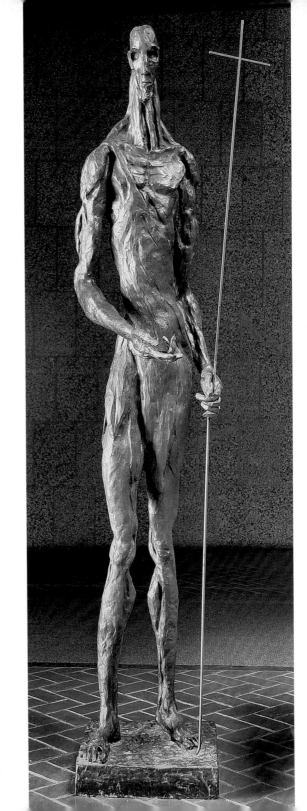

PLATE 8. Doris Caesar, *Saint John the Baptist*. Bronze, 96 inches.

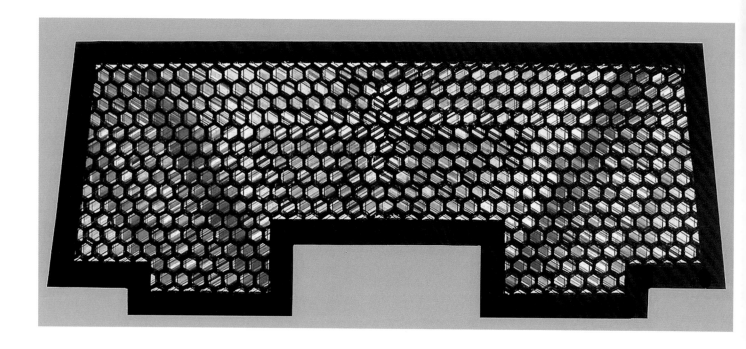

PLATE 9. Josef Albers's design for the northern window wall.

PLATE 10. The northern stained glass window by Bronislaw Bak abstractly depicts the liturgical seasons of the year.

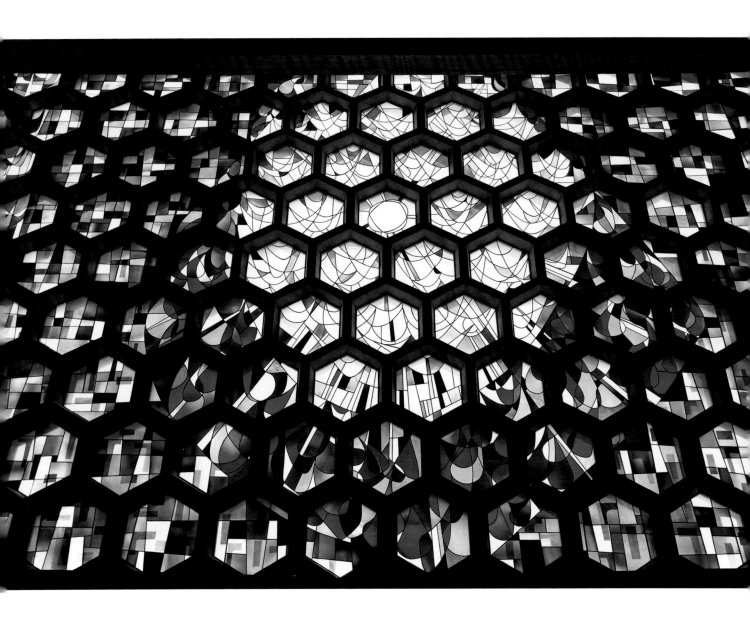

PLATE 11. The white in the central portion of the northern stained glass window symbolizes the eye of God.

PLATE 12. Gerald Bonnette's sketch and notes for the apse screen detail the role of color in the design.

PLATE 13. A new public quadrangle anchored by Alcuin Library at the left of the bell banner and the Engel Science Center at the right (visible through the legs of the banner).

PLATE 14. Proposal for an unbuilt student center by Breuer and Associates.

PLATE 15. Marcel Breuer's design for a gymnasium.

PLATE 16. Traditional and modern: the churches of Saint John's.

PLATE 17. Saint John's Abbey and University, ca. 1993. Marcel Breuer's buildings include the monastery wing behind the church, Alcuin Library and the Peter Engel Science Center facing the church, the dormitories at center right near the lake, and the Collegeville Institute for Ecumenical and Cultural Research across the lake from the dormitories at lower center.

which is first—the design or the engineering. Engineering ideas are an organic part—they are very important."[34] Breuer called this demonstrative architecture during his initial visit to Saint John's and he enjoyed more generally creating structures out of reinforced concrete:

> The most interesting developments in structural design are those using reinforced concrete. Here is a completely plastic medium—concrete for compression, steel for tension in one new material. . . . For here the material not only acts as the support of the building, but also as the enclosure, the form.[35]

In their 1962 book *Modern Church Architecture*, Albert Christ-Janer and Mary Mix Foley proposed that the fundamental difference between historic and modern architectural styles was to be found in the nature of materials, and the unique masonry material of the midcentury was reinforced concrete.[36] The explorations in concrete that Breuer and others conducted at the midcentury also necessitated a reevaluation of style.

Breuer's design approach dictated the style of the building. In a 1959 interview at Saint John's, Breuer said he believed the wide variety of materials in the present day had blurred the definitions of architectural style. "Style as we understand it, is a 'part style,' it is a form or style which is de-rived from a view of society. Structure, or practical necessity, is dependent upon available materials, not purely formal considerations."[37] During a visit to Minnesota in May 1959, Breuer lectured to more than five hundred people at the Walker Art Center and many students at the University of Minnesota, upon the request of Dean Ralph Rapson. In his "Notions about Architecture" talk at the Walker, Breuer highlighted his UNESCO, Saint John's, and Starkey House (Duluth, Minnesota) projects.[38] According to the June 2, 1959, *Minneapolis Morning Tribune*, Breuer presented his definition of modern architecture to the audience: "Modern architecture is not so much a specific period style as an attitude. It is an approach with which the designer cuts himself free from precedent, starts fresh by analyzing the functions and structural needs of a building, considers the social implications of this assignment and then applies his imagination to the project. The result is usually simple in line, striking in effect." He went on to point out that "the building will outlive the architect and will go on exerting influence on the appearance and spirit of its community for many years."[39] For Breuer, the style of the building's engineered form mattered less than its ability to sustain the ritual performed within it.

Reinforced concrete was also inexpensive compared to traditional forms of architecture. In a November 1956 letter to Abbot Dworschak, Breuer noted that when he first conceived of the design in 1953, he discussed with the American structural engineer Nicholas Farkas how much more his structure would cost compared to another "most economical construction in either steel or reinforced concrete."[40] Breuer considered Farkas to be a "conservative, practical type" of American engineer whose view of reinforced concrete structures he considered to be pessimistic at the time and critical about such buildings in comparison to steel structures. Breuer informed the abbot that the situation had changed considerably in three years, because of the Korean conflict and steel restrictions, as well as owing to the fact that American engineers were better acquainted with the reinforced concrete structure. Breuer believed that using reinforced concrete decreased the structural cost of a building like Saint John's by 4 percent and that leaving concrete exposed reduced the cost of finishing work even further. He told the abbot that if he tried to build a larger version of the old abbey church, the nineteenth-century Romanesque Revival building, it would cost him 50–75 percent more than the concrete vision he had planned. Breuer believed that a commonplace structure would not uphold the monks' goal of architectural significance as it would have "very little design expression."

Even though Breuer favored innovation and a practical and cost-effective response to function in his architectural designs, he desired to add to the history of architecture with buildings that reflected the spirit of a time and place. Breuer's intent was matched by that of the Benedictines. The new church would be an architectural masterpiece built without the trappings of traditional form or style, as Peter Hammond noted:

> The first quality that the Church must demand of an architect is complete artistic integrity: not conventional piety, and still less a familiarity with the "ecclesiastical" styles. The styles are a lie: our concern to-day must be to clothe the truths of the faith in honest modern dress—the simpler the better, provided only that the cloth is good and that it is well cut. It is better to come before God naked than in period costume.[41]

Frustrated by the variety of meanings the word *modern* could take on in relation to style, Breuer felt that "modern design or architecture is not a form or motif, but an instinct, or rather, a tendency. This tendency or instinct is a fundamental one, like our tendency for good or bad—or our tendency for beautiful or ugly."[42] Equipped with the architectural language of his own version of midcentury modernism and liturgical consultants in the Benedictines, Breuer and his team created an appropriate and functional church for Saint John's centered on a spiritual journey for the midcentury worshipper.

THE SPIRITUAL AXIS:
A JOURNEY OF THE FAITHFUL

The notion of an axial path is at the core of architecture throughout time, from the Egyptian temples to the mall in Washington, D.C., and beyond. For Christians the path is not a source or goal, as Christopher Stroik asserts, but rather a journey in their role as followers of Christ.[43] The liturgy moves worshippers down the path, while the architecture shapes the manner in which time and space are experienced in one's movement and stasis along the way. The philosophy of liturgical modernism had changed the role of the path, as architect Rudolf Schwarz noted; the less complicated reformed liturgy no longer required long processional paths of entrance and exit in a longitudinal church. The communion procession, with its "way forward, union and way back," was now important.[44] Unification, consolidation, and innovation were at the heart of the liturgy the Saint John's church would cast in concrete form.

Both the Benedictines and Breuer understood the importance of movement in a building, not just in its form and energy, but also in one's procession through the building's spaces. Breuer's design philosophy underscored space as motion and flow, where the small details no longer diverted the attention of the user, and movement through the building sustained a unified worship experience.[45] The Benedictines support of liturgi-

cal reforms, particularly the unity of the congregants and clergy during the Mass, merged nicely with Breuer's architectural philosophy as they created the spiritual axis of the abbey church.

Father Meinberg set the tone for Breuer's understanding of the axis in the modern Catholic church with his essay "The Monastic Church." In the earliest Christian times, baptism would begin a pathway that led to the altar and Eucharist and culminated in the monastic components of choir and abbot's dais:

> To the monastic church will come the choir of monks to join with the whole church in the liturgy of praise. Born to monastic life through the second baptism of their profession, they will gather daily near the altar to center their lives in Christ. Baptistry, altar, choir will form the axis of the church, and the building will thus express the sacramental polarity of the monastic life.[46]

Grounded in the renewed ritual of Catholicism, this spiritual axis took on an innovative architectural role in the new church. This process began in 1953 with the initial design followed by the presentation of the model and drawings in January 1954 (Figure 3.5). This scheme was further developed in 1956 when the church committee was formed and the design was revised, and later between 1958 and 1961, when McGough Construc-

FIGURE 3.5. Marcel Breuer and his team present their ideas to the Benedictines, January 1954. At front table (far right to left): Subprior John Eidenschink, architect Hamilton Smith, Marcel Breuer, Abbot Baldwin Dworschak, and Prior Clarus Graves.

tion led the construction of the church.[47] This spiritual axis is an active and participatory pathway through the main level of the abbey church, and it unifies laity and clergy. This dynamic, public space contrasts with the more contemplative, private devotional elements of the overall design, such as the private rooms and reliquary chapels located mostly on the lower or crypt level. The building showcases its programmatic power as a worshipper walks down the spiritual axis, starting at the bell banner, moving through the baptistery

and nave, and culminating at the high altar and abbot's throne. In discussing the design and construction of the church, it is instructive to follow the path of the spiritual axis to illuminate the interaction of the Benedictines and Breuer.

THE BELL BANNER BEGINS
THE SPIRITUAL AXIS

From the exit off Interstate 94, the main thoroughfare in central Minnesota, the abbey banner looms large across the landscape and guides visitors to the front of the church.[48] Its scale is immense, and the sensation of wanting to journey to approach it echoes the experience of the medieval pilgrim seeing, for example, the cathedral in Chartres rise above the French countryside. It is an awe-inspiring sight that enlivens the worshipper's spirit (Figure 3.6).

The portal in architecture marks the difference between inside and outside, welcomes the worshipper, and signals that something significant lies beyond.[49] The bell banner is the modern portal and marks the threshold to the spiritual axis, delineating the sacred from the profane.[50] The threshold here is reached by walking up seven stairs of local granite from Cold Spring,

FIGURE 3.6. The bell banner: a new vision for the portal and entrance to the spiritual axis.

Minnesota, onto a rectangular-cut granite-paved piazza from which the concrete legs of the banner spring. The banner's curvilinear legs embrace you in the way Bernini's square does at Saint Peter's in Vatican City, symbolically sheltering the worshipper in the motherly arms of the church. On this piazza, the worshipper has culminated the journey to the building but stands poised to start another along the spiritual axis. On the western side of the piazza a circular grouping of trapezoidal concrete blocks recalls the simple cubic stools of Rudolf Schwarz's chapel at Castle Rothenfels. The eastern L-shaped concrete benches provide another place to rest prior to entering the building. The downspouts from the baptistery roof also bring the sound of running water to the piazza, a reminder of nature and a higher power that the worshipper can meditate on before entering the building.

The bell banner's unusual form was inspired by historical architecture, including bell walls and towers Breuer had seen on sailing trips in the Greek islands in the early 1930s, as art historian Whitney Stoddard has noted, and by religious buildings in the American Southwest, as Isabelle Hyman has pointed out.[51] Yet the particular form of this tower, according to Breuer, was made possible "by our technology, by new building methods, materials, and modern engineering."[52] Breuer went through several versions of the banner before deciding on the design he would present in the 1953 church model. His earliest version featured an elongated trapezoid supported by a thin singular pillar that was two times as tall as the northern façade of the building. This sketch gave no indication of the banner's relationship to the building, as is found in the other early sketches in which the banner is placed on top of the baptistery. Breuer then began to play with the fenestration of the banner, in particular the openings needed to house the five bells from the abbey's old church.[53] In another drawing, Breuer moves away from a single support for the banner's slab to provide one at each end of a large slab. As Isabelle Hyman has noted, this choice was likely influenced by Breuer's time in Paris working on the UNESCO project, where he had a constant view of the Eiffel Tower, whose silhouette resembles the profile view of the banner.[54] Breuer playfully affirmed Hyman's assertion in an unpublished coloring book of his work held at the American Archives of Art with the caption, "They are thinking of building this in the middle of Paris."[55] In the 1953 model Breuer seemed satisfied with the form of the trapezoid punctured by two openings, the larger containing four bells and the smaller holding one (see Plate 1). These openings were essential to Breuer, for he wanted one to "see the sky" and get a sunny impression.[56] The cross, which has moved from the bottom of the form, surmounts the bells. Breuer also moved the banner from its original position on top of the baptistery to just in front of it, providing the strong liturgical entrance the building deserved.

Breuer revived this engineered portal of re-inforced concrete from traditional forms and molded the modern concrete into a cantilevered slab, a symbol he found comparable to "the archaic column, gothic arch, and renaissance dome."[57] The Benedictines informed Breuer that the central arch of the bell tower performed a function similar to the main portal of medieval churches and therefore it might deserve decorative treatment. Breuer responded that he was doubtful whether an artist could satisfactorily complete the task and "was of the opinion that decorative additions to an expressive structure might be distracting rather than effective."[58]

The form of the banner sparked discussion when Father Meinberg showed off the plans in Europe, where he traveled from September 1955 to the following September.[59] Architects Rudolf Schwarz and Hermann Baur, two of the twelve contacted for this commission, disliked the banner, and Baur wondered if it really conveyed an idea of the sacred.[60] Even those who strongly supported the design, such as the Italian Archbishop Costantini, president of the Central Pontifical Commission for Sacred Art and founder of *Fede e Arte: Rivista Internazionale di Arte Sacra* in 1953, had few good things to say when Meinberg showed him a slide of the banner.[61]

In the final design revision of December 19, 1956, Breuer was concerned with the bell banner and its visual and spatial relationship to the church entrance, as he wrote to Abbot Dworschak:

It maintains the idea of a banner with through openings for the Cross and the bells. However, the cross is now a positive form. We have made a clear distinction between the supporting parabolic structure and the actual banner. We have tried to form the supporting structure in such a way that a definitely arched passageway to the church entrance is created. Low parapet walls are meant to define the shape of the piazza leading to the atrium. They will also partly surround the supporting structure of the banner and create again a space connection with the atrium.[62]

Prior to this final version, Breuer had completed several additional studies of the banner (Figure 3.7). These drawings provide insight not only into the placement of the banner in relation to the baptistery and church but also into his interest in the sculptural form made possible by reinforced concrete. Breuer sensed a strong connection between architecture and sculpture. Both media required multiple viewpoints to fully understand a form and, in the new spirit of architecture at the midcentury, architecture was again becoming sculptural in its "three-dimensional nature of the whole and its organic details—the sun and shadow of its modulation, the contours of its structure, the surface relief and texture of its material."[63] Another version of the banner could be read as menacing, prompting associations with Romanesque fortress churches in southern France, which Breuer saw on his travels. Of all the images created for the church, these banner designs reflect most strongly Breuer's love of solids and voids, of transparency, and of the shaping of surface form with a sculptural sensibility.

For his final version Breuer settled on a banner design that combined his interest in sculpture and engineering. The church committee remarked on the new symbolic character of the banner as "forming a triumphal arch of entry surmounted by a cross like triumphal arches in ancient tradition in church structures." It stated that the revised banner "makes the cross the most prominent sign of the church structure."[64] Working with the university's art department, the design team modified the banner's oak cross several times in search of an appropriate form to signify the intention of this building as a sacred portal. And even though some of the brethren did not appreciate this new version, Breuer and his team reminded them of its practical function, as it reflected light into the church through the northern stained glass wall, and a bell tower would not be an adequate substitute for this purpose.[65]

During the cold winter months of 1958 and

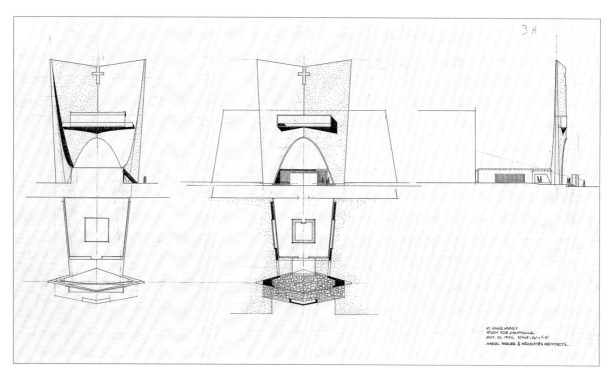

FIGURE 3.7. Breuer acts as sculptor with this October 1956 version of the bell banner.

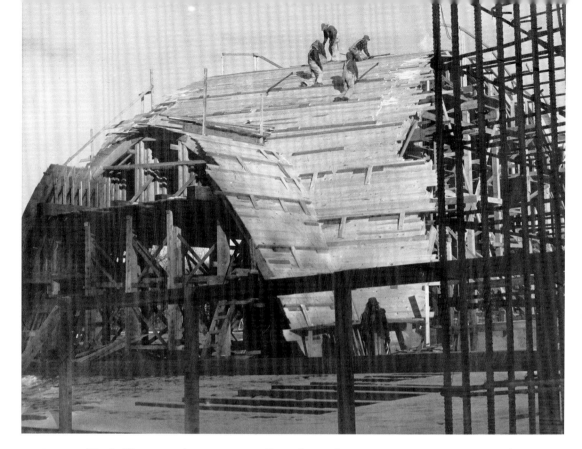

FIGURE 3.8. The bell banner under construction, December 1958.

1959, workers fabricated the banner's wooden formwork from individual pieces of wood (Figure 3.8). The slender, 112-foot-high-by-100-foot-wide banner is a cantilevered slab of reinforced concrete resting on parabolic supports that are only 2½ feet thick at the base but extend 15 feet belowground for strength. The four footings were joined to each other, forming a huge rectangle covering 5,220 square feet. It weighed 2,500 tons and was poured in place from April to November 23, 1959.

THE BAPTISTERY: A SACRAMENTAL (RE)INITIATION INTO THE CHURCH

Movement underneath the banner and toward the church doors signifies an intention to enter God's house. The brick flooring, laid in the same vertical alignment as the granite pavers, transports one easily to the doorway of dark-stained oak, which repeats the rectilinear pattern. The doorway's concrete walls act as an open narthex and atrium, directing worshippers into the

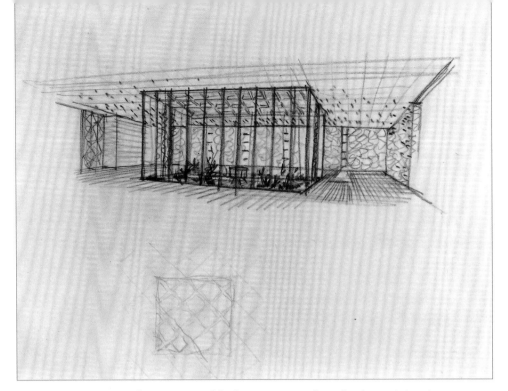

FIGURE 3.9. Breuer's early conception of the baptistery is similar to his domestic interiors.

building while sheltering them at the same time. There are three doors set in this recessed alcove: a monumental double door separated by a glass slit in the center is used for high feasts and important processions; two smaller doors of dark-stained oak are used regularly by visitors to the church. The legs of the banner overlap the baptistery and provide a strong continuity between these two components of the sacred path, while the doorway projects out to welcome the user, who is ready to enter the living Church and be born again of water and the Spirit. It is a place of acceptance into the church, and the location of the baptistery and baptismal font on the spiritual axis affirms this important element of reforms, as many baptisteries in the nineteenth and twentieth centuries were located in an area not immediately visible to someone entering a church.

An early sketch for the baptistery in the archives at Syracuse University Library reveals Breuer's skills as a domestic architect, one of the reasons why he was invited to contend for this commission (Figure 3.9). This drawing illustrates the scale of the room, the use of light to highlight key elements like the baptismal font, and the importance of nature through the use of local materials such as fieldstone. Breuer further defined the rectangular space with a full-height wooden screen around the interior courtyard, a feature similar to the bamboo screen shields found in the dining room of his own house, barriers that divided space while allowing it to flow freely through their transparency. And just as his fireplaces and stairs created sculptural focal points in his domestic designs, the baptismal font provided a sculptural center in this religious space.

In December 1956 Breuer presented the new design for the baptistery. He supported its concrete, coffered roof with two cruciform-shaped columns on either side of the sunken area containing the baptismal font. The font is on a direct axis starting with the center of the bell banner, moving through the monumental door and on toward the altar (Figure 3.10). Instead of lowering the screened area by one step on all sides as he originally intended, Breuer placed three steps on the axial ends of the sacred path only, recalling baptism by immersion as done in the early church and symbolizing the principle of dying and rising with Christ.[66] Breuer's fully screened wooden wall in his early design gave way to a half-height wall of concrete, smooth faced on the exterior and roughcast on the interior. He placed the black granite holy water fonts in the east and

FIGURE 3.10. The baptistery begins the spiritual axis within the building.

west walls, making them easily accessible to users, who recall baptism on their way into the nave as they bless themselves with the holy water. Originally Breuer located these fonts closer to the entrance door of the baptistery, but the monks asked him to move them closer to the entrance of the church, "for the use of holy water on entering the Church should be expressive of an aftermath of Baptism and not a forerunner of it."[67]

Creating the baptismal font gave Breuer another opportunity to design as a sculptor, and he reworked the baptismal font's form several times, progressing from a rectangular, two-tiered structure to a circular one carved from a single piece of dark gray granite. One workman with modern tools spent eighteen days hollowing out the circular bowl of the font. Breuer centrally located the granite baptismal font inside the concrete walls and placed planters in each corner. The plants symbolize life, as does the simple agitation in the water running through the baptismal font.[68]

Breuer's artistic highlights in the baptistery were made through the use of materials, including concrete, wood, granite, metal, and red brick. Additionally, Breuer employed light to signify the importance of the font within the space, illuminating it from above with six skylights and providing auxiliary light through the small slit windows in the central entrance door. In his domestic designs, top-lighted spaces were usually interior gardens or courtyards open to the sky, uniting the man-made house with nature. In the baptistery,

the top lighting denotes heaven, although it is a dimly illuminated version compared to the powerful light one has just left on the exterior. There is more light ahead, visible through the portal into the nave.

The design of the baptistery is sophisticated both architecturally and liturgically. Breuer's handling of materials, scale, and light creates a contemplative moment of pause for the worshipper, a signal that there is mystery in the church, a move from the darkness into the light. But most importantly, the spiritual axis becomes symbolic at this point, for the worshipper will not walk the path directly to the altar, but rather views it obliquely and from above. This movement to the side of the path also prevents a direct view of the altar as you walk around the sunken area with the font. It is not until one moves through the baptistery on the way to enter the nave that the path is retaken and the culmination is visible.

INTO THE NAVE: THE WORSHIPPER'S RESTING PLACE

The worshipper now moves into the church's main space, through a second tripartite doorway consisting of a larger center opening with two smaller doors on either side. Breuer emphasized the physicality of the portal with his use of materials: oak doors with copper insets and rough-hewn granite panels placed inside the concrete doorjambs. The nave and baptistery are further integrated by the transom-like opening above the portal, which allows visual access to the adjoining room. The portal is located between two confessionals. It is here that sinners can atone for their misdeeds before accepting Holy Communion during the Mass at the high altar.[69] At the rear of the nave the worshipper moves through a dimly lit, compressed space, with the main illumination coming from the northern stained glass window wall. This is a transitional moment, preparing one for the expanse and majesty of the church, 65 feet from ground to lantern above the altar, 180 feet across at the entrance, tapering to 87 feet wide at the monastery door 225 feet away (see Plate 2).[70] For Breuer, architecturally this was an "exciting experience" whereby one emerged "from a darker, low-ceilinged space into a light, high large space."[71] It was also a place symbolically big enough to hold God.[72]

The excitement builds as worshippers walk down the central aisle of the nave, with the lantern's warm orange and golden light illuminating them from above. The three-ton white wooden baldachin, suspended in the space with the cross immediately underneath, directs one's attention to the altar, where, according to the liturgy, life is nourished and brought to perfection through the Eucharist. It is the pinnacle of a Christian's journey as Anson's and O'Connell's texts would have pointed out. O'Connell defines the altar as a "consecrated table of natural stone in which relics of the saints are enshrined, and on which the

Christian sacrifice—the Mass—is offered."[73] The Catholic bishops of Germany emphasized the symbolic status of the altar:

> Since at the Consecration in the Mass our divine Lord becomes present upon the altar, it is, even without the tabernacle, Christ's throne on earth. And since the altar is His throne, the faithful from patristic times saw in the altar a symbol of Christ Himself, for the throne symbolizes the person of the Ruler.[74]

The first altars in early Christian churches were simple, impermanent wooden tables. These gave way to stone altars in the fifth century, when permanence of the altar was desired. The high altar at Saint John's recalls altars carved from stone.

Architecturally, Breuer's high altar design recalls the bell banner in its use of parabolic arches that lead from the ground up to a rectangular mensa. Liturgically, its central placement in the choir allows for unimpeded views from the monks and laity (Figure 3.11). The white Vermont marble contrasts strongly with the floor of red brick, dark-stained wood stalls, and gray concrete of the choir, providing a visual focal point for both seated and moving worshippers. This choice of material, based on its color, was Breuer's as there was no local granite in white.[75] Visual engagement is further ensured by its position on a circular predella, one brick taller in height than the

FIGURE 3.11. The main altar, made of Vermont white marble, centers the liturgical space.

already elevated choir, and its location under the white wooden baldachin. Sculptor James Rosati, a member of New York's abstract expressionist circle, designed the crucifix, candleholders, and tabernacle for the high altar with the guidance of the monks.

As believers sit and rest on its dark-stained oak pews, the nave gives them time to contemplate all the elements of this vast concrete room. The choir is immediately before them, visible from any seat because of its placement four feet higher than the grade of the nave, with the altar clearly in sight. The priest can celebrate Mass from both sides of this altar in order to serve the two different communities that use the space, laity and monastic choir. Four communion tables of concrete and granite visually separate the sanctuary from the choir, but do not create a barrier in the manner of a full communion rail or screen, thereby enabling the unity sought in liturgical reforms.[76] When worshippers come forward during the Mass to receive communion, they stand at these tables and obtain a different vantage point of the choir, gaining a more intimate perspective on the space. This is also a symbolic moment, as the height of these tables, positioned so that one stands rather than kneels to receive the Eucharistic host, enables an understanding of them as high altar. Finally, at the southern end of the axis, one can see the abbot's dais and throne, surrounded by the monastic choir, the lower section of which, flanking the altar, was for the lay brethren and the main area, to the sides of the throne, for professed monks and priests, where they would look back out toward the congregation. Above the choir is a screen for the apse mosaic, the final (unfinished) image for the spiritual journey.[77]

An early section drawing of November 23, 1953, reveals how Breuer initially structured space in the church (Figure 3.12). He placed a large balcony supported by double supports across the northern end of the building to accommodate the

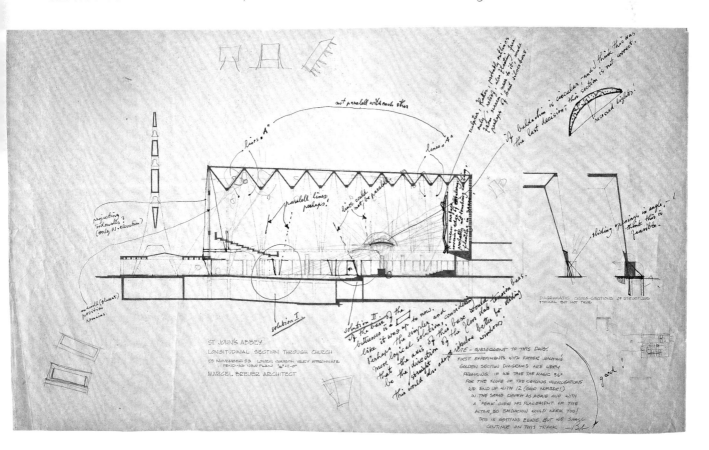

FIGURE 3.12. Section of the church, November 23, 1953.

FIGURE 3.13. The 1957 model of the church.

large number of worshippers the church would have on feast days and during the school year. He positioned the high altar and its circular balda-quin between the laity and the choir, which he organized in a semicircular fashion around the altar. The abbot's throne surmounted by a large statue of the crucified Christ terminated the de-sign at the building's southernmost end.

On December 19, 1956, Breuer and Smith met with the church committee to present their de-sign revisions. The first was the addition of a lan-tern over the altar and baldachin, a response to the artist and liturgical consultant Ade Bethune, who asked Breuer's office why there was no ocu-lus.[78] The brethren agreed with Bethune's desire to place some opening over the altar, hoping that it might "provide enough natural light for ordi-nary day-time use of choir—like the oculus of the Pantheon, Rome."[79]

As visible in the 1957 model of the church, Breuer put his own architectural stamp on changes to the building (Figure 3.13). His Mondrian-like grid façade of the 1953 design had given way to a hexagonal pattern wall. This change was likely influenced by Breuer's 1953–54 design for the De Bijenkorf department store in Rotterdam, where he used Roman travertine hexagons for the façade in homage to the beehive trademark of the well-known store. There is no indication of a religious or liturgical focus in this change; it is likely an evolution based on structural necessity and aesthetic preference.

The fabrication of the 430 hexagons for the northern window wall proved a challenging task for the construction team. Breuer intended to have them cast full concrete hexagons that they would place together with reinforcing bar to form the wall. An experimental pouring of a hexagon raised two major problems with the method (Figure 3.14). First, although oiled, the wooden formwork damaged the edges of the concrete when removed, and second, a wall of these

FIGURE 3.14. Marcel Breuer (right) and his on-site architect Val Michelson examine a full hexagon test pour.

individual units needed continuous reinforcing in order to be secure, a requirement that would hamper the artistic value of the window. Breuer, Michelson, and Hoffmeyer decided that in order to strengthen the wall, the shape poured should be that of a half hexagon. Michelson and Hoffmeyer devised a formwork that could shape seven half hexagons, four on the top and three below, and made the formwork of steel because its reuse "might prove to be more economical in the long run."[80] The fabrication of the hexagons in this way provided the stability the wall needed, and in a sense it was a non-load-bearing curtain wall, as Breuer-associated architect Murray Elmslie wrote to Chicago architect David Fredman in July 1957: "Our present thinking is that this screen wall will be structurally stable due to the internal design of the concrete sections without any structural steel back-up in the way of lateral bracing. The frame of the building is to furnish structural support so that the screen is in effect a panel wall."[81]

During the same time work on the church's enclosure walls was under way.[82] Pier Luigi Nervi engineered the building for Breuer.[83] In a December 1961 article in *Arts and Architecture* titled "The Influence of Reinforced Concrete," Nervi explained the twofold nature of concrete architecture: not only did it have a physical presence dependent on materials and technical necessity but it also moved into the realm of art in the emotion of its dimensions and materials.[84] Breuer had worked with Nervi on the UNESCO complex in Paris, including its conference hall, where a construction system of folding thin shells of concrete for the roof and walls inspired the work in Collegeville.

Breuer and Nervi altered the conference hall's design by slightly curving the long side walls on the east and west at Saint John's.[85] They also folded the long walls of the structure rather than the shorter end walls at UNESCO.

McGough Construction built the church's long side walls of the trapezoid using folded plate construction while the ends were treated as flat walls. Twelve pleated reinforced concrete folds, poured in place, are structurally continuous from the side walls through to the ceiling of the building (Figure 3.15).[86] They increase in all their dimensions—width, depth, and wall thickness—as they cross successively broader segments of the plan.[87] The longest fold spans 135 feet, measures nearly 15 feet from top to bottom, and has walls that vary between six and eight inches in thickness. According to Larry McGough, the construction team worried throughout the process, not only about where to break the concrete pours, but also about the number and location of the cold joints.[88] The construction of the roof and the east and west folded walls required a 48-foot-high temporary steel support system for the wooden formwork, making the construction site appear like a steel frame for a small office building (Figure 3.16).[89]

The concrete folds dynamically define the

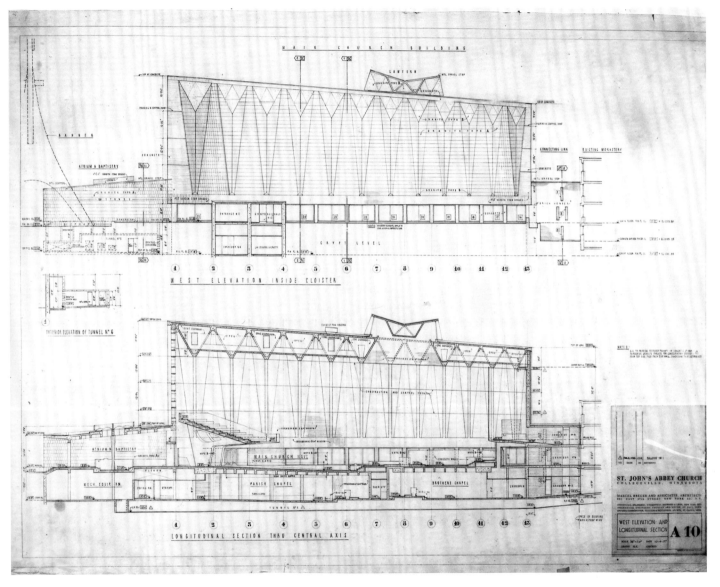

FIGURE 3.15. Elevation and section, October 1957.

FIGURE 3.16. Construction photograph from April 1959 shows the internal steel framework that supported the roof and side wall formwork during the concrete pours.

space, as they do not reach all the way to the ground but rather meet a slightly curved, horizontal support beam upheld by a series of concrete buttresses. These buttresses "controlled the view of the outside" for Breuer, and their placement defied gravity as he positioned each between the concrete folds rather than directly underneath them.[90] The space between these buttresses is filled with operable glass windows, per the client's request, to allow in air while also strengthening the gravity-defying effect of the wall's design. These great concrete folds do more than shape the space. They also improve the acoustics for the brethren's antiphonal singing and Gregorian chant.

The modified folded roof structure is composed of V-shaped walls, each about nine inches thick, forming tents ranging in height from eight to fourteen feet.[91] The V shape is inverted on the roof's plane, and the triangular space within each V provides room for the circulation of people and mechanicals. A connecting bridge runs across the folds from north to south to provide access to the mechanicals. A flat slab of concrete covers the roof's V-shaped folds, protecting them and allowing for the service of lighting and ventilation elements. After the four piers of the southern wall were poured in place and the space between each filled in with brick and cinder block (later covered with a granite veneer), workers created the roof folds by spraying concrete from a special gun

over steel reinforcements in a bottom formwork only.[92] McGough's crew shot the concrete onto an oiled wooden formwork with a zero slump, a process that uses minimal water in the mixture.[93] Breuer did not want to use this process, but Michelson and Hoffmeyer convinced him to do so because it was quicker to set and it dried harder and stronger than a conventional concrete pour. Hoffmeyer and Michelson worked with the Gun-All Corporation of Tulsa, Oklahoma, to perfect the mixture, visiting Tulsa with Pete McGough in April 1959 and testing it on-site.[94]

Given the intricacies of this project, it is no surprise that challenges arose during the construction process. The most serious one occurred in the spring of 1960, when several of the folded plate roof trusses developed active shear cracks that ran "parallel to one another at forty-five degrees and other angles radial to the span of the folded plates."[95] Upon hearing of the problem from Michelson, who had confirmed it by having Hoffmeyer patch the cracks to see if the plaster would crack or widen around the splintering, Breuer requested pictures be sent to Nervi in Rome. According to Gatje, Nervi understood the problem right away. Whereas Europe had building codes for folded plate structures, the United States did not. Nervi was sure the American engineers had credited 25 percent of the shear force to the concrete itself, which was appropriate with horizontal slabs but not with inclined ones like those at Saint John's. Breuer's office contacted their engineer, Jim Leon, of Weisenfeld, Hayward & Leon, who recalculated his numbers and, although not admitting error, suggested a series of corrective measures.[96] As his relationship with Leon grew strained, Breuer immediately consulted with an engineer he respected, Paul Weidlinger of New York City.

Breuer, the Benedictines, and McGough Construction kept things quiet as they sought a solution to the shear cracking. Cold Spring Granite's president, John Alexander, was the only outsider who knew about the problem, as his company had to reinstall the steel framework to support the roof during repairs.[97] McGough's construction workers spent the next six months drilling into the sides and tops of the folds and adding more steel and concrete, a process developed by Weidlinger and Leon.[98] An independent professional inspector analyzed the situation in September 1960 and concluded that changes made to the original design, a delay in some of the placement of concrete, and a variance between the sprayed and poured concrete mixtures were to blame for the cracks.[99] Although solved quietly and effectively, this problem could have bankrupted Breuer, as he did not have professional liability insurance at the time.[100]

Work began inside the church in January 1960, and the forms of the building tested the construction team's ingenuity at every turn. McGough's crew poured the four pillars for the cantilevered balcony, their footings rising from the basement of the building. The walls surrounding the choir were completed; the Benedictines had requested that it contain eighty stalls and be split into two sections kept close together to facilitate responsorial chanting. The choir is not screened off from the laity in any manner, but eight-foot-tall concrete walls define its southern perimeter. Support pillars for the pews and choir stalls were made. The completion of the northern window wall in the fall of 1960 signified the end of the church's exterior construction. Finishing touches could then be added. On the exterior this included the hanging of the bells and cross in the banner and the placement of granite veneer on the walls of the baptistery and church. In the building's interior, pews, stalls, altars, and a limited amount of decoration in the Lady Chapel and elsewhere were installed.

MATERIALITY AS ORNAMENT IN A MODERN CHURCH

The 1953 interior model of the church, fashioned by Meinberg and others at Saint John's, and an interior perspective color drawing held in the Marcel Breuer office archives at Syracuse University, reveal the planned decorative scheme (Figure 3.17; Plate 3). Color was key; in addition to color provided by materials such as red brick

FIGURE 3.17. 1953 model of the church's interior.

for the floors, wood for the choir stalls, and white and black marble for the altar and abbot's throne, Breuer added a gilded ceiling, white side walls, a gilt-and-blue baldaquin, and a blue background for the abbot's throne. Color also dominated the apse's figural element in the change from a sculpted crucifix of steel bicycle handlebars, as proposed by Breuer, to the colorful mosaic screen of artist Gerald Bonnette featuring the imagery of Christ Pantocrator, or Christ the Almighty and ruler of all.

Breuer intended to cover the ceiling with gold leaf and whitewash the walls, but when he saw the wonderful shades of gray and the formwork marks in the concrete, he left the walls raw and unadorned, stating that their color reminded him of Gothic cathedrals.[101] It left visible the "bones, muscles and skin" of the building, showcasing "what made the building work" in order to see its "inner logic."[102] Furthermore, the simplicity of concrete, marked only by the wooden framework's casting, not only highlights the engineered character but also acts in contrast with the building's other material elements. Waxed red brick—a material used to evoke the redbrick buildings of the nineteenth-century monastic complex—covers the floor. Breuer also planned to face the exterior with red brick, but the Cold Spring Granite Company convinced him to use their locally quarried stone. The exterior is covered with two colors of gray, sawn, rough-faced granite panels, intermixed at random and subjected to heat,

which caused the quartz particles to pop out.[103] The design also includes a dark-stained oak, brass, stained glass, terracotta tile walls, and mosaics. The abbot's dais is highlighted by a golden colored, hexagonal tile backdrop, tying it in with the much larger hexagons found on the façade of the building. The French architect Auguste Perret noted in his early twentieth-century remarks regarding the unbuilt Sainte Jeanne D'Arc, "No part of the building should be devoted to ornament only; rather, aiming always at beautiful proportions, all the structural elements of the building should be turned into ornaments."[104] At Saint John's, Marcel Breuer followed Perret's dictum and let the materials visually function as the decoration for the building.

Whereas the sacraments organized the actions of participants on the spiritual axis, the building's design visually and spatially encouraged unity in worship. The trapezoidal shape and balcony brought worshippers closer to the altar than a Latin cross plan ever could, with no seat in the abbey church located farther than eighty-five feet from the altar, even though some of the brethren, including Father Cloud, worried about the balcony making the interior feel more like an auditorium than a church.[105] The deep projections and angled surfaces of the poured-in-place reinforced concrete folds contribute acoustically by promoting a general diffusion of reflected sound instead of permitting uneven, echo-producing concentrations.[106] This enabled antiphonal activity in the building, bringing the laity into the celebration in a stronger manner than had previously been done. The skillfully designed ambo or lectern, for a priest reading the Gospel and giving the homily, or a lay reader proclaiming the word of God, was prominently placed and in direct contact with worshippers. The monastic choir understood the building in a different fashion than the laity. For them, the northern window was a constant visual element of worship, but the altar still centered the space. The building also provided a meditative element to Catholic devotion, seen mainly in the design of the crypt level, but also the Lady and Blessed Sacrament chapels.

CONTEMPLATION AND PRIVATE DEVOTIONS

While the performance of the liturgy is the central activity of the Catholic Church, Catholics are encouraged to perform private pious acts and personal devotions, as codified by the Second Vatican Council's *Sacrosanctum Concilium.* This decree commended the popular devotions by the Christian faithful, encouraging them to be in harmony with the liturgical seasons.[107] Two types of private devotional spaces are found at Saint John's. The first is for the laity and takes place in the Lady Chapel and the Blessed Sacrament Chapel, both located on the periphery of the spiritual axis on the main floor of the church, and the reliquary

chapel of Saint Peregrine on the lower level. Marian devotions date back to the early church and in the mid-twentieth century the devout prayed to the Virgin as the "Mother of the Catholic Church."[108] A more modern development is the practice of praying before the tabernacle holding the body of Christ, usually in a Blessed Sacrament chapel. Usually taking place in a separate chapel but also sometimes at the altar of the church, this practice is a merciful work intended to console the heart of Jesus for sins against him by the less devout. A reliquary chapel, like that of Saint Peregrine, contains the remains of one or more saints and since before the early days of the church has provided a place for veneration, as worshippers hoped to adore Christ more fully by praying to his strongest followers.

The second type of individual devotion is for the monastic brethren. Individual private chapels located on the lower level of the building accommodate the many priests at Saint John's for their daily celebration of the Mass. The lower level also has a brothers' chapel for the saying of prayers in English rather than Latin. Although these spaces are significant in purpose for the Catholic user, their location off the spiritual axis reaffirms the importance of the Mass and unified participation for a spiritually rewarding life. And just as the upper level of the church is multifunctional in use, with laity in the nave and monastic brethren in the choir, the lower level also serves more than one user.

THE CRYPT LEVEL

For visitors wishing to attend Mass in the parish chapel or to venerate relics, Breuer provided an entrance to the basement level of the church from the baptistery. McGough Construction spent the summer of 1958 pouring the foundations of the church, enclosing the basement or crypt of the church by November 1 of that same year. The final designs for the basement include, from north to south on the central axis (Figure 3.18): a mechanical room under the baptistery; a reliquary chapel of the second-century boy martyr, Peregrine; a parish chapel; a sacristy; and a brothers' chapel dedicated to Saint Benedict. Thirty-four private chapels line the eastern and western sides of the space.

The northernmost chapel of the crypt level is dedicated to Saint Peregrine and holds the remains of the martyr, which were moved from the old church (see Figure 4.1).[109] The monks linked Breuer's modern space with tradition, calling it "reminiscent of the ancient custom of erecting tombs over martyrs" and relating the niches in the walls to those in the catacombs, but "instead of containing the bodies of saints they contained parts of their bones."[110] Originally Breuer intended this space to contain the private chapels, changing it at one point to a crying room for the lower parish chapel with a full wall of glass separating it from the worship space.[111] But the

monks asked Breuer if he could rethink the crying room as a chapel dedicated to Peregrine, because a space for relics would follow in the tradition of past churches and fulfill Benedict's exhortation in the Rule to "keep death daily before one's eyes."[112] Both the sketches and the final built version of the chapel reveal the influence of Breuer's summer visit in 1956 to Le Corbusier's pilgrimage chapel, Notre Dame du Haut in Ronchamp, France.[113] He wrote of his journey to Abbot Baldwin:

> By the way, I went to see Corbusier's chapel in Ronchamp, France. Though it is on top of a hill without a road to it, and it was a day of pouring rain and storm, there was veritable pilgrimage to the chapel; architects, students, people interested in art, or in church architecture. However mixed the reactions were, including my own, everyone felt, so far as I could learn, that the building of the chapel was justified. I spent several hours there, listened to many conversations, and also talked with a number of people, and I could not detect even a trace of regret that Corbusier was chosen to design the chapel.[114]

The southern wall of Notre Dame du Haut consists of irregularly sized windows punched out of a thick concrete-and-stone membrane and filled with clear, colored, and painted glass. Like Le

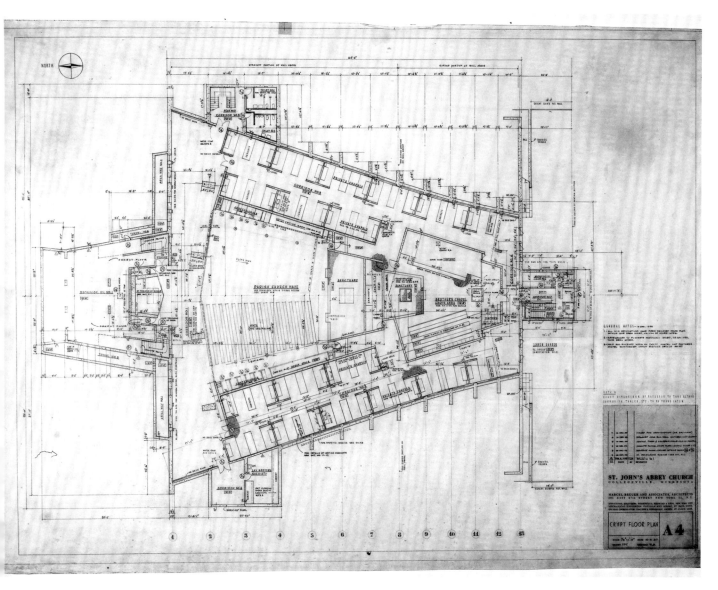

FIGURE 3.18. Plan of the crypt or lower level of the abbey church.

Corbusier, Breuer appreciated the plasticity of a malleable material like concrete to create solids and voids and provide depth and shade. His sketches for the chapel reveal this interest in their forms and intense shading. However, where Le Corbusier filled his openings with glass, Breuer's randomly shaped and sized openings are niches filled with additional relics.[115] Breuer's use of concrete to provide a simplistic backdrop for the elaborately ornamented reliquaries exemplified the modernist emphasis on functionality. In the modern space, decoration came in the qualities of the materials themselves. The chapel's smooth and polished concrete has a surface comparable to that of granite, the hardest and most beautiful and durable of materials.[116] The red brick floor provides a useful color contrast. A slatted wooden screen separates the chapel from the adjacent parish chapel and provides security for the precious relics when closed.

Breuer's love of irregular openings did not end with the completion of Saint Peregrine's chapel. On both sides of the northern wall adjacent to the chapel he used a random pattern in the windows that bring in light to the northern end of the lower level, an area that functions as a vestibule for the parish chapel. Like the other chapels on this level, Assumption Chapel's low ceiling height and lack of natural light create an atmosphere of intimacy and inwardness (Figure 3.19). Its shape is trapezoidal and a single aisle separates two sets of pews, which can seat 450 worshippers.

The altar of black Cold Spring granite is located at the southern end of the chapel, adjacent to a sacristy, which serves both Assumption and Saint Benedict's Chapels. Confessionals, storage, and crying rooms line the side aisles. Simplicity is key. Eighteen-sided pillars of concrete are painted white, as is the ceiling. "Breuer blue" colored can lights hang from the coffers, and Pennsylvania red oak is used here and throughout the building for pews, stalls, and other elements.[117]

On the eastern and western sides of the lower level are thirty-four private chapels for the use of the priests to celebrate their daily Mass. The church needed a large number of altars because concelebration of the Mass was not allowed at the time of its completion.[118] Therefore, each of the more than two hundred priests was required to individually celebrate Mass every day, making a large number of altars necessary. Sensing a possible shift with regard to concelebration, the monks tried to plan ahead and eliminate the private crypt chapels from the design, even sending one of their own, Father Godfrey Diekmann, to Rome to ask for permission to concelebrate the Mass.[119] The Vatican denied their request. Consequently the crypt was lined with the chapels, each dedicated to a different saint or saints.

Breuer's 1953 visit to the Abbey of Maria Laach played an important role in the placement of the private altars at Saint John's. During this trip he noticed that some of the private altars were located in the main body of the church, and he

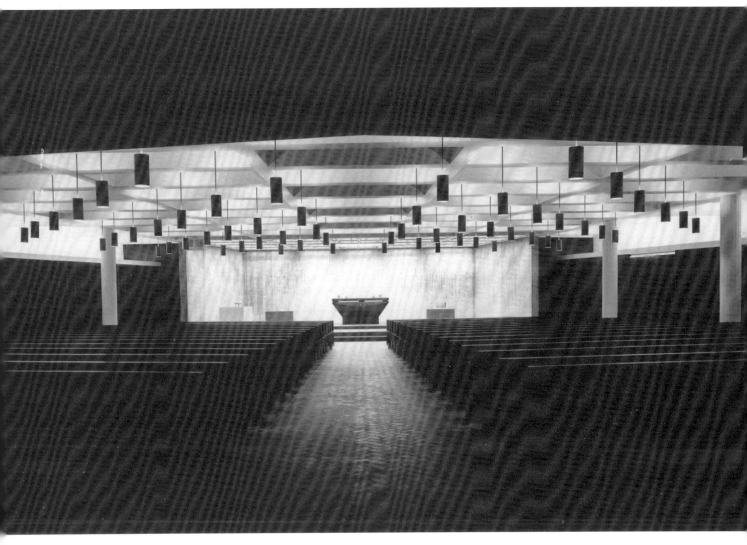

FIGURE 3.19. Assumption Chapel, the parish chapel.

sought permission from Saint John's brethren to place private altars in inconspicuous places in the upper level. The monks did not like this solution because they wanted to keep the focus on the main altar. They also preferred that all private altars in the basement chapels be separate from one another so as not to be disturbed by whatever function might be going on in the lower parish church.[120] This request led to the placement of seventeen chapels on both the east and west sides of the crypt, each separated by wooden cabinets that act as mini-sacristies for storing vestments and other accoutrements needed for the Mass. Breuer's typical chapel design, as exemplified in the space dedicated to Saint Thomas Aquinas, reveals a platform of red brick supporting an altar surmounted by a baldachin of sorts—a wooden screen covering the light source four feet above the altar (see Plate 4). The walls were painted white and the ceiling covered in cork for noise reduction.[121] For these private chapels the brethren requested fixed and permanent altars completed in the simplest manner possible.[122] The altar was the centerpiece of each space; Breuer fashioned fifteen of the altars and Kacmarcik the remaining nineteen.[123] Each chapel was filled with art appropriate to the chosen saint or saints. Breuer provided a credence table and lavabo dish in each chapel and additional lavabos in the hallway.

The private chapels led to the southern end of the crypt where Breuer located the brothers'

chapel dedicated to Saint Benedict (see Plate 5). The Benedictines had requested a separate chapel for the lay brothers to recite the short breviary in vernacular English independent of the choir monks. As he did in the Assumption Chapel, Breuer designed Saint Benedict's Chapel in the shape of a trapezoid. But instead of placing the altar at the short end of the trapezoid facing the pews, as in Assumption, Breuer located the altar on the long end of the trapezoid and projected it into the body of the chapel, running the pews and stalls for 120 persons parallel to the long side walls. Breuer placed the altar on a brick platform and positioned it in front of a wooden screen painted in his signature blue. As they did for the parish chapel, the Benedictines originally requested that the altar in Saint Benedict's Chapel be situated so the Mass could be celebrated *versus populum*.[124] But their hopes were not realized and the altar was moved to a position on the backside of the predella, adjacent to the sacristy wall, and the celebrant said the Mass with his back to the brothers.[125] Color again shines through. The ceiling panel above the altar is covered in gold leaf, and the floor is a combination of waxed red brick in the aisles and cork under the pews and stalls.

Materiality is most evident in the Lady Chapel and the Blessed Sacrament Chapel on the west and east sides of the upper level of the building, respectively. The Lady Chapel enshrines the

Mabon Madonna, a twelfth-century Burgundian wooden statue that represents Mary as the throne of wisdom. Its schematic treatment of the human form contrasts nicely with the modern backdrop of a gold leaf ceiling, walls of blue mosaic, concrete, terracotta flue tiles, a black-and-gray granite floor, and wooden kneelers and bench (see Plate 6). Lighting in this small space is complex. The southern rectangular slit window provides a strong light during the day, with the square terracotta tile screen wall between the chapel and the nave allowing additional light to filter in. Users accessed the Blessed Sacrament Chapel from a doorway in the eastern cloister wall. Its decorative program is less complex than that of the Lady Chapel. A redbrick floor, dark-stained wood, and walls of white-painted concrete define the space. Breuer creates intimacy in these spaces by lowering the ceiling height to eight feet, encouraging individual prayer and contemplation.[126] The Lady Chapel is the best example of Breuer's design philosophy regarding color, pattern, and texture, where all elements are used in a disciplined manner for a successful architectural product.[127]

Just beyond the Blessed Sacrament Chapel is the entry to one of the enclosed cloister walks to the monastic enclosure and private monastic space. The monks gain access to their meeting space, the chapter house, from this eastern cloister walk. The chapter house serves three

functions for the Benedictines. Its primary purpose is as a meeting hall with seating for 160 that would "express the community, permit participation in discussion, and permit easy access to the table of the Abbot for voting."[128] It also acts as a lecture hall and choir rehearsal space. Breuer positioned the first chapter house directly south of the church near the monastic dormitory. Although the monks were pleased with this location, Breuer asked if the chapter house could become a separate space as it had begun to get in the way of the church design.[129] The monks approved, citing the fact that many European monasteries had a separate chapter house. Breuer then proposed a more circular building before settling on an angular shape, trapezoidal like that of the church. The location of the chapter house as built was farther north along the eastern walkway. A concrete framework covered with Cold Spring granite created the form. Seating is on the diagonal, with the abbot's throne located at the apex of the diamond (Figure 3.20). Inside, McGough's team painted the chapter house's cork walls and plaster concrete ceiling white. Color is provided through light, either by the blue can light fixtures or through diagonal-shaped colored plastic panels of red, orange, blue, yellow, turquoise, or gold in the coffers.

Two cloister gardens occupy the interstitial space between the church and chapter house/cloister walk on the east and the church and

FIGURE 3.20. The chapter house.

cloister walk on the west. Breuer interpreted this space in a modern way, placing a triangular garden on either side of the church, rather than using a singular rectangular garden as was commonly found in medieval monasteries. From a user's standpoint, the cloister gardens are unsuccessful, as their size and location prevent them from providing a meditative walking space for the monks. Discussion at one point called for fountains in these gardens, but the idea was deemed inappropriate on theological and functional levels. Placing fountains here would distract from the baptismal font, deemphasizing the role of the sacrament. Church committee member Benedict Avery also found it "undesirable to have jetting waters in these gardens" as they were "not intended to draw attention to themselves from within the church."[130] The hallway walls of the cloister walk were made of terracotta flue tiles, which Breuer called a "perforated wall or a veil—a masonry veil to the cloister."[131] It seems that these tiles fulfill three important design elements for Breuer. First, they are geometric in nature and Breuer believed that "shapes, developed geometrically, have something necessary about them. Besides emotional appeal, they have logical ap-

peal."[132] Second, they allow for a fascinating play of light and shadow, and finally, they tie aesthetically into the local farming culture and bring a regional, vernacular sensibility to the building, a nod to Breuer's ability to make modernism more meaningful at the mid-twentieth century.

A NEW SPACE FOR WORSHIP

With the completion of the church's structure, Breuer and his associates, the Benedictines, and builders McGough Construction achieved the physical form necessary for the new liturgical vision. The spiritual axis ordered the worshipper's way to heaven, both literally in its architectural form but also symbolically in its many important visual vantage points. Private devotions took their place on the building's periphery. The use of brick, concrete, wood, copper, terracotta tiles, and granite provided architectural variety to a building that upheld liturgical unity. Now Breuer and the Benedictines needed to continue their collaboration and focus on filling the building with the necessary liturgical art. But this time, they would all need the help of a specialist, a liturgical coordinator named Frank Kacmarcik.

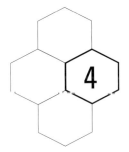

A MINISTRY OF ART

The Decorative Program of the Abbey Church

Breuer's abbey church fulfilled the Benedictines' vision for a modern vessel that would embrace the reformed liturgy. The bell banner delineated a line between the profane and sacred worlds. The building's layout emphasized the role of the sacraments in worship along a spiritual axis from the baptistery to main altar. Its open plan allowed worshippers to focus on the altar and the visual culmination of monastic choir and abbot's throne around it. Breuer's design also accommodated a chapel where the lay brothers could say their prayers in English. Nevertheless, the concept was incomplete without liturgical art to support the ritualistic actions that occurred within the architectural framework.

Art has always served as a visual representation of Catholic teachings, and the Benedictines have been creating art in service of the ritual of the Mass and monasticism for sixteen centuries.[1] Through the financial support of royalty and other wealthy landowners, monks and monk-artists collected and produced art, including illuminated manuscripts and prayer books, frescoes, wall paintings, sculpture, chalices, fonts, and tabernacles, at places such as Cluny and Maria Laach.[2] Saint John's brethren followed in the tradition of their medieval counterparts, founding an art department in the late nineteenth century that fashioned ecclesiastical art from local materials such as oak and brick.

This chapter considers the continued partnership of Breuer and the Benedictines in the furnishing of the church with liturgical art, including sculpture, painting, altars, shrines, stained glass, and a baptismal font. The close collaboration among Breuer, his liturgical consultant and artist Frank Kacmarcik, and the Benedictines builds on a twentieth-century tradition of sacred art commissions in which works from the world's leading artists, many of whom were not devoutly

FIGURE 4.1. The altar and shrine dedicated to Saint Peregrine showcase a variety of solids and voids in concrete and granite.

or at all Catholic, communicated clearly the message and goals of the church. According to James Cardinal Lercaro, it is the artist who has "the power of sensing—even anticipating—unconsciously perhaps, but with keen sensitivity, the attitudes, the tendencies, the aspiration of the moment and making himself their interpreter."[3]

In the mid-twentieth century, artists interpreted the world stylistically through a multitude of lenses. Modernism was one approach, promoted by such papal decrees as Pope Pius XII's 1947 encyclical *Mediator Dei* or "On the Sacred Liturgy":

> Recent works of art which lend themselves to the materials of modern composition should not be universally despised and rejected through prejudice. Modern art should be given free scope in the due and reverent service of the Church and sacred rites, provided that they preserve a correct balance between the styles, tending neither to extreme realism nor to excessive "symbolism," and that the needs of the Christian community are taken into consideration rather than the particular taste or talent of the artist.[4]

The pope encouraged a use of modern materials such as aluminum, copper, and steel, because they could dictate new forms. Five years later the Holy See followed with instructions to the bishops on sacred art, recognizing that every period of art is valuable, including modern. Sacred art's primary goal, however, is to "enhance the beauty of the house of God and foster the faith and piety of those who gather."[5] Breuer had a general vision for the church's furnishings, believing that "not every piece of art would have to be done according to contemporary form" and that "a variety of styles might be interesting." He also agreed that artists could be selected by an art consultant and not necessarily from a competition.[6]

Because of this project's size, which included the furnishing of the main church, baptistery, and thirty-seven chapels, it was important to hire a liturgical coordinator well versed in art and liturgy. The German Catholic bishops' 1947 directives stated that it would "be a mistake . . . to entrust the decoration of the church . . . to the arbitrary action of a transient pastor or of a donor, or to the risk of mere haphazard."[7] Breuer also thought that an artistic partner would be useful, so he suggested that Saint John's art instructor Frank Kacmarcik fill the role, and the Benedictines concurred.

The documentation of this collaboration at Collegeville is important to the history of sacred art scholarship. The archival sources indicate just how well versed the Benedictines were in contemporary art and architecture, and how well connected they and Kacmarcik were with liturgical leaders, the Vatican, and groups like the Catholic Art Association. Because of this, they filled the building with meaningful art by some of the preeminent artists of the time. They also contributed to a climate that accepted modern art into a religious setting, following the lead of groups like the Liturgical Arts Society of America.

THE LITURGICAL ARTS SOCIETY AND THE RISE OF MODERN LITURGICAL ART

The Liturgical Arts Society championed the creation of an American worship space that responded properly to twentieth-century liturgical reforms. From its inception in September 1927, Maurice Lavanoux (1894–1974), an architectural draftsman from the well-regarded Boston firm of Charles Maginnis and Timothy Walsh, led the group.[8] He edited the society's journal, *Liturgical Arts*, publishing it largely by himself four times a year from its premier issue in 1931 until its demise in the fall of 1972. *Liturgical Arts* upheld Lavanoux's view that the church could best be served by a liturgical environment that was shaped in response to the liturgy itself.[9] Lavanoux laid out his goals in the first editorial:

1. To understand the relationship of the arts to worship, as elucidated by leading clerical and lay authorities
2. To present the history of Catholic art
3. To show practical, detailed expositions of the liturgical requirements governing the construction and decoration of Churches

4. To provide descriptions of excellent modern work in architecture and the decorative arts, particularly in America

5. To share notes on such rare and important ancient objects exhibited in museums, or currently offered for sale, as will be useful in suggesting modern adaptation

6. To offer a bibliography of publications in the field

Through numerous articles in *Liturgical Arts*, Lavanoux fostered a mutual relationship for religious art and architecture and liturgical reforms.[10] Topics covered in these essays were broad, including concrete churches, the effects of light and color, and bibliographies on the evangelists. Lavanoux and the Liturgical Arts Society agreed, however, that the forms used to shape liturgical notions were not to be historical, and they demanded modern forms honestly expressed through their materiality and simplicity.

Lavanoux traveled across the globe, from Asia to Europe, experiencing and promoting modern art. His time in Vatican City helped solidify a strong American presence in liturgical reform prior to the onset of the Second Vatican Council in 1962. He stayed well informed of European developments through visits with liturgical leaders such as Abbot Lambert Beauduin at the Abbey of Mont-César. He also corresponded with Abbot Ildefons Herwegen of Maria Laach, who had published a *Liturgical Arts* essay in which he argued that religious art's essential role was to uplift worshippers: "The art of the sanctuary, therefore, does not exist for its own sake, but is purposive. Through its achievements—architecture, painting, sculpture, music—it aims to transport the faithful from what is sinful, or profane, or tinged with the cares of everyday life, to what is pure, blessed, divinely joyous."[11] Lavanoux considered Father Romano Guardini's 1927 *Spirit of the Liturgy* a "keystone for his own work" in the United States and required reading for all interested in liturgical reform.[12]

Another important influence for Lavanoux was the French Dominican priest, Father Marie-Alain Couturier (1897–1954).[13] Couturier edited the influential journal *L'Art Sacré* from 1937 until 1954, using it as a platform to argue that "the precise ideas and goals of ecclesiastical art should be pondered and presented by the church, but then the church should step back and let free the genius of the artist (which exists independent of Christian faith and yet is not without its own mysterious lines to the transcendent and the mystical)."[14] It is clear that a vision like Couturier's could create art of great power, but without a knowledgeable patron to explain and uphold its use in the church, it could also facilitate a disaster. Couturier opened the door to non-Christian artists completing works for the church, as he felt the most talented artists in the world could achieve the spiritual in their art, regardless of their religious preference.

Lavanoux promoted Couturier's call for modernism to all elements of Catholic sacred space. Couturier's commission of artists for French projects, including the Chapel of our Lady of All the Graces in Assy (1945–47), the Dominican Convent Chapel of the Rosary at Vence (1947–51), the Church of the Sacred Heart at Audincourt (1950–52), and Notre Dame du Haut in Ronchamp (1950–55), set a new standard in religious design. At Assy architect Maurice Novarina's 1937 chalet-style sandstone chapel supplemented the worship spaces of the important Plateau d'Assy sanatorium system.[15] Assy's priest sought his friend Couturier's help in completing the interiors by commissioning a range of modern artists. Pierre Bonnard, Georges Braque, Marc Chagall, Fernand Léger, Jacques Lipchitz, Jean Lurçat and his student Paul Cosandier, Henri Matisse, Germaine Richier, and Georges Rouault, among others, designed tapestries, mosaics, murals, and stained glass for the chapel.[16] Novarino also designed the church at Audincourt, where the windows and altar panel completed by Léger were inextricably linked with the shape of the building. Auguste Perret's design for the chapel at Vence served as a backdrop for Matisse's artwork.[17] Although the local Catholic hierarchy often criticized works in these buildings, these projects raised an awareness of sacred modern art in the years after World War II.[18] It was no longer satisfactory to fill buildings with prefabricated statues or objects by second-rate artists.

While the brethren at Saint John's had already established themselves as leaders in the broader liturgical reform movement, they recognized Lavanoux's expertise in the field of liturgical art and consulted him frequently during the design of the abbey church and its furnishings, even sending Breuer and his team a brochure on the society.[19] They listened keenly to his promotion of artistic projects, both at home and abroad, as they began work on the artistic component of Saint John's Abbey Church. They were well aware that an artist's religious background did not matter and that they could balance tradition and innovation as they completed the venture. But with the approximately fifty or more pieces needed for the building, they needed someone to manage the project. Enter Frank Kacmarcik.

LITURGICAL AND ARTISTIC CONSULTANT FRANK KACMARCIK

The first mention of the need to hire a liturgical and artistic coordinator came in the fall of 1953 in a letter from Father Cloud Meinberg to Breuer:

> I feel that there should be someone consulted now in the early stages of the planning of the church on the possibilities of

integrating painting, sculpture, etc. in the very architectural masses in such a way that they will really belong to the building, be a development of its thinking and growth, be thoroughly modern, and yet at the same time, fully traditional in iconographic content.[20]

For five years Breuer and his office ignored this request and worked mainly with the Benedictines to construct the building as a vessel of the liturgy. Finally in the summer of 1958 Breuer's concern for the success of the artistic program within his building prompted him to contact Abbot Dworschak and request assistance. The abbot responded with the name of the liturgical consultant, Frank Kacmarcik (Figure 4.2).[21]

Kacmarcik was born in St. Paul, Minnesota, in 1920 to first-generation Slovak–Polish Catholics. Both his parents had a strong appreciation of craftsmanship and hard work; his father was a furniture upholsterer and refinisher, and his mother was very interested in handicrafts. Kacmarcik studied art at the Minneapolis College of Art and Design on a scholarship from 1938 to 1941 before

FIGURE 4.2. Liturgical coordinator Frank Kacmarcik.

entering Saint John's Abbey as a novice. At Saint John's the mentorship of Brother Clement Frischauf (1869–1944), a monk-artist and one of the last remaining members of the Beuronese school of painting, influenced Kacmarcik greatly.[22]

After serving the United States in World War II, Kacmarcik went back to school, studying for another year at the Minneapolis College of Art and Design as well as at two Parisian schools, the Académie de la Grand Chaumière and the Centre d'Art Sacré, where he pursued a standard academic training in painting.[23] During these formative years, Kacmarcik also developed a better understanding of unity in all the artistic elements of a church from other influences, including the work of Augustus Welby Northmore Pugin, Ralph Adams Cram, and Eric Gill.

Saint John's University hired Kacmarcik as an art instructor in 1950, a position he would hold until 1954, when he left the institution and established himself as an independent liturgical art consultant. He was an advocate for modernism and played a major role in convincing the Benedictines, particularly Abbot Dworschak and Father Meinberg, that modern art and architecture were appropriate solutions to their building needs.[24] He became well known for his application of modern art to modern worship space; as priest and liturgical scholar Robert Tuzik has pointed out, "Much of the progress that has been made in architecture and the arts in this country can be attributed to Frank Kacmarcik."[25]

Kacmarcik described the role of a liturgical consultant as

a very difficult one, especially if he is an artist like myself. His role is not to impose his personality on the building. He should act more as a teacher, making the architect more than he would be if the consultant were not there, the pastor more of a pastor, and the people's role more active.[26]

He characterized his work as "a ministry of art" and himself as a "deacon preaching visual theology."[27] He went on to state:

The furnishings, the vessels, the utensils that we use in worship must have a profundity, a *gravitas*, an inner content, nothing frivolous about them. . . . That is why we need art consultants, not just for buildings and spaces, but for all the things we use in worship: for furnishings, for vessels, for vesture, for objects.[28]

According to Kacmarcik, the most successful consultants pursued a broad mandate of artistic and architectural involvement as they encouraged Catholics to embrace the new communal nature of the church. Kacmarcik's ability to sustain a career as a liturgical art consultant was due not only to his tenacity and will to see things done correctly, but also to his visual acumen, artistic insights, and a Catholic reform movement that encouraged the unification of church space and decorative arts in the postwar years.

KACMARCIK, THE ART COMMITTEE, AND BREUER

The Benedictines hired Kacmarcik as the liturgical and artistic consultant in December 1958. Kacmarcik had been corresponding with Breuer as early as the fall of 1953, recommending two sacred artists, Jean Lambert-Rucki of Paris and Gerald Bonnette of Vermont, who could help Breuer make the art of the church "an integral part of the whole architectural concept spiritually and aesthetically."[29] During his tenure as coordinator Kacmarcik made several trips to Breuer's office, always concerned with how Breuer's architectural language could be used for sacred space. After a May 1957 visit he wrote to Breuer, "I am still very concerned as to how and whether a sacral character can be achieved in the completion of the new church. It is this that will make this project different from UNESCO and other contemporary works."[30] Breuer replied: "As far as the sacral character of the church is concerned, I feel that we're are on the right track, and all that we need is some confidence. I should have said, a great deal of confidence and I assure you I am very conscious of this."[31] Kacmarcik was intent on carefully guiding Breuer through this process and even more intent on using modern art by

modern artists whenever possible, as long as the Benedictines agreed. Knowing that this would be a difficult task, Kacmarcik even wrote a prayer of support:

Lord God, our Father, send us wise makers of sacred forms to adorn a visible house for Your invisible glory. Enlighten us, and let us choose the ones who have received wisdom from You to do this work with all humility, reverence and perfection. . . . Show us to find the ones who that same Holy Spirit will guide and strengthen for their task. Be mindful, Lord, of these artists, and stand by them in the work they have undertaken for Your glory. Strengthen their souls in their struggle to create new and living forms. Defend them against the lure of cowardly solutions, falsity, insincerity and servility to worldly standards. May they be sanctified in their work, may their work itself be holy, and may it raise all hearts to you in prayer. Amen.[32]

By January 1960, the monks agreed that modern art did have a place in the new building, and after years of working in somewhat piecemeal fashion with artists, they formed an art committee consisting of Fathers Benedict Avery and Joachim Watrin. They were responsible for "all new vestments, rugs and furnishings," as well as the theological content of each piece.[33] Three sources appear regularly in their correspondence with the architect and artists, and aided their understanding regarding furnishing the church: the German bishops' "Directives for the Building of a Church" (1947), Peter Anson's *Churches: Their Plan and Furnishing* (1948), and John O'Connell's *Church Building and Furnishing* (1955).[34] These documents provided historical and contemporary information on church building and furnishings. Additionally, the artistic (and architectural) work at the abbey was guided by papal decrees, including Pius XII's "On the Sacred Liturgy" of November 20, 1947, and the Holy Office's "Sacred Art" instruction of June 30, 1952.[35]

ALTAR DESIGNS BY MARCEL BREUER AND FRANK KACMARCIK

The Benedictines commissioned several artists to complete the necessary imagery for the church, including Marcel Breuer, whom they encouraged to design some of the church's liturgical furniture. Anson's and O'Connell's texts would have upheld the significance of the altar as the most important piece of art in the church. O'Connell defines the altar as a "consecrated table of natural stone in which relics of the saints are enshrined, and on which the Christian sacrifice—the Mass—is offered."[36] The Catholic bishops of Germany emphasized the symbolic status of the altar:

> Since at the Consecration in the Mass our divine Lord becomes present upon the altar,

it is, even without the tabernacle, Christ's throne on earth. And since the altar is His throne, the faithful from patristic times saw in the altar a symbol of Christ Himself, for the throne symbolizes the person of the Ruler.[37]

Breuer wanted a cube-shaped high altar, but the brethren requested one that was rectangular and more like the early Christian table. Breuer's high altar design imparts architectural and liturgical significance as it integrates into the overall design of the building. As was mentioned in chapter 3, architecturally it recalls the bell banner, and liturgically it is a focal point for the monks and laity with its central placement in the apse. Workmen fashioned the altar on-site and from the baldachin above it suspended a silver Greek cross that provided both the brethren and the laity with a view of this symbolic reminder of Christ as the priest celebrated Mass both *versus populum* and facing the monastic choir (Figure 4.3). Sculptor James Rosati of New York finished the crucifix, candleholders, and tabernacle for the high altar.[38] The monks sent the sculptor a letter describing the liturgical purpose of each item in the Mass and included a four-page essay on the historical and contemporary importance of the crucifix. The brethren also requested that Rosati fashion a crucifix that had artistic interest on each side, since the Mass would be celebrated from both sides of the altar. He fulfilled their wishes by

FIGURE 4.3. Workmen position the high altar, May 1961. Photograph by field superintendent Ted Hoffmeyer.

placing a corpus on the choir side of the cross and an abstract jeweled pattern on the opposite side facing the laity.[39]

In his designs for the church's additional altars, Breuer maintained unity of the building project through the choice of form, the trapezoid, and materials such as granite and concrete. Granite, quarried from nearby Cold Spring, Minnesota, and inlaid into the concrete, composed the ambo and communion rails in the upper church. In the lower church, Breuer used Cold Spring polished granite in the parish and brothers' chapels, while in Saint Peregrine's altar shrine he combined a granite mensa set in concrete with a bush hammered concrete base (see Figure 4.1). His most creative expression in altar design, however, came in the completion of the private crypt chapels.

CRYPT CHAPELS: ART AND ARCHITECTURE

With over two hundred priests on-site at Saint John's, the need for space for each to say his required daily Mass was great. Breuer and his team used the eastern and western sides of the crypt or basement level for thirty-four private chapels for this need, each filled with art appropriate to the saint or saints of its dedication (Figures 4.4 and 4.5).[40] Each saint provides a vital link to important events in the church and in Benedictine monasticism.[41] Relics are included in each of the chapels, another connection to the past.

The money for these chapels came in part from contributions beyond the abbey. The abbey sent brochures soliciting donors for the chapels in March and April 1958.[42] The monks were calculated in designating saints of dedication, as they did not want to refuse inappropriate gifts or create a haphazard situation later on. Patrons could fund a chapel (to be decided on by the Benedictines) as a memorial to a loved one, with payment plans that allowed for installments rather than giving all the money up front. The brethren dedicated all the chapels in a ceremony on July 19, 1961, and invited all funders to attend.

The brethren likened the altar designs of Breuer and Kacmarcik to the simple, wooden early Christian altars.[43] Breuer's altar design for chapel two devoted to Saint Henry is one of his most interesting, consisting of a single support that starts out as an ellipse but meets the two-color granite mensa as a rectangle (Figure 4.6). On Saint Francis of Assisi's chapel altar he left the granite rough and supported the mensa with two trapezoidal-shaped legs that recall the overall plan of the church (see Plate 7). The brethren called Kacmarcik's design for the altar in Saint Ansgar's chapel, where two square blocks of granite provide a base from which four simple legs rise to meet the rectangular table, his heaviest and most elaborate, noting its character as Romanesque.[44] In the altar designed for the American saint Isaac Jogues's chapel, Kacmarcik

FIGURE 4.4 (*left*). The hallway of the western crypt chapels.

FIGURE 4.5 (*below*). The private chapel prototype.

FIGURE 4.6 (*facing*). Breuer's design for the private chapel altar dedicated to Saint Henry.

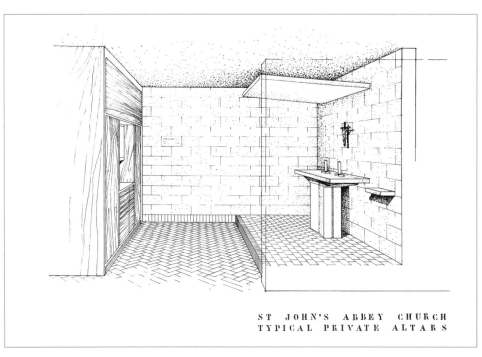

ST JOHN'S ABBEY CHURCH
TYPICAL PRIVATE ALTARS

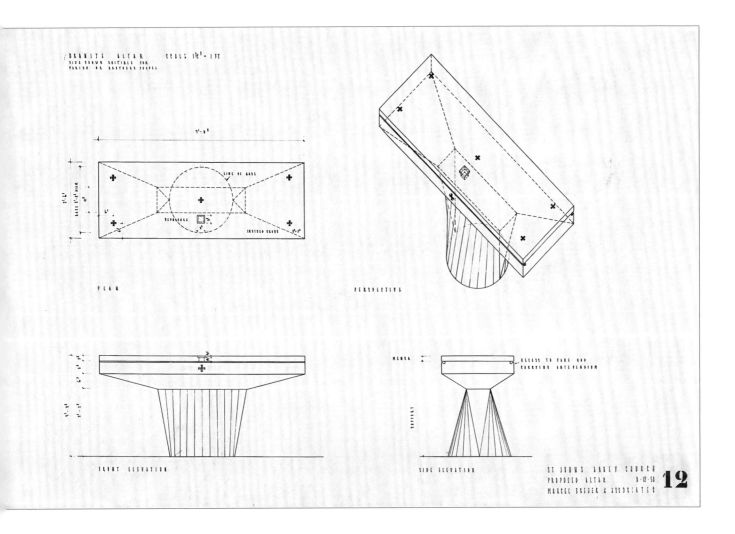

GRANITE ALTAR   SCALE 1½" = 1FT
SIZE SHOWN SUITABLE FOR
PARISH OR BROTHERS CHAPEL

PLAN

PERSPECTIVE

FRONT ELEVATION

SIDE ELEVATION

ST JOHNS ABBEY CHURCH
PROPOSED ALTAR   9-12-53
MARCEL BREUER & ASSOCIATES

12

emphasized the nature of the material, enframing a rough-hewn granite pillar within two smaller polished pieces as a support for the mensa.

ART IN THE CRYPT CHAPELS

In addition to designing altars for the private chapels, Kacmarcik also aided the monks in procuring art for each space. In late February 1960, the abbey began inviting artists to create art for the crypt chapels. They asked for art that would "utilize the living, creative forms of our own day" and would be "in harmony with the monumental character of the architecture. At the same time it should convey a profound sense of the sacred. It is art with rich theological content—with a Godward rather than a subjective, sentimental orientation—which will, we believe, best reflect Christian tradition as it has found expression in the great churches of the past."[45] In April 1961 more than twenty artists received a detailed letter from the abbey asking them to design specific art for the building. These letters described how the monks sought art that fit into the "virile architecture" of the building, as Abbot Dworschak described it to artist Peter Watts of England.[46] Writing to the Italian artist Mario De Luigi, Dworschak further characterized Breuer's architecture:

> Marcel Breuer's strong and dynamic architecture is marked by a vital character and an almost austere simplicity. These are a challenge to the artist to produce a contemporary sacred image possessing a gravity and a profundity that are truly creative and universal—an image free of the sentimentality that has so seriously marred religious art since the Renaissance, depriving it of its Godward, sacred character. The ideal is to portray the Saint in his essentially spiritual presence in the Church today/in the praying Church rather than merely to recall an incident from his earthly life.[47]

Furthermore, the art, like the architecture, must be fashioned of the "living creative forms of our own day" and also "convey a profound sense of the sacred."[48]

The abbot's letter pursued the goal of commissioning modern, simple art, appropriate to present-day worshippers, from artists of all faiths. Maurice Lavanoux reminded the brethren during a visit with the art committee in May 1960 that they "needed to embrace artists of all faiths, not only to promote ecumenism and charity, but also to find the truly talented designers."[49] The artists selected came from England, Germany, Italy, Panama, Switzerland, Missouri, New York, Rhode Island, and even from within Saint John's membership. They were Jews, atheists, Catholics, and Protestants. The brethren kept Breuer abreast of their progress in furnishing the church. A portion of Breuer's office files, archived in Special Collections at Syracuse University, is filled with copies of artists' brochures and the Benedictines' correspondence with various artists.

A commission for artwork usually started with a recommendation by the arts committee or the liturgical coordinator for a particular artist to complete a piece in a specific medium.[50] For instance, Kacmarcik endorsed the well-known Jewish artist Leonard Baskin of New York to make a work in wood for the crypt chapel of Saint Thomas Aquinas.[51] The abbot then sent a letter to the artist seeking his commitment. Baskin was flattered by the offer but was also candid about his artistic fee: "I fear you will be adding to your financial burdens if you employ me. My work in the New York marketplace sells for atrocious sums and I am not in a position to alter that state of affairs."[52] The Benedictines hired him anyway, and the abbot sent a letter laying out the iconography and historical background on Saint Thomas, suggesting books to read, including the saint's own *Summa Theologica*.[53] He also stated the reasons for dedication, in this case, because the monks wanted to include leaders from other religious orders such as the Dominicans. Saint Thomas was also the patron saint of schools, a critical element of life in Collegeville. The packet included a blueprint of the chapel illustrating its architectural setting, colors, and the location of the intended artwork.

The ideas of the art committee and Kacmarcik had a direct bearing on the aesthetic component of the commission, and in the case of Baskin, the abbot relayed to the sculptor specific ideas of how he might conceive the artwork. The letter mentions that since the space had an altar with a crucifix over it, perhaps the piece could depict Saint Thomas praying before it, given his lifelong devotion to the crucified Christ. "The Saint could be shown standing in prayer, turned somewhat in the direction of the altar crucifix . . . and perhaps with hands reaching forward slightly. Such a representation would also represent the mystical quality of his prayer."[54] The monks hoped to see sketches of the work in case details about iconography or theology needed to be discussed. Baskin refused to send a sketch of the saint but did allow the Benedictines refusal of the final piece.

Baskin's thirty-nine-inch-high walnut statue captures the sprit of the Benedictines' intentions for liturgical art to support the chapel's saintly theme (Figure 4.7). The artist stated that he sought a "straight forward monumentality as befitting the author of the Summa and a man of great physical stability."[55] Saint Thomas Aquinas's hands are clasped in prayer and design details are kept to a minimum, recalling the French sculptor Auguste Rodin's *Balzac* of the late nineteenth century. The brethren had not specified a style for the work; they wanted a "virile" and sacred piece that would communicate Thomas's passion for Christian theology to the viewer.

Established international artists also completed work for the Benedictines. In 1954 the Parisian artist Jean Lambert-Rucki contacted the

FIGURE 4.7. Leonard Baskin, *St. Thomas Aquinas*. Walnut, 39 inches.

monks about providing art for the building, and he received commissions to complete art for two private chapels.[56] Father Godfrey Diekmann's reply to Lambert-Rucki's letter encouraged his involvement, stating that many of the monks thought he was "the most qualified Catholic sculptor to execute the decoration of the church."[57] After Lambert-Rucki's successful completion of the figures of Saints Joachim and Anne, on August 17, 1960, Abbot Dworschak asked him to consider doing additional work in wood, perhaps a figure of Saint Vincent de Paul or Saint Cloud, and a crucifix.[58] Nine days later he accepted the commission for a three- to four-foot-high statue in oak with little color.[59] He also included sketches of his ideas, based on directions the monks had sent. The monks assigned him Saint Cloud, a grounding of the art in its locale, with the city of St. Cloud only a short drive away. They even asked him to change the church the saint held in his sketch to represent the town's cathedral, the local diocesan headquarters. They included a photograph of the cathedral and told Lambert-Rucki to interpret the building freely.[60] The next version of Lambert-Rucki's Saint Cloud figure did not meet with the monks' approval, and they requested a "strong and virile" version.[61] Within two months the brethren were satisfied with Lambert-Rucki's work. The statue and crucifix arrived in Collegeville in late May 1961 and were installed in the private chapel before the consecration of the church in August (Figure 4.8).

Artists with ties to Saint John's also completed work for the building, including 1953 university alumnus Gerald Bonnette, whom the brethren hired to design art for the chapel dedicated to Saint Francis of Assisi (see Plate 7).[62] The monks kept a dossier of Bonnette's work, and Josef Albers, Marcel Breuer, Walter Gropius, and Richard Neutra had all noted its quality, even when he was a student.[63] Bonnette's inspiration for the seraphic polychrome wooden crucifix was "Francis' vision of the winged seraph revealing Christ to him. Isaiah had the original vision of seraphim (angels) with their six wings and their cry of 'Holy, holy is the LORD of hosts.'"[64] The eyes in the wings signify God's all-seeing power. The cost for crucifix and figure was $1,200, and they were delivered to the abbey in February 1960.

THE LADY CHAPEL AND THE BAPTISTERY

Like the crypt chapels, two spaces in the upper church showcase the important relationships between art and religion, tradition and innovation. The Lady Chapel reveals how historical art can be merged with modern design. The chapel's focus is on Mary as the throne of wisdom, seen in the thirty-six-inch-tall, walnut with polychrome, twelfth-century Burgundian Madonna sculpture. Kacmarcik secured its donation from patrons James B. and Mary Frost Mabon of New York City and placed it in the colorful modern setting of the Breuer-designed chapel on the main floor

FIGURE 4.8. Jean Lambert-Rucki's wooden figure of Saint Cloud, 36 inches, polychromed oak.

of the church, a place for private devotions as we saw in chapter 3 (see Plate 6).

In the baptistery, architect and artist united in a design that created a renewed awareness and appreciation for the visitor of the central sacrament of baptism with modern artistic forms. As we saw earlier, the central font was supplemented by one of the most prominent sculptural pieces commissioned for the church, Doris Caesar's statue of the abbey's namesake, Saint John the Baptist (see Plate 8).[65] Kacmarcik and the abbey began corresponding with Caesar about the commission early in 1959. Abbot Dworschak stressed its importance as *the* statue of the church's patron thereby securing its prominent position within the building.[66] Upon Caesar's acceptance of the commission, Kacmarcik reaffirmed the significance of the work to the artist, calling this piece "the most important commission" and hoping that "the final work will be a great and true work of sacred art."[67] As they did for the small chapels, the Benedictines carefully guided this commission, informing Caesar of the liturgical and historical importance of the work by sending her a short text and articles. Abbot Dworschak and Subprior Eidenschink visited Caesar in Connecticut in March 1959 and viewed the finished clay model in order to approve it before she did the final cast in bronze. Upon completion of the statue, she described it as "beautiful," with the patina already "mellowed into a very fine dark brown."[68] Saint John the Baptist stands ninety-six inches high and its elongated, somewhat distorted form is expressionistic. Caesar shipped the statue of Saint John to Collegeville in June 1961 so that Breuer could position it during a visit. She reported her pleasure at the approval of her work to Abbot Dworschak:

I have heard from Mr. Breuer that the two bronzes arrived and that the statue of St. John is magnificent, placed in the Baptistry. I am very happy that he and Hamilton Smith and Frank Kac[marcik], all of whose opinion I value highly, feel that the figure has strength, beauty and power in this great architectural setting.[69]

The fellowship experienced by the abbot, Breuer, and Caesar was special and indicative of how collaboration could create great art for the building.[70] However, Abbot Dworschak and Marcel Breuer's working relationship was significantly tested over another major artistic element of the building, the northern window wall.

THE DEBATE OVER THE NORTHERN WINDOW WALL OF STAINED GLASS

Generally, the monks accepted Breuer's ideas for the church, as they were the product of considerable dialogue with the community. In the case of the design for the stained glass in the 430 hexagons of the northern wall, an expanse of glass 178 feet wide by 65 feet high, patron choice trumped the architect's vision. Breuer intended to have the design completed by his former Bauhaus classmate, Josef Albers (1888–1976).[71] Albers was born in Germany and had studied art in Essen and Munich before entering the Weimar Bauhaus in 1920, where he became friends with Breuer. After completing his studies, he joined the Bauhaus faculty teaching and eventually ran the furniture workshop. When the Nazis closed the Bauhaus in 1933, Albers moved to the United States and became head of the art department at the newly founded Black Mountain College near Asheville, North Carolina, where he remained until 1949. From 1950 to 1958 he served as the head of the art department at Yale University.

In the fall of 1955 Albers completed the five-by-eleven-foot White Cross window in the abbot's private chapel at Saint John's (Figures 4.9 and 4.10). The window design was first and foremost practical, reducing light and glare in the chapel.[72] Artistically Breuer encouraged Albers to be abstract and nonrepresentational, hoping the window would "apply purely architectural forms, textures and colors."[73] The chapel window was a natural outgrowth of Albers's research into color theory, particularly his *Homage to the Square* series initiated in 1950.[74] Images in this series placed colors in the shape of a square while varying or re-peating the hue, forcing the viewer to evaluate art in a new way with pure color. Albers did not mix colors but rather put them on the canvas straight out of the tube and made color superior to form.[75] In the abbot's chapel, however, color is enhanced by form for Albers; as he later said about it, "mathematical form and measurement, its radial and static symmetry, I believe improves its mystic atmosphere and vibration."[76] The White Cross window provided a three-dimensional version of the *Homage* series but with white rectangles, using the mullions of the eleven-foot-wide factory window to further divide the space in a rectilinear fashion, as Albers described:

> The resulting substructure of overlapping rectangles permitted me to arrange three adjacent shades of opalescent white in such a way that the rectangles appear not only translucent (visible through each other) but also in different distance.[77]

He went on to detail the unifying action of the cross's thin white lines: "Above a ground of indistinct distance, light accumulates toward the middle and culminates in the whitest light of the extended cross, the center, extending wide arms to the farthest ends."[78] The accumulation of a bright white light was made possible by new fabrication techniques, facilitated by Corning Glass Laboratories in New York.[79] Each piece of glass, directly

FIGURE 4.9 (*left*). Josef Albers's White Cross window in the abbot's private chapel.

FIGURE 4.10 (*below*). Detail of Albers's White Cross window.

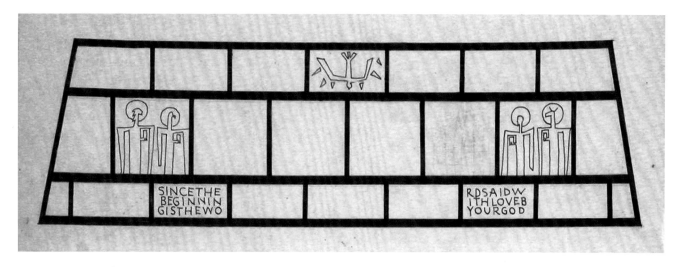

FIGURE 4.11. Gerald Bonnette's design for the stained glass in the northern window.

set in mullions rather than the usual divisions of leading, was photosensitive. Unlike traditional stained glass, it did not require direct sunlight as reflected light could illuminate the window on cloudy days and at night.

In his earliest designs for the church of December 1953, Breuer drew inspiration from the UNESCO project and included a Mondrian-inspired grid-like tracery scheme of concrete rectangles and squares on both the northern and southern ends of the church, with the northern wall finished in textured glass of various transparencies and the southern end in concrete block painted a deep blue and pierced with small glazed blue lights. Breuer had granted the Benedictines' request that artist Gerald Bonnette design a pat-

tern for the northern window (Figure 4.11). When the reworked church plans were presented in May 1957, Breuer changed the northern wall to a pattern of 430 concrete hexagons filled with glass.[80] As discussed in chapter 3, Breuer used the hexagon in his design for De Bijenkorf department store in Rotterdam in 1953.[81] Discussion began in the summer of 1958 regarding completion of the great northern wall of stained glass. Breuer anticipated a varied use of color, with translucent glass applied at the edges and transparent glass in the middle to better view the bell banner from inside the church.[82] He also believed that the design needed to be integrated with the overall building, reflecting its form in geometry and simplicity.

The expanse of the northern wall presented an artistic opportunity and challenge. Everyone understood the importance of this commission, including Abbot Dworschak, who stated that the northern wall "provides a wonderful opportunity for stained glass of noble proportions."[83] The Benedictines did not want the window program to represent a major iconographic theme, but insisted it should use abstraction to create an appropriate mood for the interior of the church.[84] As in the work of Dominikus Böhm and Rudolf Schwarz, light, color, and the atmosphere they provided were essential elements of religious design for the Benedictines.

Given the artistic weight of the window to the building, it was crucial to find the right artist. Immediately, the Benedictines were led to one of the world's most prominent stained glass artists, the Frenchman Alfred Manessier.[85] They discussed his work in their early meetings and deemed him the artist "most competent to design this window for our Church."[86] Manessier had completed stained glass commissions in many churches, including All Saint's in Basel with architect Hermann Baur.

Abbot Dworschak's letter to Manessier requested a sketch of his ideas and outlined the important considerations for the commission.[87] First, each pane of glass was to be set into a hexagon with a 9½-inch reveal on the interior and 14½-inch on the exterior. The second and third considerations involved the design complications arising from the structure of Breuer's building, including the lack of direct light due to the northern orientation of the window and the need to respect architectural elements already in place, including the bell banner and interior balcony. The theme of the window was the liturgy, as Abbot Dworschak explained:

> The central portion represents the Mass,
> a lifting of the mind and heart to God; the
> side portions represent the liturgical year
> in its different liturgical seasons of Advent,
> Christmas, Lent, Easter and Pentecost.[88]

But as he was courting Manessier, who would bow out of the process after citing its limitations, Abbot Dworschak had another designer working on the problem in Collegeville, the Polish artist Bronislaw Bak (1922–81).[89] Bak, a survivor of German labor and concentration camps during World War II, studied art in postwar Germany under German expressionist painters at Mannheim and Koblenz before moving to the United States with his family in 1952. He became a stained glass window designer at the Michaudel Stained Glass Studio in Chicago before his 1958 appointment as a faculty member of Saint John's art department (Figure 4.12).[90]

On September 11, 1958, Abbot Dworschak wrote a letter to Hamilton Smith introducing Bak to the Breuer office, informing them that Bak was eager to complete a sketch for the window and the abbey had agreed to let him do so.[91] Smith, and subsequently Breuer, who was traveling in France at the time, must have been surprised, for the letter went on to state that not only had the sketch been completed, it had also been unanimously approved by the community. As Abbot Dworschak explained:

> Mr. Bak has actual experience in stained glass windows, and he said that if he were fortunate enough to be commissioned to do the window, he would plan to hire two glass cutters and make the window here under his supervision. He would purchase the glass required from Germany and from France, and one type, I believe, from this country, and he was fully confident that making the window here would be much better than having it cut elsewhere or manufactured elsewhere and then shipped here. He felt that the artist, whoever he may be, must supervise the manufacture of the window, for only in that way could he select and choose the exact piece of glass required in each instance.[92]

FIGURE 4.12. Bronislaw Bak at work on stained glass at Saint John's.

Fabrication of the window on-site had many advantages. First, it was fiscally responsible, particularly if the brethren could provide some of the needed labor. It would also be a useful

FIGURE 4.13. Bronislaw Bak with a cartoon for the center portion of the northern window.

instructional tool for the university's art department. But most importantly for the Benedictines, it solidified their impression of Bak as a dedicated artist who would put into place every piece of glass and monitor every move made in the construction of the window. Bak had the added benefit of being an insider in the Benedictine community, which was important for the brethren. Bak's fashioning of the window also followed the Benedictine tradition of inspirational and powerful sacred art and architecture, as Susan Hedahl has pointed out:

> Both enriching and complicating the conversations of the Church Committee was the fact that of all arts connected with church building, that of the art of stained glass window-making had been borne with special pride of the Benedictines through the centuries.[93]

Even though the brethren entertained several notable stained glass designers, they continued to promote Bak as their choice. Pressure from the abbot to accept Bak's designs led Breuer to take a "wait and see" attitude, and he provided Bak both encouragement and criticism during late 1958. Encouraged by Bak's designs, Breuer supported the abbot's decision to award him the commission of the north window, believing that "this work will turn out very well. As I understand, he is already working in glass on a number of hexagons and I am anxious to see his experiments on

my next visit to Saint John's."[94] But Breuer was unaware of what was really going on in Collegeville. During the first five months of 1959, Kacmarcik informed Breuer that he was "concerned with all the haste and also some rather political moves" occurring with the project, and he felt Bak's work was not "the standard we should have."[95] As the liturgical consultant, Kacmarcik wanted a window that would be a "really dynamic and creative solution" to the problem, and he made his concerns known to the Benedictines and the architects in March with his "Critical Observations and Recommendations for the Great Window of the New Abbey Church."[96]

In May 1959 Breuer finally examined Bak's design firsthand and rejected it, disappointed that the artist had not heeded his comments and recommendations. He then asked the monks to solicit a design from Albers, whose White Cross window had been so well received. Soon a small head-to-head competition developed between Albers and Bak.[97] Bak continued to rework his design, incorporating suggestions from Breuer and others in his preparation of a full-scale cartoon (Figure 4.13). At the same time Albers inquired about an appropriate theme for the window, asking the church committee if the "presentation of a text of a significant prayer would be liturgically desirable."[98] Albers had the support of the liturgical consultant Kacmarcik and the architect Breuer, who even escorted Albers to the abbey on November 12, 1959, for the presentation of his window design.[99] Bak had the support of the monks. But who would design the church's largest artistic element?

Albers's design echoed the architectural nature of the bell banner and building plan with its strong trapezoidal-shaped central element and use of diagonal lines (see Plate 9). Its red, yellow, and orange color scheme would visually provide warmth to the building. A white cross, reminiscent of the abbot's chapel window, filled the center space and clearly communicated the presence of God. Like Albers, Bak created a work that was abstract but much more complicated in design and cooler in tone (see Plate 10). Bak used an abundance of colors, including reds, blues, and purples, in his attempt to bring the symbolic colors of the liturgical season together in a cohesive whole.[100]

The two designs were judged not only by the architect and client but also by the American stained glass master Emil Frei Jr. Frei supported Albers and was pleased with his sketch because it "respected fully the forms of the structure."[101] But Frei advised the brethren that their architect should make the final decision. The Benedictines did not heed his advice and, after a lengthy discussion on the matter, called for a vote of the church committee to select the winner on November 25, 1959. The count was seven to five in favor of Bak. Displeased with the outcome, Breuer told the abbot that the window was an "organic part of the architecture" that belonged in

the "architect's domain just as much, or probably more, than to the domain of the artist."[102] Hamilton Smith found Bak's design "lacking an organic principle that would have aesthetically kept the window in harmony with the church."[103] Smith went on to state that Breuer's advice to Bak over the past months was not heeded and Bak was unable to successfully complete such a large-scale project, for he was more interested in making "individually over-wrought panels which do not relate in color, value or line to each other or to the original overall design sketch."[104] Frank Kacmarcik was even more vehement in his displeasure. He stated that the acceptance of Bak's design was a "serious compromise of artistic standards and integrity" and the only solution to the problem was to "smash the window."[105]

Breuer, Smith, and Kacmarcik were fighting for the larger artistic integrity of the abbey church. Puzzled by Breuer's lack of confidence in the Benedictines' ability to judge the situation, Abbot Dworschak stated:

> If you felt that we did not have sufficient competence to judge the merits of the work of Mr. Bak and if you had told us this, I think most of us would have been willing to withdraw and let the decision rest with you and those more competent to judge.[106]

Obviously there had been a breakdown in communication between Breuer and the Benedictines. Yet there were other reasons why Bak's design was selected. It was financially practical, as by this point the abbey had secured donations for 100 of the 430 hexagons, and they wanted the window to be finished at the church's consecration. Some involved in the process, such as architect Robert Gatje, believed that Albers's manner annoyed the fathers, particularly his professorial lectures on the virtues of using a light-diffusing prismatic glass, similar to that used in his design for the abbot's private chapel window.[107] Meanwhile, Bak's inclusive approach fulfilled the Rule of Saint Benedict's call for artisans of the community "to practice their craft with all humility" while "fending off idleness by daily manual labor" through his offer to train the brothers in the making of his colored glass.[108]

Work on the glass window took place on-site over the course of eighteen months. In an unused dairy barn on campus, Bak fashioned the window in 125 hues of handblown glass imported from France, Germany, and England. Six brothers aided Bak: Adrian Cahill, Andrew Goltz, Richard Haeg, John Kruz, David Riegel, and Placid Stuckenschneider. Bak focused his design on the symbolic white eye of God at the center, surrounded by swirling red flames (see Plate 11). On either side of the central area are shafts of green with red, recalling the tree of life and the fruit of the spirit. When viewed from the interior of the building, the window's church year theme begins on the left side with Advent depicted in shafts of yellows and tans. Multicolored stars proclaim Christmas joy. Easter, represented immediately to the right of the center, uses purple glass to signify the passion of Christ. Christ's resurrection is symbolically portrayed through the continuous upward lines of color in the overall window. The final shaft at the far right uses yellows and browns to mark his ascension. Overall, the window is balanced in color, and a patterned background of blues, grays, and greens separates thematic areas.

Even today, Bak's window is still a source of debate for the monks and scholars.[109] Many at Collegeville wonder how Albers's window would have changed the space and feeling of the church. Albers's lantern windows, glowing their brightest orange and yellow at high noon, provide an intriguing clue of what the northern window might have been.

UNFINISHED LITURGICAL ART: THE SCREEN MOSAIC

Given the sizable amount of art commissioned for the church and its many chapels, it is not surprising that portions of the artistic program were not complete by the consecration date of the church. One of the commissions left unfinished was the second-largest artistic display in the upper church, the intended mosaic for the apse screen. This loss is due to the difficulties associated with the northern window. Its fraught design process left the brethren and the architect with little desire to engage in another large-scale artistic commission, one that would have dramatically reinforced liturgical and aesthetic notions owing to its location above the altar and choir.

The screen behind the altar was intended to be functional and decorative, acting to conceal the organ while reaffirming the reformed liturgy of the church. Breuer was interested in the design from the start, as he included a plan for a crucified Christ made out of handlebars in his November 1953 section of the building (see Figure 3.12). Breuer's notations detail his plans for the crucifix: "Sculpture, flatter, probably outlines only, relief, also floating free from screen, near to it, made perhaps of bent silver bars."[110] Completing the sculpture of bent silver bars harks back to Breuer's experiments with tubular steel furniture design at the Bauhaus in 1925.

Breuer reevaluated the apse screen in December 1953 on the advice of Gerald Bonnette. Kacmarcik had recommended that Bonnette, then living in New York City, help Breuer in procuring liturgical art. Bonnette spent a week with the office to develop the "Church iconographically," as Hamilton Smith noted.[111] He argued that a Christ enthroned theme would be best, as it would draw less attention during worship and allow the main altar to remain prominent, a necessity for the liturgical nature of this building.[112] Bonnette also pointed out that axial placement of

the image meant that the baldachin would block the viewpoint of many worshippers. Breuer then changed the theme to the Pantocrator or ruler of all and flattened out the imagery on a large mosaic screen fronting the organ balcony. Breuer's iconography recalled the apse of the old abbey church, which had been painted with this same theme in 1939.[113]

Presented to the community in 1954, the model's design included the iconographic theme of Christ Pantocrator. The monks secured Bonnette for this vision and sent his sketch and notes on to Breuer (see Plate 12). In May 1955 the monks acknowledged Lambert-Rucki for sending in a sketch for the apse screen decoration, with a Christ in glory theme or Parousia.[114]

With the church under way it became clear that the time had come to consider completion of the apse screen, and the brethren created a subcommittee and began the search for an artist in November 1959.[115] The subject matter was the Parousia "with one very large figure (Christ in glory) and several smaller ones." The smaller figures were to include Mary, Saints John the Baptist, Benedict, Scholastica, and angels. Father Benedict Avery's letter explained the iconography to the artists and Breuer's office as being a traditional theme in the Byzantine East and Latin West for the first thousand years of church iconography.[116] He also cited the tympanum at the Romanesque church in Vézelay, France, as an excellent depiction of this theme. The Benedictines liked the liturgical significance of this imagery because, as Father Avery noted, "The apse-theme of 'Christ in glory' points, then, to the goal of all worship, which is the goal of the redemption itself: the transformation of the world into the kingdom of God, in the Spirit."[117] The work was to be representational and nonabstract, a contrast with the modern design of the church. If an artist chose to submit a design, his or her work would be judged by an outside committee with Saint John's reserving the final right to accept or deny their selection.[118]

With the spiritual theme in place, the abbey could begin its search for an artist to complete the screen. While only two artists were considered for the northern stained glass window wall, the subcommittee took a contrasting approach and compiled a list of thirty-three potential artists for the apse screen mosaic. The brethren solicited names from the editors of the world's five leading liturgical art journals—*L'Art Sacré, L'Art d'Église, Das Münster, Liturgical Arts,* and *Chiesa e Quartiere*—while rounding out the list with several artists of their own choice.[119] Leading sacred artists such as Alfred Manessier and Gerald Bonnette were included on the list, as was Frank Kacmarcik. Again, the designer's religious affiliation proved to be an issue. Early in the selection process, the committee discussed the ability of a non-Catholic to complete the work, and a

couple of its members thought the artist needed to be a Catholic. Father Meinberg said that this would "eliminate most of the possible artists of ability," and the subcommittee agreed that the artist needed to be a believing Christian at the very least.[120]

The December 1959 letter sent to the editors of the sacred art journals also outlined the requirements of the competition and included architectural drawings of the screen from Breuer's office. The overall size of the screen was 39½ feet wide by 33½ feet high. While Breuer intended to place the mosaic on an aluminum grid, he changed it to steel to support the weight of the tesserae. In consulting with the Holtkamp Organ Company, Breuer's office learned that 70 percent of the total surface of the grid should be open or uncovered by the tesserae in order for the organ to get the proper amount of air. Therefore, only 30 percent of the screen's surface could actually be covered by the artwork, as Abbot Dworschak stated:

The arrangement of the 30% may be in any areas of the screen; it is quite possible that openings may be left within the actual design itself—in fact this seems desirable to us. The representation in the apse screen will appear as a mosaic in a light curtain which has open and partly closed areas and would take on a sculptural quality, thus also becoming active in the design.[121]

The abbot intended that the artists would use this restriction of 70 percent to formulate their designs. This was a hindrance to many of the artists who found it nearly impossible to create a design on just 30 percent of the screen.

In May 1960 the commission of the apse screen mosaic began to fall apart. Without consulting the rest of the subcommittee or the abbot, Father Diekmann sent a letter on behalf the abbey to a final list of eighteen artists. Several of the brethren, including fellow art committee member Father Avery, were upset with Diekmann's action. Avery wrote the abbot a terse letter listing the many reasons for his anger over Diekmann's "inexcusable blunder."[122] He was upset with Diekmann for speaking on behalf of the community when doing so was the abbot's prerogative. He also expressed frustration that Diekmann had gone beyond the sole responsibility of the committee to work out the theology for the apse screen. But most of his anger was focused on how the artists were invited and how they would present their work for consideration. Instead of researching their work in the reference library's five-volume lexicon of internationally recognized artists, Father Diekmann requested that each artist send reproductions of his or her work. Father Avery felt that this process, along with the letter's lack of a theological statement for the screen, made the Benedictines look like amateur patrons. The brethren wanted to establish a professional competition with a group of experts selecting the winner. This process had

not been followed for the northern window wall commission, and that situation was still fresh in committee members' minds. Breuer and his associates also weighed in on how the apse screen commission should be awarded. In a December 11, 1959, letter to Father Eidenschink, Hamilton Smith stated that the firm "believed that the artists invited to submit designs for the apse-screen should be required by competition rules to come to St. John's."[123] He went on to state that the artists needed to experience the space of the church and talk directly not only with members of the community but also with the architect. Ensuring a successful design was key for both patron and designer.

Decision making on the apse screen, labeled by Abbot Dworschak as "the most important work of iconography in the new church,"[124] languished for financial reasons until early in 1966, when Breuer's office received a package from the managing director of the Instituto Internazionale di Arte Liturgica, Giuseppe Giacomini, containing a wax sketch of the screen done by Marcello Mascherini.[125] Abbot Dworschak's reply to Giacomini shows the impact the northern window commission had on the abbey's relationship with its architect:

As in all other matters pertaining to the new Abbey Church, we believe that we should follow the advice of our architect, Mr. Breuer. It was his opinion that your suggestion for the apse screen in the Abbey Church would be over-powering, that it would over-shadow the altar of the church, which should be the main focus of attention. After Mr. Breuer had given us his reasons for this opinion, I considered the matter with my advisors and they came to the unanimous conclusion that Mr. Breuer's opinion was correct.[126]

For this artistic commission, Breuer's opinion was clearly communicated. The brethren, determined not to make the same mistake they had with the northern window, put off the completion of the mosaic and put their money toward other buildings on campus. Today the unfinished screen is covered with red fabric that sets a simple yet colorful tone over the altar.

Even without the completion of the apse screen, Saint John's set a new example of artistic collaboration in the furnishing of the abbey church. Breuer, the Benedictines, and the liturgical coordinator, Frank Kacmarcik, commis-

sioned modern art that possessed "a devotional approachability, gravity, and universality—strong images free of the sweetness and sentimentality so common in religious art since the Renaissance."[127] The Benedictines found their building's architecture and much of the art within it to be vigorous, strong, and masculine in its associations and innovative in its forms. Yet they mixed in traditional elements, like the Mabon Madonna, as a result of the discussions, consultations, and collaboration. This art upheld the veneration of saints and the rites of the liturgy.

Kacmarcik's role was so integral to this project that when Breuer designed a house for him in St. Paul, Minnesota, in 1961, he told the liturgical coordinator that there was no bill for his work, for Saint John's Abbey Church would not be as it was without him.[128] A year later, Kacmarcik would leave the house Breuer created for him and return to Saint John's, where he resided as a cloistered oblate until his death in 2004.

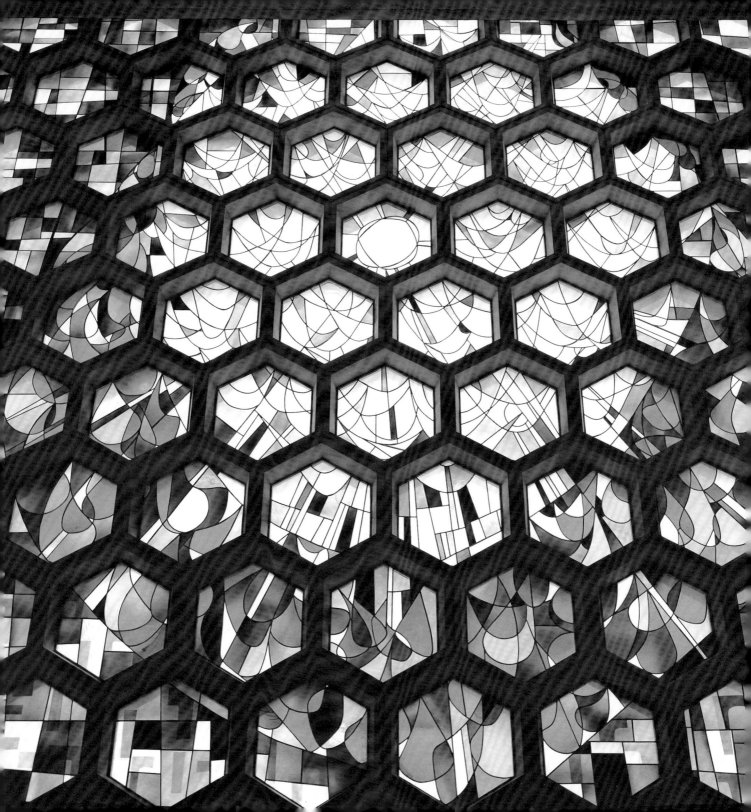

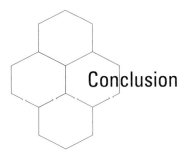

Conclusion

A MODERN LITURGICAL DESIGN FOR THE AGES

Father Cloud Meinberg informed Hamilton Smith shortly after the consecration of the abbey church: "Crowds continue to pour through the church—and no signs of stopping. The church is working out extremely well in use, for which of course, we are very happy."[1] For many scholars and religious, this was the important element in its design; as Peter Hammond stated, "The task of the modern architect is not to design a building that looks like a church. It is to create a building that works as a place for liturgy."[2] Profiles and reviews of the new building published in more than twenty religious, popular, and architectural journals accomplished the Benedictines' goal of making their church a visible paradigm of modern liturgical space.[3] The design and construction of the church came at a crucial time not only for religious architecture in America but also for Catholicism, as Saint John's Abbey Church was completed the year before the Second Vatican Coun-

cil reconsidered the role of the faith in a modern world. Among the ideas and notions reevaluated were artistic concepts for a modern church, and the brethren in Collegeville were once again well connected to the process of reform.

SAINT JOHN'S AND THE SECOND VATICAN COUNCIL (1962–65)

Upon his death in 1938, Father Virgil Michel's leadership in early twentieth-century liturgical reform passed to his protégé, Father Godfrey Diekmann, a member of the abbey church's subcommittee on the apse screen mosaic.[4] Like Michel, Diekmann had studied at the right schools (Saint Anselm's in Rome and the Abbey of Maria Laach in Germany) to gain a proper understanding of the liturgy, and he knew many of the movement's leaders. During his forty-five-year stint as editor of *Worship*, Diekmann became one of the key

players in the liturgical revival, using the journal to spread the word to bishops and parish priests. Diekmann also participated in the broader reform movement through liturgical conferences, serving as a member of the North American Liturgical Conference in the 1940s and 1950s and attending many of the international conferences, including those held at Mont César in 1954 and Assisi in 1956.[5] Diekmann's service to and unparalleled understanding of liturgical reform prompted those preparing for the Second Vatican Council to obtain his assistance as a *peritus*, or expert adviser, on liturgy to the council.

The Second Vatican Council called for the full and conscious participation of the faithful through a spiritual renewal of the church and a reconsideration of its place in the modern world.[6] Pope John XXIII began preparations for the council on January 25, 1959, and established a committee for the liturgy in June of 1960. The council commenced on October 11, 1962. Its most important document for liturgical and artistic purposes was the *Sacrosanctum Concilium* or "Constitution on the Sacred Liturgy," promulgated by Pope Paul VI on December 4, 1963, at the end of the second session.[7] "The Constitution on the Sacred Liturgy" emphasized the Church as a liturgical assembly and encouraged the restoration of community worship. This required a reconsideration of liturgical space and art according to chapter 7 of the constitution, "Sacred Art and Sacred Furnishings." With regard to architecture the constitution stated, "And when churches are to be built, let great care be taken that they be suitable for the celebration of liturgical services and for the active participation of the faithful."[8] This necessitated a plan that facilitated worship by placing the altar at the center of the church, where the priest as the representative of Christ celebrated the Mass amidst the laity and clergy. The council's renewed interested in the sacraments brought about architectural elements such as the spiritual axis at Saint John's.

The Benedictines and Breuer worked together to design and build the church of Saint John the Baptist from May 1953 through August 1961. Therefore the Benedictines had already contemplated many of the artistic and liturgical notions considered by Vatican II, with Father Diekmann communicating directly with Church leaders. Unity and inclusion for Catholics during the Mass were key concerns of reformers. Collegeville priest Father Alered's essay on the orientation of the high altar informed the abbot and subprior that their church allowed for celebration both ways. This made "it easier for the people to familiarize themselves with the ceremonies of the Mass, and it also helps to establish *rapport* between the celebrant and congregation, so important for pastoral liturgy."[9] Although the priest still remained the vital link to God, lay members' role in the Mass increased when they were asked to read the scriptures during the Mass. The brethren and Breuer anticipated this and interpreted

FIGURE C.1. The transitional space at the back of the church provides access to seating in the balcony.

it visually at Saint John's by fashioning an ambo with an inset stand/holder for the Bible, prominently displaying it to the congregation.

At Saint John's, Breuer's trapezoid unified worshippers. The absence of a communion rail or screen, which was replaced by four communion tables of concrete and granite, more fully promoted openness in the building. Father Diekmann sought out advice on the use of tables, writing to French liturgical expert Père Gy for his opinion:

> We have definitely planned to eliminate the communion rail. We figure that it has come to denote in people's minds not merely the distinction between sanctuary and nave, that is between priest and people, but actually separation. And we feel that this is most undesirable, particularly because Communion itself is the sacrament of union, and for it to be distributed at a symbol of separation seems most inappropriate.[10]

Gy deemed there to be nothing canonically wrong with using the tables, and so they were built of bush hammered concrete and granite, with the materials becoming the decorative element. This modern artistic sensibility was supported by the council:

> The Church has not adopted any particular style of art as her own. She has admitted styles from every period, in keeping with the natural characteristics and conditions of peoples and the needs of the various rites. Thus in the course of the centuries she has brought into existence a treasury of art which must be preserved with every care. The art of our own times from every race and country shall also be given free scope in the Church, provided it bring to the task the reverence and honour due to the sacred buildings and rites.[11]

The art of the church may be modern, but it was immediately becoming historical with modernism's incorporation into the long lineage of religious styles.

As the twentieth century progressed, the pace of design innovation quickened, and not all the abbey church's architectural features would serve their intended purpose after 1965. In addition to visual engagement with the altar in the church's open plan, another way to engage the layperson was to say the Mass in the local vernacular rather than Latin, a topic the council discussed and approved in the first session.[12] A precouncil ruling supporting the vernacular would have eliminated the need for Saint Benedict's Chapel on the lower level of the church, a place where the lay brothers said their prayers in English. After Vatican II, Saint Benedict's chapel became a place the monks went for private prayer outside the regular offices and mass.

In addition, decrees of the council would have

eradicated the need for the private chapels in the crypt, as they enabled concelebration at various types of gatherings.[13] This was followed up with the May 7, 1965, decree from the Sacred Congregation of Rites, "The Concelebration of the Mass and Communion under Both Kinds," which allowed concelebration on a much broader scale, for it emphasized the unity of the priesthood and laity, with all coming together at one altar.[14] Father Diekmann anticipated concelebration when he traveled to Rome specifically to ask about its potential decree. When Church leaders informed him that concelebration was not going to be allowed, the crypt chapels were put into place. Within two years after the church's dedication, however, the Church permitted concelebration and the chapels became obsolete, although priests were still encouraged to say Mass individually. Appropriately, Saint John's Abbey was one of the places designated in 1964 for experimentation with the rite of concelebration.

BREUER BUILDINGS AT SAINT JOHN'S: FULFILLING THE ONE-HUNDRED-YEAR PLAN

Breuer's architectural commitment to the Abbey of Saint John the Baptist was greater, however, than just his design for the acclaimed abbey church. He was tasked with reshaping the entire monastery and university over a period of one hundred years. As *Time* magazine reported at the inception of the project, there was no rush:

The whole project may cost about $8,000,000, and since the sum is far beyond St. John's likely early means, its completion may be far in the future. But Abbot Baldwin and his black cowled brothers are in no mad rush. "After all," he said last week, "what are a few generations to the Benedictines?"[15]

Many different building types were needed to house the growing academic units and monastery. After the presentation of the comprehensive plan, the monks employed Breuer to complete the monastic dormitory in 1955 (Figure C.2).[16] He also provided plans for four student residences, beginning in 1957 with his design for Saint Thomas Hall. The 1965 scheme for the halls named for Saints Bernard, Boniface, and Patrick illustrate again the solidity of his concrete design, complete with sunshades to protect the building's western façade.

Breuer displayed his architectural ingenuity in another manner through the design of Alcuin Library (1964–66), named for Alcuin of York, an eighth-century monk who was the patron of Saint John's fifth abbot, Alcuin Deutsch. Two reinforced concrete trees with twenty-seven-foot centers, each weighing 132 tons, support the 860-ton roof (Figure C.3). There is seating for 620 students, six seminar rooms, a listening room, an audiovisual auditorium, a smaller auditorium, twenty study rooms, one hundred carrels in the stacks and fifty freestanding carrels around the

FIGURE C.2 (*facing*). The first Breuer design, completed in 1955, was the monastic dormitory (in foreground).

FIGURE C.3 (*above*). Concrete trees inside Alcuin Library.

library. The exterior of the concrete building was faced with granite panels, featuring insets of terracotta field tile. The Mondrian-inspired window around the entry doors recalls the first proposal for the church's northern wall. Granite, concrete, and field tile provide a continuity across the open plaza or public quadrangle that unites the church, library, and science hall (see Plate 13). The Engel Science Center, named after another abbot, was designed in 1964 and built from the fall of 1965 through August 1966. It was, along with the library, part of phase two of Saint John's ten-year, now $12 million building program.[17] It provided 100,000 square feet of space for 800 students.

Other buildings completed by Breuer and his associates include the 1967–68 Ecumenical Institute, founded to encourage religious and cultural diversity as scholars search for the meaning of Christian identity and unity. This is Breuer's most domestic-like building on campus, a series of apartments centered on a small gathering space with a simple chapel. Hamilton Smith designed the Bush Center/Hill Monastic Manuscript Library in 1974, a facility for medieval studies research and home to the workings of the present-day Saint John's Bible. Not all Breuer's designs were built, however. His 1966 proposals for a student center and gymnasium or palaestra did not fit into the plans of the Benedictines at the time (see Plates 14 and 15). Over the next decades, a range of architects, including Hugh Newell Jacobsen, Dan Kiley, and Vincent James, were commissioned to design an art gallery, landscape plan, and guesthouse, respectively. In some cases these structures respond directly in form and detail to Breuer's buildings, including the 1998 addition to the science building by Greg Friesen of CSNA Architects of Denver and Lee Tollefson of Rafferty, Rafferty and Tollefson from St. Paul. But no matter how many buildings are erected in Collegeville, the abbey's church is still the campus anchor and a visible reminder of how great architecture can be created in partnership.[18]

THE INSPIRATION OF SAINT JOHN'S ABBEY CHURCH ON BREUER'S DESIGN OF SACRED SPACE

Breuer's church was a successful fulfillment of the brethren's liturgical ambitions. It was also a triumph of his career, as Saint John's became the foundation for a number of Breuer's subsequent religious spaces. In fact, his first two religious commissions following Saint John's were granted specifically because of his work on the abbey church. The trademarks of Saint John's—the bell banner, the spiritual axis, concrete, stained glass, and the hyperbolic paraboloid—all manifest themselves to some degree in these buildings.

In 1954 the Benedictine Sisters of Annunciation Monastery in Bismarck, North Dakota, decided that their monastic community needed a more suitable setting. Aware of his ongoing work

FIGURE C.4. Annunciation Monastery, Bismarck, North Dakota.
The chapel is located at center right of the monastic complex.

in Collegeville, they asked Breuer for his assistance.[19] With the help of Frank Kacmarcik and Ray Hermanson, the local architect on the Saint John's project, they presented Breuer with their ideas, and he agreed to design their convent, stating, "Perhaps we might build a little jewel."[20]

Breuer and Smith completed the master plan in 1954, and construction began in two phases, lasting from 1958 to 1963. The isolated, wind-swept site, with its rolling hills, ravines, tall grasses, and view of the Missouri River, helped determine Breuer's design of the monastery.[21] In a metaphorical effort to have the buildings on top of the plateau protect each other from blowing away in the wind, Breuer kept them close together in a "social island . . . a cultivated area, landscaped and controlled."[22] Like at Saint John's, the bell banner announced the abbey's presence as a sacred space, framed against the hills of the Missouri River Valley (Figure C.4). The banner's twisted planes and its concrete formwork marks made it rough and rugged like the terrain.

As seen at Saint John's Abbey Church, a spiritual axis organized the path to the altar in Annunciation's main chapel. This time, however, the banner shifted off the axis. A fountain just outside the door to the chapel's narthex replaced a baptismal font on the spiritual axis, reflecting the building's functional difference from the church of Saint John's. Breuer used half-hyperbolic paraboloid shells of concrete to create the chapel. He faced the shell's exterior with local fieldstone and a buff-colored brick. He had the interior painted white, as he had planned for Saint John's. Breuer also learned from his experience with the stained glass window in Collegeville and commissioned an artist immediately to fabricate the windows. He did not hire Albers, but worked with members from his own firm, who set one-inch-thick pieces of colored and clear glass into a stucco framework on both sides of the nave (Figure C.5). In the case of Annunciation, glass is used aesthetically rather than symbolically, preserving the architect's control of a complete sacred vision.

BREUER'S RELIGIOUS ARCHITECTURE

Frank Kacmarcik, Breuer's artistic coordinator at Saint John's, had recommended him not only for the North Dakota project but also for the 1960 commission to design Saint Francis de Sales, a parish church in Muskegon, Michigan. In this work, Breuer used the concept of the bell banner from Saint John's and Annunciation for the building itself (Figure C.6).[23] The banner on the east wall, the west wall, and the roof were each trapezoidal-shaped planes connected by hyperbolic paraboloid side walls. A cross hangs on the main façade, rather than within it as at Saint John's, and the bells are located in a canopy above it.

Breuer and Kacmarcik shaped the space around liturgical requirements, but because the banner was now the façade of the church, the baptistery begins the sacred axis of the church. Breuer set the baptistery within a low, mastaba-like building inside a forecourt with low walls. Breuer loved the simplicity, size, and massiveness provided by the stone construction of Egyptian architecture, a historical influence as he innovated new forms in the twentieth century.[24] Like Saint John's, he placed the baptismal font into a recessed area and compressed the height of the baptistery's ceiling. He also moves visitors into the church under a balcony before he releases them into the space, this time rising eighty-five feet high in the sanctuary. Clear light enters from above, and stained glass is only to be found in small panels on either side of the entry into the nave from the baptistery.

Saint Francis exemplifies one of Breuer's most important design contributions, an engineered space that defies conventional wisdom yet supports the liturgy. As Breuer stated:

FIGURE C.5. The side walls of the main chapel at Annunciation Monastery contain glass designed by Breuer and Associates.

How much this building affects those who see and enter it, how much it signifies its reverent purpose, will depend on the courage its designers manifest in facing the age-old task: to defeat gravity and to lift the material to great heights, over great spans—to render the enclosed space a part of infinite space. There the structure stands—defined by the eternal laws of geometry, gravity and space.[25]

Breuer's church was, like the great pyramids or the medieval cathedrals, powerful, expressive, and massive. Modern architecture, like its earlier counterparts, seemed able to withstand the test of time, and Breuer's ability to design impressive sacred spaces had been established. These spaces could be created for various faiths, such as the 1961 design for the unbuilt Temple B'nai Jeshrun in New Jersey, as well as plans for a Protestant church dedicated to Saint Luke in New York (1964). The freestanding towers of Saint John's and Annunciation were the source for the banner at the unrealized Kent Girls School Episcopalian chapel in Connecticut (1967), and for the more simplified version of a tower at the Franciscan convent in Baldegg, Switzerland (1968–72). Breuer also used the banner as a building motif for an unbuilt parish church outside Rome in Olgiata, Italy (1968).[26]

THE MODERN CHURCH: A LITURGICAL VISION

The Benedictines of Saint John's took a very active role in all stages of this commission, concerned from the very beginning with the proper architectural and symbolic representations of their religious ideals. In Abbot Baldwin's view, one central issue was the matter of style:

> We had . . . to decide whether our spiritual purposes could best be served by copying traditional architectural styles or by seeking fresh forms available to twentieth-century architects using twentieth-century materials.[27]

The selection of twelve modern thinking architects indicated that fresh forms of the twentieth century were the appropriate solution for the Benedictines at midcentury. The decision to secure Marcel Breuer signified the respectability of a modern religious spirit in architecture, which would manifest itself in the great abbey church, arguably one of the finest examples of Catholic architecture in the United States. Additionally, it encouraged the Benedictines of the viability of modernism as the architectural idiom for other monastic projects. For example, just one year after the final designs were approved for the abbey church, Gyo Obata of Hellmuth, Obata and Kassabuam (HOK) designed the Priory Church of Saint Mary and Saint Louis for the Benedictines

FIGURE C.6. Saint Francis de Sales Church, Muskegon, Michigan. The banner has become the building.

FIGURE C.7. The church of Saint John the Evangelist, Hopkins, Minnesota, 1965.

outside St. Louis, Missouri (1958–62).[28] Obata's church placed the altar at the center of a circular plan covered by three tiers of parabolic arches, forms inspired by modern architecture and engineering. A central oculus illuminated the altar with bright clear light, highlighting its importance in the modern liturgy. As Prior Columba of Saint Mary and Saint Louis stated, "The paradox that Benedictines, who are the most traditional of people, should build in a contemporary style, is no paradox at all. If we examine history, we find that is what they have always done."[29]

At a more vernacular level, the new architectural form of the liturgy entered many parishes in the United States through the work of Frank Kacmarcik because of his collaborations with

Breuer. The Church of Saint John the Evangelist in Hopkins, Minnesota (1965), was designed with his concept of a gathering space. Although the liturgy dictates the form of the church, all of its parts flow together to allow easy transitions from worship to socialization and fellowship (Figure C.7).[30] In the 1980s Kacmarcik would redesign the chapel at Saint Benedict's Monastery in Saint Joseph, Minnesota, the Benedictine sister house and educational partner to Saint John's. He placed the altar in the center of the building under its dome, allowing the building's form to order the unsuccessful placement of liturgical furniture, as noted by Kevin Seasoltz.[31] Successful or not, the form needed for Catholic worship had changed after the Second Vatican Council. The Benedictines of Saint John's Abbey were responsible, in part, for this reconsideration.

BUILDING A MODERN ABBEY CHURCH FOR THE AGES

Five decades later, the abbey church remains a testament to the Benedictines' faith, their order, and their promotion of a renewed liturgy, appropriate to the public they were serving (see Plate 16). Yet, in their traditional humility, they never have forgotten the men who worked with them to create their modern version of a heavenly Jerusalem. As Abbot John Klassen noted in his comments on the fortieth anniversary of the church's dedication:

Today we have especially grateful hearts for the collaboration between Marcel Breuer and his skilled associates, and the creative spiritual imagination of this monastic community; for the engineers and the contractor who made sure the building would stand; for the local carpenters, steel workers, and other skilled craftsmen who constructed it; and to all the people who have and continue to pray with us in this church. We pray that we may have the courage and wisdom to take this spiritual legacy and move forward into the future with boldness and confidence.[32]

The power of this place, its church, and the people who built it will endure for generations (see Plate 17). The liturgical concerns evaluated and presented in the church's design facilitated an emphasis on unity that became the cornerstone of religious architecture after the Second Vatican Council, when modern building methods and materials were added to the traditional lexicon of church design. The Benedictines used Breuer's creative, engineered concrete forms to uphold the prestige and forward-thinking architectural nature of their order, just as their Gothic counterparts had done centuries before. But the work of Breuer and his associates went beyond just a reaffirmation of monasticism: it was also the cornerstone of a liturgically reformed American and international Catholic architecture.

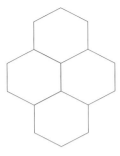

NOTES

INTRODUCTION

1 The consecration of a Catholic church is a three-part event that usually takes place on the same day, but special dispensation from the Sacred Congregation of Rites enabled part one to be held on the evening of August 23, 1961, with completion of the consecration the following day. Breuer was present on the second day.

2 Sacred Chrism is olive oil scented with balsam that is blessed by a bishop and used for many kinds of sacraments and blessings in the Catholic Church.

3 Dworschak, "Marcel Breuer," 1.

4 Wilfrid R. Ussner, Port Moody, to Abbot Baldwin Dworschak, Collegeville, August 30, 1954, Office of the Abbot. New Church and Monastery Building Records, 1952–81 (bulk 1953–62). Saint John's Abbey (Collegeville, Minn.), box 5, folder 5 (further references to this archive will be shortened to SJA).

5 Peter F. Anson, Banffshire, Scotland, to Father Godfrey Diekmann, Collegeville, August 12, 1954, SJA, box 5, folder 5.

6 Evans, "St. John's Abbey Church," 517.

7 Ibid., 521.

8 Lavanoux, "Collegeville Revisited," 47.

9 Father Anthony J. Jacobs, Oxnard, to Abbot Baldwin Dworschak, Collegeville, July 22, 1954, SJA, box 5, folder 5. The article Jacobs was referring to was "A Benedictine Monastery."

10 Reverend Clifford Howell, S.J., Grantham, Leicestershire, to Brother Godfrey Diekmann, O.S.B., Collegeville, August 2, 1954, SJA, box 5, folder 5.

11 Beatrice Starr Jenkins, Santa Fe, to Abbot Baldwin Dworschak, Collegeville, July 25, 1954, SJA, box 5, folder 5.

12 Hughes, *The Monk's Tale*, 169.

13 My work adds to scholarship on midcentury sacred building production, joining Meredith Clausen on Pietro Belluschi (1992), Kathleen James-Chakraborty on Erich Mendelsohn and Dominikus Böhm (2000a), Susan Solomon on Louis Kahn's synagogues (2009), Timothy Parker on Roman modern churches (2010), Joseph Siry on Frank Lloyd Wright's Beth Shalom synagogue (2011), Anat Geva on Wright's sacred design (2012), Vincent Michael on Barry Bryne (2013), and Robert Proctor on midcentury Catholic churches in Britain, among others. Forthcoming work by Mary Brunstrom will document the midcentury work of the St. Louis–based architects Joseph D. Murphy and Eugene Mackey. A broader look at sacred space and the American landscape will be provided by

Gretchen Buggeln's forthcoming *Churches for To-day: Modernism and Suburban Expansion in Post-war America.*

14 Niebling, "Modern Benedictine Churches." Nie-bling published his dissertation findings in two articles in the *American Benedictine Review*: "Mo-nastic Churches Erected by American Benedic-tines Since World War II," parts 1 and 2. Seasoltz, "Contemporary Monastic Architecture and Life in America," 320. Encouraging for the continued study of the modern monastery was the session "Building the Kingdom" chaired by Ayla Lepine and Kate Jordan at the 2013 Society of Architec-tural Historians annual meeting. See http://www.sah.org/docs/conference/sah_13_program_final_web_2.pdf?sfvrsn=0 (accessed August 3, 2013).

15 "The 1962 AIA Honor Awards."

16 Gatje, *Marcel Breuer*, 89.

17 The seven sacraments are Baptism, Confirmation, the Eucharist, Penance, the Anointing of the Sick, Holy Orders, and Matrimony.

18 I coined the term "spiritual axis" based on Father Cloud Meinberg's 1953 essay on the monastic church, originally delivered to the community of Saint John's on September 29 and sent to the office of Marcel Breuer and Associates shortly thereafter. See chapter 3 for a discussion of the design, con-struction, and use of this axis.

19 Barry Bergdoll, "For Great Buildings, Get a Great Client," *New York Times*, July 21, 2002, http://www.nytimes.com/2002/07/21/weekinreview/21BERG.html?tntemail1# (accessed July 21, 2012).

20 As quoted in the sidebar titled "Ham Smith's Description of Breuer's Approach to Design," in Young, "The Design and Construction of Saint John's Abbey Church," 118.

21 Hull was reviewing Williams, *Houses of God.*

22 "Art: The New Churches," *Time*, December 26, 1960, http://www.time.com/time/magazine/article/0,9171,895154,00.html (accessed July 21, 2012).

23 Hammond, *Liturgy and Architecture*, 13.

24 Hitchcock and Johnson's *The International Style* and its associated show at the Museum of Modern Art in 1932 included only one religious space, J. J. P. Oud's church in Kiefhoek, Holland. The 1992 edi-tion of Frampton's *Modern Architecture* contains only four church illustrations out of 336 buildings. Curtis's *Modern Architecture since 1900* incor-porated only forty-four religious spaces in its 862 images, a mere 5 percent. The list could include Jencks's *Modern Movements in Architecture* and Benevolo's *History of Modern Architecture*, among others.

25 Midcentury modern churches have been included in surveys of American religious building such as Kennedy's *American Churches*, which provides many excellent photographs but very limited com-mentary. Williams's *Houses of God* and Chiat's *America's Religious Architecture* are based largely on vernacular examples ordered geographically in a guidebook fashion, offering little in the way of an analytical, comprehensive look at religious space. Several key texts were published during the midcentury, most notably Christ-Janer and Mix Foley's *Modern Church Architecture*. A selection of additional works published on the subject includes Biedrzynski, *Kirchen unserer Zeit*; Getlein and Getlein, *Christianity in Modern Art*; Gieselmann and Aebli, *Kirchenbau*; Hammond, *Liturgy and Architecture*; Hammond, *Towards a Church Archi-tecture*; Henze and Filthaut, *Contemporary Church Art*; Macguire and Murray, *Modern Churches of the World*; Meier, *Recent American Synagogue Architecture*; Mills, *The Modern Church*; Pichard, *Modern Church Architecture*; Seasoltz, *The House of God*; and Short, *Post War Church Building.*

26 As Vidler has pointed out in *Histories of the Imme-diate Present*, scholars like Giedion, Pevsner, and Hitchcock already were historicizing modernism by the 1940s, making it clear that modernism could be a style of choice for clients like the Benedictines. See discussion in Vidler, 5–6. For another discus-sion on the theorization and stylization of modern-ism see Goldhagen, "Something to Talk About."

27 This discussion of religious art in sacred space builds on scholarship by McDannell, *Material Christianity*; Morgan and Promey, *Visual Culture of American Religions*; Heller, *Reluctant Partners*; and others.

28 Spaeth, "Worship and the Arts," 166.

29 Jungmann, "Church Art," 68.

30 See, e.g., Couturier, "Religious Art and the Modern Artist." Couturier was also the publisher of the journal *L'Art Sacré*, which published many articles on the subject.

31 White, *Art, Architecture, and Liturgical Reform*, 116.

32 Luxford, *The Art and Architecture of English Benedictine Monasteries, 1300–1540*, 31.

1. BRICKS AND BROTHERS

1 General monastic histories include Brooke, *The Monastic World, 1000–1300*; Dunn, *The Emergence of Monasticism*; and Lawrence, *Medieval Monasticism*. Histories of the Benedictines include Butler, *Benedictine Monachism*; Daly, *Benedictine Monasticism*; Kardon, *The Benedictines*; Knowles, *The Benedictines*; and Van Zeller, *The Benedictine Idea*.

2 Fry, *The Rule of St. Benedict in English*.

3 Ibid., chapter 39, "The Proper Amount of Food," and chapter 40, "The Proper Amount of Drink."

4 See Horn and Born, *The Plan of St. Gall*; Price, *The Plan of St. Gall in Brief*; and Sanderson, "The Plan of St. Gall Reconsidered."

5 For more on Suger's church see Crosby and Blum, *The Royal Abbey of Saint-Denis from Its Beginnings to the Death of Suger, 475–1151*; Panofsky, *Abbot Suger on the Abbey Church of St.-Denis and Its Art Treasures*; and Kidson, "Panofsky, Suger, and St. Denis."

6 "The Monastic Church," delivered by Father Cloud before the community on September 29, 1953. SJA, box 5, folder 19.

7 Beales, "Joseph II and the Monasteries of Austria and Hungary," 228.

8 Braunfels, *Monasteries of Western Europe*, 224.

9 Beales, *Prosperity and Plunder*, 117.

10 Curran, *The Romanesque Revival*, 83–93.

11 See Barry, *Worship and Work*, and Rippinger, *The Benedictine Order in the United States*.

12 For more on Wimmer see Oetgen, *An American Abbot*, and Oetgen, *A History of Saint Vincent Archabbey*.

13 Rothan, "The German Catholic Immigrant in the United States (1830–1860)," 66. At the opening of the Civil War, 68.3 percent of the foreign-born residents of central Minnesota were Germans.

14 As Benedict said in the prologue to the Rule, "We intend to establish a school for the Lord's service." For more on the priests' role in missionary work see O'Neill, "The Development of a German-American Priesthood," 145–55.

15 A good portion of the money came from Bavarian donors as Abbot Wimmer had just returned from a trip to Germany. Barry, *Worship and Work*, 23.

16 After rising, the brethren attended Matins and Lauds of the Divine Office, meditated for thirty minutes, and went to Mass. Prime, Terce, and Sext of the Divine Office was at 6:00 a.m.; 10:45 a.m. was time to examine one's conscience, eat, and adore the Blessed Sacrament. At 11:45 a.m., the monks were present at None of the Divine Office, and the remainder of the afternoon was devoted to work and teaching, until 4:30 p.m., at which time Vespers and Compline were sung. The hour from 5:00 to 6:00 p.m. was set aside for spiritual reading. For more on this initial settlement see Tegeder, "The Benedictines in Frontier Minnesota."

17 The layout of the original buildings is taken from textual descriptions in Barry, *Worship and Work*, 83, and Tingerthal, "St. John's First Abbey Church."

18 The abbey's missionaries did not discriminate and provide services only to German Catholics. They also served other ethnic groups in the area, including Irish Catholics.

19 Barry, *Worship and Work*, 105. The school was

divided into three parts: elementary, collegiate, and theological.

20 Ibid., 398n17.

21 Klenze, *Anweisung zur Architektur des christlichen Cultus*. See Watkin, "The Transformation of Munich into a Royal Capital by Maximilian I Joseph and Ludwig I," 10. According to Watkin, Klenze believed that a revival of early Christian architecture for sacred space preserved some of the spirit of the classical and also reversed things that had gone wrong with the architectural decorative excesses of the baroque and rococo.

22 For more on Gärtner see Curran, "Friedrich von Gärtner's Farb- und Ornamentauffassung und sein Einfluss auf England und Amerika," and Hederer, *Friedrich von Gärtner, 1792–1847*. Gärtner's architecture was influential in Europe and America because of his position as professor at the Academy of Architecture in Munich and his numerous design publications, such as Gärtner, *Sammlung der Entwürfe ausgeführter Gebäude*. Architectural historian Kathleen Curran credits the building of the Ludwigskirche as the introduction of the style, known in the United States as the Romanesque Revival. The Romanesque Revival became popular in ecclesiastical buildings in the 1840s after noted American architect Richard Upjohn (1803–1903) designed the first Romanesque Revival church in Brooklyn, New York, the Church of the Pilgrims (1844). See Kathleen Curran, "German Rundbogenstil and American Round-Arched Style," 357, and Curran, *The Romanesque Revival*, 51–57 and 83–93.

23 Roemer, *Ten Decades of Alms*, 54.

24 Curran, *The Romanesque Revival*, 84.

25 For the history of the society see Theodore Roemer, *The Ludwig-Missionsverein and the Church in the United States (1838–1918)*, 67, and Joseph A. Schabert, "The Ludwig Missionsverein."

26 Roemer, *The Ludwig-Missionsverein and the Church in the United States (1838–1918)*, 110.

27 From 1858 to 1883 the Ludwig Mission Society sent 20,760 gulden and 8,500 marks to Saint John's Abbey and its three dependencies, including money for the 1868 building of the brick monastery. See ibid., 67.

28 Hampton, "The Church Architecture of Adolphus Druiding," 21–27, and Hampton, "German Gothic in the Midwest," 61–64.

29 The diocese founded Assumption Church in 1854 for the German Catholics of St. Paul. The cornerstone was laid on August 15, 1855, and the diocese turned the building over to the Benedictines of Saint John's in 1858; they remained until 1912. It served as the state's largest and most important German parish. The Ludwig Mission Society provided money for the project and likely influenced the choice of Reidl as its architect and the Ludwigskirche as the architectural model. For more on the architecture of the building see John D. Milner, "Church of the Assumption (Roman Catholic)."

30 The parish added the classically inspired cupolas in the early 1900s.

31 Barry, *Worship and Work*, 142.

32 Ibid., 153.

33 This structure would have stretched across the entire northern side of the present-day quadrangle.

34 Barry, *Worship and Work*, 89.

35 Lamprecht (1838–1922) studied at the art academy in Munich before moving to Cincinnati, Ohio, in 1867. There, he collaborated with the Benedictine Covington Altar Stock Building Company, supplying works to churches and monasteries across North America. He moved to New York in 1871. For more on Lamprecht see Bénézit, *Dictionnaire des peintres, sculpteurs, dessinateurs et graveurs*, 6:411; Gerdts, *Art across America*, 2:185; Merrill, *German Immigrant Artists in America*, 151; and Annemarie Springer, *Nineteenth Century German-American Church Artists* (2001), http://maxkade.iupui.edu/springer/index.html (accessed July 22, 2012).

36 Misch emigrated from Germany with his parents in 1850, settling in New York and working with his father in the stained glass–making trade. In 1864 he opened his own glass-making business in Chicago. For more on Misch see Andreas, *The Encyclopedia of Chicago*, 3:100.

37 Shuster, "Catholic Culture in America," 12–13,

38 For a discussion of the missionary work of Saint John's brethren, see Hilary Thimmesh, "Plowing the Fields, Scattering Good Seed upon the Earth," in *Saint John's at 150*, 58–69.

39 Mitchell, *History of Stearns County*, 1:267. Saint John's was the first Catholic college founded in the state with its seminary dating to March 1857. The number of religious would grow to 140 priests, 41 clerics, 21 lay brothers, and 10 novices in 1921. By 1927 Saint John's was the largest Benedictine house in the United States, surpassing its motherhouse of Saint Vincent's in Latrobe, Pennsylvania.

40 Thimmesh, "A Time to Plant and a Time to Grow," in Thimmesh, *Saint John's at 150*, 8. See this entire chapter and in the same volume, Farry, "A Scientific, Educational, and Ecclesiastical Institution," 31–44, for an excellent overview of the abbey and its connection to the world in education and monastic leadership.

41 This history of the liturgical movement is based on information from Bouyer, *Life and Liturgy*; Crichton, *Lights in Darkness*; Klauser, *A Short History of the Western Liturgy*; Koenker, *The Liturgical Renaissance in the Roman Catholic Church*; Pecklers, *The Unread Vision*; Reid, *The Organic Development of the Liturgy*; and David Torevell, *Losing the Sacred*. A sacrament is an outward sign instituted by Christ to give inward grace. Virgil Michel described the role of the sacraments in an unpublished manuscript titled "Philosophical and Theological Bases of the Liturgical Movement": "Baptism is the birth into this life; Confirmation the attainment of maturity. Penance and Extreme Unction [Anointing of the Sick] restore the lost life

or heal its wounds and strengthen its weaknesses. Holy Orders and Matrimony provide for the propagation of the Christ-life on earth." Marx, *Virgil Michel and the Liturgical Movement*, 53.

42 For more on Guéranger see Johnson, *Prosper Guéranger (1805–1875)*.

43 At the outbreak of the French Revolution only 50 of 130 bishoprics were using the Roman liturgy decreed by the Council of Trent. The rest returned to pre-Tridentine liturgy heavily informed by national traditions. See Klauser, *A Short History of the Western Liturgy*, 119.

44 *L'année liturgique* contained historical information about and explanations of ceremonial practices, poetry, and sermons to aid the reader in understanding the liturgical year.

45 *Motu proprio* signifies that the pope decided personally on the ideas presented, rather than with the advice of the cardinals or others. Pope Pius X, "The Restoration of Church Music," cited in Seasoltz, *The New Liturgy*.

46 Ibid., 4.

47 For more on Beauduin see Bouyer, *Dom Lambert Beauduin*; Haquin, *Dom Lambert Beauduin et le renouveau liturgique*; and Quitslund, *Beauduin*.

48 Cited in Tuzik, *How Firm a Foundation*, 25, and taken from Beauduin, *Liturgy*, 44–46.

49 Reid, *The Organic Development of the Liturgy*, 83.

50 Maria Laach, founded in 1093, had been dissolved in 1802 only to be reestablished in 1892 by the Benedictines from Beuron Abbey, founded in 1863 by two of Guéranger's followers, Maurus and Placidus Wolter.

51 Hughes, *How Firm a Foundation*, 128.

52 Crichton, *Lights in Darkness*, 153. In early Christian times the altar was situated in such a way that the priest could face the people. According to Reverend Theodor Klauser and others, it is commonly agreed that beginning in the sixth century altars began to be placed against the rear wall of parish churches, moving the priest behind the altar with his back

toward the laity. By 1000 CE this configuration was commonplace. The liturgical movement encouraged a return to the ancient practices in order to unify the congregation and celebrant. Klauser, *A Short History of the Western Liturgy*, 100–101.

53 Casel, *The Mystery of Christian Worship and Other Writings.*

54 Guardini, *The Spirit of the Liturgy*; http://www.ewtn.com/library/liturgy/sprlit.txt (accessed June 3, 2013). For more on Guardini see Hoffman, "Portrait of Father Guardini," 576; Krieg, *Romano Guardini*; and Lypgens, "Romano Guardini, a German Priest." According to liturgical scholar Alcuin Reid, Guardini's ideas in *The Spirit of the Liturgy* "underpinned most of the activity of the Liturgical Movement." Reid, *The Organic Development of the Liturgy*, 92.

55 *Jungbrunnen* means "fountain of youth." On the Quickborn movement see Lord, "Neu-Deutschland and German Catholic Youth," and Tyldesley, *No Heavenly Delusion?*, 23–27.

56 Tuzik, *How Firm a Foundation*, 42. Most of these students were college age. The work at Rothenfels ended in 1939, when, after nine years of infiltration, the Nazis confiscated the buildings.

57 Krieg, *Romano Guardini*, 80.

58 For more on Parsch, see Schnitzler, "Parsch, Pius," 10:903. Online *New Catholic Encyclopedia* available at http://go.galegroup.com/ps/ (accessed June 3, 2013).

59 Parsch, *The Liturgy of the Mass*, ix.

60 Reid, *The Organic Development of the Liturgy*, 111.

61 For more information on Michel see Franklin, *Virgil Michel*; Leonard, "The Liturgical Movement in the United States"; and Marx, *Virgil Michel and the Liturgical Movement*. For more on the liturgical movement in America see Koenker, *The Liturgical Renaissance in the Roman Catholic Church*, and Pecklers, *The Unread Vision.*

62 Rippinger, *The Benedictine Order in the United States*, 185–86.

63 Beauduin began teaching courses in fundamental theology, apologetics, ecclesiology, and liturgy at Saint Anselm's in 1921. Beauduin's emphasis on the nature of the church as the Mystical Body of Christ greatly influenced Michel.

64 Marx, *Virgil Michel and the Liturgical Movement*, 28. For more on the travels of Michel see ibid., 24–48.

65 Beginning with the December 1951 issue, *Orate Fratres* was renamed *Worship*. The Liturgical Press at Saint John's is still publishing *Worship*, and it remains a leading journal on liturgical issues. The first issue of *Orate Fratres*, with a cover designed by English Catholic artist Eric Gill, was mailed to eight hundred people. Thirty years later its success supported a subscription rate of five thousand copies, with a breakdown in 1954 circulation as follows: clergy, 38.8 percent; laity, 26.72 percent; institutions, 22 percent; nuns, 11.6 percent; and publications, .88 percent. See Barry, *Worship and Work*, 270. For more on the history of *Worship* see http://www.saintjohnsabbey.org/our-work/publishing/worship-magazine (accessed June 8, 2014).

66 In 1889, Saint John's established a printing house, publishing materials in English and German.

67 Himes, "Eucharist and Justice."

68 *Proceedings: 1940 National Liturgical Week*. Catholic leaders modeled the American Liturgical Week conference on the *Semaines Liturgiques*, held annually since 1912 at the Abbey of Mont César in Louvain, Belgium, Dom Beauduin's home monastery.

69 Marx, *Virgil Michel and the Liturgical Movement*, 33.

70 *Liturgical Arts*, first published by the Liturgical Arts Society in October 1931 in New York City, was an important source of information on American and European trends in liturgical art and architecture. For more on its significance see chapter 4.

71 Michel, "Architecture and the Liturgy," 13.

72 Ibid., 17.

73 For more on these renovations see Maeder, "St. John's First Abbey Church (II)."

74 For more on Beuronese art see Hauser et al., *Sacred Art*.

75 Marx, *Virgil Michel and the Liturgical Movement*, 33.

76 Michel, "Architecture and the Liturgy," 14.

2. THE TWELVE APOSTLES

1 Eighty-seven monks resided at Saint John's in 1880, the time of the dedication of the first church, and by 1921, when Saint John's became involved with the reformation of the liturgy, there were 168 members of the abbey. Catholic Church, *Ordo for the Liturgy of the Hours and Mass in the Churches and Oratories of the American-Cassinese Federation*.

2 Members of the building committee included Abbot Baldwin Dworschak, Fathers John Eidenschink, Gerald McMahon, Godfrey Diekmann, Hubert Dahlheimer, Joachim Watrin, Lancelot Atsch, Alfred Deutsch, Michael Marx, Benedict Avery, Cloud Meinberg, Colman Barry, Florian Muggli, and Jeremy Murphy.

3 SJA, Meinberg file. Meinberg came to Collegeville in 1939 and chaired the art department from 1949 to 1957, teaching classes on architecture and specializing in sacred design.

4 Senior Council meeting minutes, March 4, 1953, SJA, box 5, folder 1.

5 Meinberg renovated the Stella Maris Chapel on the southeast side of Lake Sagatagan at Saint John's in 1943. According to Kacmarcik, Abbot Dworschak was very interested in the arts and even worked as an artist making pottery, but he had little knowledge of modern art and architecture. Author's conversation with Frank Kacmarcik, June 20, 2002, at Saint John's.

6 Thimmesh, *Marcel Breuer and a Committee of Twelve Plan a Church*, 2.

7 The March 7, 1953, letter is located in SJA, box 2, folder 13, and all quotations in this section are taken from it.

8 For more on the Bauhaus and its impact in the United States see Bayer, Gropius, and Gropius, *Bauhaus*; Bernhardt, Harms, and Schoeller, *Bauhaus*; Forgács, *The Bauhaus Idea and Bauhaus Politics*; Franciscono, *Walter Gropius and the Creation of the Bauhaus in Weimar*; Hochman, *Bauhaus*; James-Chakraborty, "From Isolationism to Internationalism"; and Jordy, "The Aftermath of the Bauhaus in America." The Nazis closed the Bauhaus in 1933 as many of its teachers, including Gropius, Mies van der Rohe, Albers, and Breuer, were either on their way to or about to leave for the United States, where they would continue the educational process for American students.

9 James-Chakraborty, *German Architecture for a Mass Audience*, 3. In her essay "From Isolationism to Internationalism," James-Chakraborty points out that American acceptance of modern architecture was the result of many forces, including economic factors like the Great Depression, World War II, and American culture, which had embraced regional works by Frank Lloyd Wright prior to modernism's arrival.

10 The parabolic arch is economical as it requires the smallest amount of material with a given load, and it has a small section with less reinforcing than another arch supporting any given load.

11 Forty, *Concrete and Culture*, 169.

12 Bruggink and Droppers, *When Faith Takes Form*, 8.

13 Breuer, "Architectural Details," 121.

14 Concrete is an artificial stone-like material made by mixing cement and various aggregates, such as sand, pebbles, gravel, and shale, with water and allowing the mixture to harden by hydration. Although concrete's employ as a building material dates back to ancient times (the Roman Pantheon [118–28 CE], for example, has a mass concrete dome), its rise in application as a twentieth-century phenomenon was facilitated by the discovery that steel and concrete have the same coefficient of expansion and therefore could work together to span great distances. For more on the role of concrete in

architecture see key studies by Collins, *Concrete*; Forty, *Concrete and Culture*; and Onderdonk, *The Ferro-Concrete Style*.

15 Byrne, "A Philosophy of Design for Concrete," 54–55.

16 Forty, *Concrete and Culture*, 172.

17 Collins notes that Paul Cottancin's method differs from the contemporary methods for reinforced concrete. His system used pierced bricks threaded with steel rods in compression members and rods in reinforced cement (i.e., rods embedded in a mixture of sand and cement without any stone aggregate) for tension support. Collins, *Concrete*, 116.

18 For more on Perret's philosophy of design see Collins, "The Doctrine of Auguste Perret."

19 Perret used five shapes in creating these walls—a cross, a circle, a diamond within a square, a half square, and a quarter square.

20 Onderdonk, *The Ferro-Concrete Style*, 177.

21 Ibid., 180.

22 Hammond, *Liturgy and Architecture*, 52. In 1918 the parish priest of Raincy, Abbé Félix Nègre, consulted several ecclesiastical architects about the design of the church, but he was unable to settle on an architect because their designs were too expensive for the parish coffers of 600,000 francs (see Onderdonk, *The Ferro-Concrete Style*, 155). He then contacted Perret because of his reputation for cheap and effective concrete architecture, and although Perret had not built an ecclesiastical space prior to this work, he was hired and provided a worship space for 2,000 people at far less cost than the ecclesiastical designers. See Christ-Janer and Mix Foley, *Modern Church Architecture*, 11. The total cost of the church in 1924 was $120,000, equal to $1,663,663 in 2014. Perret designed additional churches using reinforced concrete, including Saint-Thérèse, Montmagny, France (1925), and Saint Joseph's in Le Havre, France (1953–57). The church in Le Havre was part of the town's reconstruction after World War II, during which the seaport had been bombed

more than one hundred times. It would be useful to conduct additional research on the economies of concrete. Is it really more cost effective over the life of the church, from construction costs to regular maintenance? Another venue for future research could investigate the parallels between this commission and the church at Saint John's. Both had very engaged patrons, neither architect had designed a religious space prior to each work, and they both used concrete—although Perret might have appreciated its economical value more than Breuer. In 1963 Hamilton Smith estimated the costs of Saint John's Abbey church at $2,169,500, the equivalent of $16,808,094 in 2014. Hamilton Smith, "Interpretation of Saint John's Abbey Church Building Costs for Future Estimating Purposes," March 27, 1963, Syracuse University Library Archives, Marcel Breuer Papers, box 114, folder 4. Further references to this archive will be indicated as SUL.

23 Pecklers, *The Unread Vision*, 236.

24 Hammond, *Liturgy and Architecture*, 157. For more on the significance of the building as it relates to the new liturgy see Gieselmann, *New Churches*, 12; Harwood, "Liturgy and Architecture," 54; Henze and Filthaut, *Contemporary Church Art*, 22; and Maguire and Murray, *Modern Churches of the World*, 14–16.

25 Schnell, *Twentieth Century Church Architecture in Germany*, 34–35.

26 James-Chakraborty, *German Architecture for a Mass Audience*, 64. Like other reformers, van Acken called for the moving of the altar into the body of the church, where it would better facilitate his *Messopferkirche* or "church of the mass sacrifice concept" whereby worshippers were co-sacrificers with the priest.

27 Onderdonk, *The Ferro-Concrete Style*, 214.

28 James-Chakraborty, *German Architecture for a Mass Audience*, 68.

29 Henze and Filthaut, *Contemporary Church Art*, 23.

30 Debuyst, *Modern Architecture and Christian Cel-*

ebration, 45; Debuyst's emphasis. For more on Schwarz see Hasler, *Architektur als Ausdruck*; Pehnt and Strohl, *Rudolf Schwarz 1897–1961*; and Schwarz, *Kirchenbau*.

31 See Rudolf Schwarz, *Kirchenbau*, 37–46.
32 Tuzik, *How Firm a Foundation*, 43–44.
33 See also Schwarz, *The Church Incarnate*, and Mies van der Rohe, ibid., vii.
34 Schwarz, *The Church Incarnate*, 28.
35 Ibid.
36 "Maurice Lavanoux, Tenacious Commentator," 5. For more on the Liturgical Arts Society see chapter 4.
37 Lavanoux, editorial, *Liturgical Arts* 2, 2 (second quarter 1933): 49.
38 Ibid., 49–50.
39 Ibid., 50.
40 Mumford, "A Modern Catholic Architect."
41 Chappell and Van Zanten, *Barry Byrne and John Lloyd Wright*, 35. For more on Byrne's role in Catholic church design see Vincent Michael, "Express the Modern: Barry Byrne in 1920s Europe," *Journal of the Society of Architectural Historians* 69, no. 4 (December 2010): 536–37, 545–52.
42 Michael, *The Architecture of Barry Byrne*, 73.
43 Vincent Michael, "Continuity and Clarity: The Postwar Designs of Barry Byrne," presentation at the Society of Architectural Historians annual meeting in the session "Rebirth of Solids," Richmond, Va., 2002.
44 Lavanoux, "Saint Patrick's Church, Racine, Wisconsin," 98.
45 Ibid.
46 Byrne, "A Philosophy of Design for Concrete," 54.
47 Michael, *The Architecture of Barry Byrne*, 101.
48 Byrne, "Plan for a Church," 58.
49 Ibid.
50 Cram's ideas can be found in (among others) *The Gothic Quest*, *American Churches*, *Church Building*, *American Church Building of Today*, *The Catholic Church and Art*, and *My Life in Architec-*

ture. Vincent Michael outlines the debate between Cram and Byrne in *Commonweal* about traditional vs. modern. Michael, "Express the Modern."

51 McNamara, "Modern and Medieval," 75.
52 Crichton, *Lights in Darkness*, 157.
53 Pope Pius XII, *Mediator Dei*, part 199; cited in Seasoltz, *The New Liturgy*, 157.
54 Seasoltz, *The New Liturgy*, 157.
55 Ibid., 156.
56 The German bishops established a liturgical commission in 1940. See Ruff, *Sacred Music and Liturgical Reform*, 239–40.
57 See Klauser, "Directives for the Building of a Church." Klauser was Rector Magnificus of the University of Bonn.
58 "Churches: Must the Church Build in the Gothic?," 63.
59 Architecture training at Saint John's started as an outgrowth of its math department. Father Gilbert Winkelman founded the department in the early decades of the twentieth century, teaching courses in architecture, mechanical and freehand drawing, theory of construction, and other aspects of engineering and mathematics. He was also an architect, attending classes in the summer at the Armour Institute of Technology in Chicago. He designed churches in Avon, Swanville, and Foxhome, Minnesota, as well as in Rugby and Fort Totten, North Dakota. The 1924 *Sagatan* yearbook mentions that ecclesiastical architecture was an important part of the curriculum. English, religion, mathematics, freehand drawing, water coloring, designing, history of architecture, elements of construction, and physics made up the two-year program. Father Cloud Meinberg was one of the instructors along with Winkelman. Gilbert Winkelman file, SJA, box Z 50, and *Record* (October 1, 1918).
60 "Chronology," *Record* 67 (May 1961): supplement, 6, and Frank Kacmarcik, conversation with author, Collegeville, Minnesota, August 25, 1999.

61 Schwarz, *The Church Incarnate*, 10.

62 Rudolf Schwarz, Cologne, to Abbot Baldwin Dworshak, Collegeville, March 25, 1953, SJA, box 2, folder 10.

63 Pichard, *L'art sacré modern*, 64. For more on Baur see Brütsch, Hofmann, Humbel, et al., *Hermann Baur 1894–1980*; and Mainberger, *Kirchenbauten von Hermann Baur und Fritz Metzger*.

64 Hermann Baur, Basel, to Abbot Baldwin Dworschak, Collegeville, April 7, 1953, SJA, box 2, folder 1.

65 For more on Bosslet see Bosslet, *Vom Zeichnen und Bauen*; Brülls, "Albert Bosslet (1880–1957)"; Brülls, "Deutsche Gotteshäuser"; Hoffmann and Steinlein, *Albert Bosslet*; Jöckle, "Albert Bosslet (1880–1957)"; "Obituary Albert Bosslet"; and Kahle, *Deutsche Kirchenbaukunst des 20. Jahrhunderts*, 66–68.

66 Senior Council meeting minutes, March 4, 1953, SJA, box 5, folder 4.

67 Kramreiter worked for Böhm in Cologne from 1928 to 1932. For more on Kramreiter see "Architettura religiosa contemporanea in Austria"; "Chiesa della pace a Vienna (Quellenstrasse)"; Parsch and Kramreiter, *Neue Kirchenkunst im Geist der Liturgie*; and Kramreiter, *Die Schottengruft in Wien*.

68 Abbot Baldwin Dworschak, Collegeville, to Pius Parsch, Klosterneuburg, March 10, 1953, SJA, box 2, folder 6.

69 Robert Kramreiter, Vienna, to Abbot Baldwin Dworschak, Collegeville, March 24, 1953, SJA, box 2, folder 6.

70 Books by Sharp include *The Anatomy of a Village*, *English Panorama*, *Exeter Phoenix: A Plan for Rebuilding*, and *Town Planning*. For more on Sharp see Kathryn Stansfield, *The Poetry of Planning*, and the online archive of Sharp's work at http://catless.ncl.ac.uk/sharp (accessed June 14, 2012). For work that places Sharp's oeuvre in context with the Garden City movement and Corbusian planning strategies, see Pendlebury, "The Urbanism of Thomas Sharp." This article is from an issue of *Planning Perspectives* devoted to Sharp's designs.

71 Sharp, *Exeter Phoenix*, 11.

72 Thomas Sharp, Oxford, to Abbot Baldwin Dworschak, Collegeville, March 20, 1953, SJA, box 2, folder 11.

73 Ronald Roloff, O.S.B., "Building Committee Minutes," April 20, 1953, SJA, box 5, folder 4. Senior Council Committee minutes of April 20, 1953, indicate a concern about the cost of bringing the Europeans to Collegeville for a preliminary survey.

74 For example, see Abbot Baldwin Dworschak, Collegeville, to Hermann Baur, Basel, April 24, 1953, SJA, box 2, folder 1.

75 For more on Belluschi see Carroll, "Reconciling Modernism and Tradition"; Clausen, *Pietro Belluschi*; Clausen, *Spiritual Space*; Ross, "The 'Attainment and Restraint' of Pietro Belluschi"; and Stubblebine, *The Northwest Architecture of Pietro Belluschi*.

76 Pietro Belluschi, Cambridge, to Abbot Baldwin Dworschak, Collegeville, March 17, 1953, SJA, box 2, folder 2. All quotes in this paragraph are taken from this source.

77 Clausen, *Spiritual Space*, 13.

78 Belluschi, "Architecture To-day," 21.

79 Clausen, *Spiritual Space*, 72.

80 For more on Saarinen see Olivarez, "Churches and Chapels," 266–75; Roman, *Eero Saarinen*; Saarinen, *Eero Saarinen on His Work*; and Saarinen, *Eero Saarinen*.

81 Saarinen, "The Changing Philosophy of an Architect."

82 For more on Christ Church see "Christ Church"; Christ-Janer and Mix Foley, *Modern Church Architecture*, 146–53; and "A Different Gem in a Homely Setting."

83 For the Twenty-Five Year Award see Mary E. Osman, "The 1977 AIA Honor Awards"; and more recently the American Institute of Architect's traveling exhibition *Structures of Our Time: 31 Buildings*

That Changed Modern Life. The building was also added to the National Register of Historic Places in June 2001.

84   Eero Saarinen, Bloomfield Hills, Mich., to Abbot Baldwin Dworschak, Collegeville, April 1, 1953, SJA, box 2, folder 9.

85   Herm Sittard, "Church for the Twentieth Century."

86   For more on Neutra see Hines, *Richard Neutra and the Search for Modern Architecture*; Lamprecht, *Richard Neutra*; McCoy, *Richard Neutra*; Neutra, *Life and Shape*; Neutra, *Richard Neutra, Promise and Fulfillment, 1919–1932*; Neutra, *Nature Near*; and Sack, *Richard Neutra*.

87   McCoy, *Richard Neutra*, 13.

88   Richard Neutra, Los Angeles, to Abbot Baldwin Dworschak, Collegeville, March 13, 1953, SJA, box 2, folder 8.

89   "Notes and Observations on the Visits of Mr. Neutra and Mr. Gropius," March 30, 1953, SJA, box 2, folder 8. All information on Neutra's visit is taken from this source.

90   Frank Kacmarcik, conversation with author, Collegeville, June 20, 2002.

91   Gropius and Neutra had first met on May 14, 1928, in California during Gropius's first trip to the United States. For more on Gropius see Fitch, *Walter Gropius*; Giedion, *Walter Gropius*; Isaacs, *Gropius*; and Nerdinger, *Walter Gropius*.

92   For more on Beaux-Arts-based methods in the United States see Draper, "The Ecole des Beaux-Arts and the Architectural Profession in the United States"; Esherick, "Architectural Education in the Thirties and Seventies"; and Drexler, *The Architecture of the Ecole des Beaux-Arts*.

93   Walter Gropius, Cambridge, to Abbot Baldwin Dworschak, Collegeville, March 16, 1953, SJA, box 2, folder 8.

94   "Notes and Observations on the Visits of Mr. Neutra and Mr. Gropius," March 30, 1953, SJA, box 2, folder 8.

95   The McCormick Office Building was designed in

1953 while Gropius was working with The Architects Collaborative (TAC). Arthur Myhrum was the associate on the project.

96   Ronald Roloff, "Minutes of the Building Committee," April 20, 1953, SJA, box 5, folder 4.

97   Biographical information on Murphy is limited but growing. Because of his time as dean of the College of Architecture at Washington University (St. Louis, Missouri), their collection holds information on his life and career. Washington University art history PhD candidate, Mary Reid Brunstrom, is currently at work on a dissertation on Murphy's career, focusing on his partnership with Mackey Jr. and the churches they built together for the Catholic archdiocese in St. Louis. I am grateful to Mary for her insights into Murphy and his work.

98   Information on Murphy's visit is taken from "Notes and Observations on the Visit of Joseph Murphy," April 14, 1953, SJA, box 2, folder 7.

99   Ibid., comments by Father Cloud Meinberg. Murphy designed the structure around two steel trusses that enabled a span in the nave from narthex to sanctuary of 120 feet.

100   Blake, "The House in the Museum Garden, Marcel Breuer, Architect."

101   "Marcel Breuer, Teacher and Architect." Among the domestic aspects of Breuer's work the article addressed were the subdivision of rooms according to use; the use of materials to soften a stern geometry; bright color accents; stairs and fireplaces as sculpture; consistent detailing; intimate open spaces; and the fact that his houses reach for a view of nature.

102   Isabelle Hyman, "Breuer and the Power of Concrete," paper delivered June 22, 2002, at Saint John's Abbey. Although Breuer's architecture would become sculpture through his wonderful handling of concrete, he only completed one public commission for sculpture, *The Athlete*, located at Saint John's Abbey. See Figure 2.16. For more on Breuer's relationship with Hungary see Mate Major, "Mar-

cel Breuer and Hungary." For more on Breuer see Gatje, *Marcel Breuer*; Hyman, *Marcel Breuer, Architect*; and Wilk, *Marcel Breuer*.

103   Hyman, *Marcel Breuer, Architect*, 40.

104   Architecture was the last course taught at the Bauhaus, for Gropius considered it to be the pinnacle of all the arts. As Andrew Saint has pointed out, the Bauhaus was "primarily an arts-and-crafts school in which during Gropius's time the architectural strain ran thin. No true architectural course was taught there for the first eight years of its existence." Saint, "The Battle of the Bauhaus," 117. For more on the educational philosophy of the Bauhaus see Bergdoll and Dickerman, *Bauhaus 1919–1933*.

105   Marcel Breuer, New York City, to Abbot Baldwin Dworschak, Collegeville, March 14, 1953, SJA, box 2, folder 14.

106   "Notes and Observations on the Visit of Mr. Breuer to Saint John's," April 20, 1953, SJA, box 2, folder 14. Quotes by Breuer in this discussion of his visit are taken from this source.

107   Sittard, "Church for the Twentieth Century," 25.

108   Leake, *Egyptian Architecture*.

109   Howarth, *Marcel Breuer*, 19.

110   Information on Byrne's ecclesiastical projects may be found in Chappell and Van Zanten, *Barry Byrne and John Lloyd Wright*, 22–37, and Michael, *The Architecture of Barry Byrne*. For a discussion of Byrne's involvement with liturgical reforms see White, *Art, Architecture, and Liturgical Reform*, 156–59.

111   Byrne liked concrete for its unification of science and architecture and for its beauty of form and finish.

112   Barry Byrne, Evanston, to Abbot Baldwin Dworschak, Collegeville, March 17, 1953, SJA, box 2, folder 4.

113   Abbot Baldwin Dworschak, Collegeville, to Barry Byrne, Evanston, April 2, 1953, SJA, box 2, folder 4.

114   Barry Byrne, Evanston, to Abbot Baldwin Dworschak, Collegeville, April 13, 1953, SJA, box 2, folder 4.

115   Abbot Baldwin Dworschak, Collegeville, to Barry Byrne, Evanston, April 26, 1953, SJA, box 2, folder 4. In subsequent correspondence Byrne asked to remain in consideration for any future work at the abbey.

116   Ronald Roloff, "Minutes of the Building Committee," April 21, 1953, SJA, box 5, folder 4.

117   "Notes and Observations on the Visits of Mr. Neutra and Mr. Gropius," March 30, 1953, SJA, box 2, folder 8.

118   Gropius was a religious man, however, as I learned from his daughter, Ati, in October 1999, when I interviewed her at their house in Lincoln. She said that her father did not have a religious preference but that he was a very spiritual man who through his architecture sought a safe place for people by the provision of an appropriate space for living, his key to the spirit of life. She also said that at Christmas her father read stories to her from the Bible in front of the fireplace at the house in Lincoln. Ati also considered Gropius to be more spiritual than Breuer. Ati Gropius, conversation with author, Lincoln, Mass., October 30, 1999.

119   Wilk, *Marcel Breuer*, 15.

120   Former architectural partner Robert Gatje considered Breuer to be a humanistic Protestant. He also believes it unlikely the Benedictines knew about Breuer's Jewish origins. See Gatje, *Marcel Breuer*, 90.

121   Confirmed by Dion Neutra, conversation with author, Minneapolis, October 16, 2000.

122   "Notes and Observations on the Visit of Mr. Breuer to Saint John's," April 20, 1953, SJA, box 2, folder 14.

123   Isabelle Hyman, conversation with author, New York City, April 22, 1999.

124   Abbot Baldwin Dworschak, quoted on p. 3 of press pack for the Saint John's Abbey and University Church Consecration, August 24, 1961.

125   Marcel Breuer, New York, to Abbot Baldwin Dworschak, Collegeville, April 28, 1953, Archives of American Art, Marcel Breuer Papers, AAA_breumarc_5718_192_001; http://www.aaa.si.edu/

collections/marcel-breuer-papers-5596 (accessed June 1, 2014). Further references to this archive will be cited as AAA. This letter gets into some of the costs that would be outlaid for the comprehensive plan—$20,000 without developing the church and $30,000 to include it. Breuer's team would complete this all by December 15, 1953.

126 Abbot Baldwin Dworschak, memo to the community, April 23, 1953, SJA, box 2, folder 13.

127 Senior Council meeting minutes, March 4, 1953, SJA, box 5, folder 1.

128 Tenoever, "Edward J. Schulte and American Church Architecture of the Twentieth Century," 14. Interest in Schulte is on the rise. On April 17–18, 2010, the Architectural Foundation of Cincinnati held a symposium on Schulte. For more on Schulte see McNamara, *Heavenly City*, 142–43. Schulte also wrote "The Cathedral" in 1956 and the book *The Lord Was My Client* in 1972.

129 Tenoever, "Edward J. Schulte and American Church Architecture of the Twentieth Century," 12.

130 Edo J. Belli, "Interview with Edo J. Belli," interview by Betty J. Blum, Chicago, November 3, 1983, Art Institute of Chicago, 1–52. http://digital-libraries .saic.edu/cdm/ref/collection/caohp/id/451.

131 Maurice Lavanoux, New York City, to Abbot Baldwin Dworschak, Collegeville, March 16, 1953, SJA, box 5, folder 5.

132 Emil Frei, St. Louis, to Abbot Baldwin Dworschak, Collegeville (n.d.; March 1953?), SJA, box 5, folder 5.

133 Ibid.

134 Spade, *Oscar Niemeyer*, 126.

135 Philip Kennicott, "Niemeyer and the Sweep of History," *Washington Post*, October 5, 2008. http:// articles.washingtonpost.com/2008–10–05/news/ 36916785_1_pampulha-oscar-niemeyer-brazilian -identity (accessed August 3, 2013).

136 See Le Corbusier, *The Chapel at Ronchamp*; Pauly, "The Chapel of Ronchamp as an Example of Le Corbusier's Creative Process"; Pauly, *Le Corbusier*; and Stoller, *The Chapel at Ronchamp*.

3. BUILDING THE SPIRITUAL AXIS

1 Breuer intended to "shadow build" at Saint John's, eliminating the old buildings once the new version of it was completed. Costs prevented this from happening. Senior Council meeting minutes, March 4, 1953, SJA, box 5, folder 1.

2 Breuer's 10 percent fee was based on the American Institute of Architects New York chapter's schedule of architect fees. Saint John's also had to reimburse the architect for 50 percent of the structural engineering fees, or $8,750.00, due to the special character of the structure. Marcel Breuer, New York, to Abbot Baldwin Dworschak, Collegeville, February 1, 1954, AAA_breumarc_5718_195_001; http://www.aaa.si.edu/collections/marcel-breuer -papers-5596 (accessed June 1, 2014).

3 Supreme Congregation of the Holy Office of the Vatican, "Instruction of the Church on Sacred Art," June 30, 1952. http://www.traditioninaction .org/HotTopics/c029_Instruction.htm (accessed June 9, 2014).

4 For more on Michelson see the Val Michelson papers at the Northwest Architectural Archives, University of Minnesota; Mack, "From Russia, with Visions of Modernism"; and Hawley, "Russian Architect Val Michelson's Life 'Was like a Novel.'" In 1962 Michelson designed Saint John's Preparatory School and in 1965 he completed the Benedictine monastery of St. Paul's for women in Maplewood, Minnesota. Both buildings used reinforced concrete as their primary building material.

5 Although they were fourth-generation descendants of builders in Ireland, the McGough family, led by father Peter with his sons Charlie, Leo, Larry, Greg, Tom, and Pete, had just started the company in 1956. The abbey church was a breakthrough project for them. For more on McGough see Johnson, "McGough Construction—Still Prospering after Five Generations." Mechanical engineers were Gausman and Moore, Inc., from St. Paul, Minnesota. Cold Spring Electric completed the electrical

work. Joseph Tuohy & Sons of Chatfield, Minnesota, built the church seating. Weidner Plumbing & Heating of St. Cloud provided plumbing, heating, and ventilation for the building. The lighting consultant was Stanley McCandless, and the acoustical consultant was S. K. Wolf. AAA, reel 5738.

6 Florian Muggli, Collegeville, to Hamilton Smith, New York City, March 3, 1958, SUL, box 104, file 1. Smith's comments were written on the letter before it was passed on to Breuer.

7 There were four bidders for the project, and McGough came in the lowest at $1,663,000. The abbey rejected the bid, however, as they were not ready to undertake construction at that time, owing to financial reasons. About six months later, Fred Hughes, the abbey's lawyer, called and asked them to come up and talk about the project. The McGough family realized the revolutionary nature of the building and decided to take $100,000 off a projected profit of $160,000. Larry McGough still feels this was a real bargain for the publicity the building brought to the company. Victoria Young interview with Larry McGough, June 1, 2011, Roseville, Minnesota.

The base bid of the church included everything except thirty-nine altars; lavabos; glass for the north wall; choir stalls, pews, and seats in the chapter house; organs; screen at the south end of the church; the Stations of the Cross; cabinet work; vestment cabinets in the private altar chapels and larger sacristies; confessionals; new roads and parking lots; cloister gardens and bells. Abbot Baldwin Dworschak, memo to members of the community, November 6, 1957, SJA, box BA 6.

8 All the men associated with this project still speak of the importance of Hoffmeyer and his ability to get things done. Robert Gatje, Hamilton Smith, and Larry McGough, roundtable discussions at Saint John's Abbey in October 2001 and June 2002. Hoffmeyer would state about the project: "This is a job that separates the men from the boys. Most any contractor can do an ordinary building; but there

are few that will tackle a job like this one." Sittard, "Church for the Twentieth Century," 65.

9 The Universal Atlas Cement Company of New York City provided all the concrete for the project. They also paid for the 1957 model of the church, using it in their own publicity. The advertisement originally appeared in *Time* magazine on May 20, 1957. See also Schweitz, "Saint John's Abbey Church."

10 Abbot Baldwin Dworschak to the community, April 15, 1958. SJA, box BA 6.

11 "Project Record Book: Preliminary Costs May 1960," SUL, box 102, folder 7, and telegram from Abbot Baldwin Dworschak, Collegeville, to Hamilton Smith, New York City, April 22, 1958, SUL, box 104, folder 1. Recall Hamilton Smith's 1963 estimated costs of Saint John's Abbey Church at $2,169,500. Hamilton Smith, "Interpretation of St. John's Abbey Church Building Costs for Future Estimating Purposes," March 27, 1963, SUL, box 114, folder 4.

12 McGough Construction Co. of St. Paul, brochure, ca. 1973, SJA, box 3, folder 3. Over 416,000 feet of lumber was used during the construction of the church.

13 Information on the monastic workforce is taken from Millete, "St. John's New Abbey Church," 79–80.

14 Marcel Breuer, "List of Information Needed for the Comprehensive Study of St. John's," April 27, 1953, AAA, reel 5257.

15 Father John Eidenschink to the community at Saint John's, June 4, 1953, SJA, box 2, folder 13.

16 This binder is now in SUL, box 70, folder 6. The history of the parishes is called "Our Parishes: The Plants Take Root" and can be found in SUL, box 70, folder 9. The nineteenth-century church did not impress Breuer. He characterized it as "low to mediocre" in quality. Frank Kacmarcik, conversation with author, Collegeville, Minnesota, June 20, 2002.

17 "Daily Schedule of Priest Members of St. John's

Abbey, Collegeville, Minnesota," AAA, reel 5257. The Office and Mass times included Prime at 4:45 a.m., Mass at 5:45 a.m., Tierce, Sext, and None at 11:40 a.m., Vespers and Compline at 5:30 p.m., and Matins and Lauds at 7:30 p.m.

18 It is not uncommon for designers to become quickly familiar with the workings of a faith. See Joseph Siry's work on Frank Lloyd Wright's Beth Shalom Synagogue for an excellent discussion on Wright's crash course in Judaism. Siry, *Beth Shalom Synagogue.*

19 SUL, box 70, folder 6.

20 Hamilton Smith, "Notes from *Benedictine Monachism,*" SUL, box 70, file 6.

21 SUL, box 70, file 6.

22 Both Anson's and Reinhold's books are referred to frequently in the correspondence between Breuer and the Benedictines, not only in the design process, but also during construction. Reinhold published many articles in *Worship.* For more on Reinhold see Upton, *Worship in Spirit and Truth.*

23 SUL, box 114, folder 4. See also the copy at SJA, box 5, folder 19. In a December 31, 1955, letter from Meinberg to Breuer, Meinberg suggests more readings for the architect: "By separate mail I am sending you a copy of the Plan Issue of *The Record.* I do not know if you ever received a copy—there was an earlier one that was only partly devoted to the plans which I think you did receive. In case you have not seen this issue before there are several articles that may interest you, e.g., 'Dogma and Concrete' and 'Building on the Holy Rule.' I am also enclosing a copy of the Jan. '55 issue of *Worship* because of the article 'Church Art' of Fr. Jos. Jungmann's—this is an excellent article, one of the best I have ever seen. I personally cannot agree with the idea that architecture is a 'representational art,' but otherwise the article is fine." AAA, box 3, reel 5712.

24 Father Cloud Meinberg, Collegeville, to Marcel Breuer, New York City, December 31, 1954, AAA, box 3, reel 5712.

25 Frank Kacmarcik has recounted how Fathers Cloud Meinberg and Joachim Watrin discussed Benedictine architecture, particularly Maria Laach, with Breuer and Smith during the early visits. Frank Kacmarcik, conversation with author, Collegeville, June 20, 2002.

26 SUL, box 70, folder 5.

27 Gatje, *Marcel Breuer,* 47, 51, and 59.

28 Sittard, "Church for the Twentieth Century," 62.

29 "Story of a Church and Connected Problems," SUL, box 70, folder 6.

30 SUL, box 70, folder 4.

31 In a letter from Hamilton Smith to Watrin of December 1953, Smith noted that this was never their intention, stating that the "present shape came about partly in answer to your requirements and partly as a matter of 'feel.'" He went on to say that since they were so close to the golden section with the plan, they were "tempted to make the building a plan form dominated by the Golden Mean." The architects did bring the final plan's measurements into accordance with the golden section. Hamilton Smith, New York, to Joachim Watrin, Collegeville, December 2, 1953, SJA, Watrin file.

32 Traditionally Catholic churches were laid out on an east–west line, with the eastern end containing the sanctuary and altar so that the clergy and laity would face the direction of the rising sun, as Christ was often referred to in the liturgy. Saint John's understood that there were exceptions to this practice and that no ecclesiastical law mandated an east–west orientation. The first abbey church, although placed on an east–west line, had the altar on the west end. Site conditions usually dictate a building's orientation. For more see Father Cloud Meinberg, "Orientation of Church," SUL, box 114, folder 4.

33 Howarth, "Marcel Breuer," 260.

34 Sittard, "Church for the Twentieth Century," 62.

35 Breuer, *Marcel Breuer,* 70–71.

36 Christ-Janer and Mix Foley, *Modern Church Architecture,* 4.

37 Uldrich, "Architect and Psychologist," 2.

38   The lecture was held May 26, 1959. See the Walker invitation, *Star Tribune* article of May 31, 1959, and letters from Rapson's assistant and Forrest Selvig, assistant curator of the Walker in AAA, box 4, reel 5714.

39   "The New Red Line" in the *Minneapolis Morning Tribune*, June 2, 1959, AAA, box 4, reel 5714.

40   Marcel Breuer, New York City, to Abbot Baldwin Dworschak, Collegeville, November 20, 1957, SJA, box BA 6.

41   Hammond, *Liturgy and Architecture*, 157.

42   Marcel Breuer, "Defining Modern Architecture," undated typescript in AAA, reel 5718.

43   Stroik, *Path, Portal, Path*, 52–53, 55.

44   Schwarz, *The Church Incarnate*, 177.

45   Breuer, *Marcel Breuer*, 60.

46   Father Cloud Meinberg, "The Monastic Church," SUL, box 114, folder 4.

47   On October 11, 1956, Abbot Baldwin established a fifteen-member church committee, appointing himself as chair and subprior Father John Eidenschink as the vice-chair. Other members of the committee included all the members of the building committee with the addition of Father Hilary Thimmesh; see chapter 2, note 2. The committee members saw their role not as that of decision makers but rather as communicators. They were a formal means of offering the architects suggestions for the building of the church, both from within their own ranks and from the Benedictine community at large. SJA, box 5, folder 6. See Thimmesh, *Marcel Breuer and a Committee of Twelve Plan a Church*.

48   Breuer proposed a banner at the roadside—a mock-up of a portion of the folded side walls—but for financial reasons the monks said no.

49   Stroik, *Path, Portal, Path*, 52–53, 55.

50   Mircea Eliade, the well-known historian of religion, made a clear distinction between the sacred and profane worlds in his 1959 book, *The Sacred and the Profane*.

51   Stoddard, *Adventure in Architecture*, notes that

Breuer became enamored with the thin facades carrying bells on his travels through the Greek islands in 1931–32 (98). He liked their asymmetry and play of light and shadow. Hyman mentions in *Marcel Breuer, Architect*, a photograph in the Breuer archives at Syracuse and the American Archives of Art of San José, Laguna Pueblo, New Mexico, on which Breuer had labeled "adobe wall with bells reminiscent to concrete banner of St. John's church" (222). AAA, reel 5257. Furthermore, an advertisement in the November 1954 issue of *Harper's Bazaar*, located in the Breuer office files, depicts the flat wall of an unknown church with five different sized bell openings. *Harper's Bazaar* (November 1954): 135. SUL, box 114, folder 3.

52   *Walker Art Center Design Quarterly* 53 (1961): 5.

53   The bells were originally cast in 1879 and range in weight from 2,100 to 6,600 pounds.

54   Hyman, *Marcel Breuer, Architect*, 222.

55   AAA, box 7, reel 5718. The coloring book dates from December 1962.

56   Sittard, "Church for the Twentieth Century," 62.

57   Breuer, *Marcel Breuer*, 71.

58   Val Michelson memorandum, Collegeville, to Marcel Breuer, New York City, October 8, 1958, SUL, box 102, folder 10.

59   Meinberg visited 150 towns and cities in Italy, Switzerland, Germany, Belgium, France, and Spain. He photographed and sketched buildings, shared the plans, and met with architects, artists, and members of religious communities.

60   Father Cloud Meinberg, "European Observations on Our Church Plans" (n.d.; ca. September/October 1956), 5–6. SJA, box 5, folder 5.

61   Meinberg, "European Observations on Our Church Plans," 3.

62   Marcel Breuer, New York City, to Abbot Baldwin Dworschak, Collegeville, October 16, 1956, SJA, box 2, folder 18.

63   Marcel Breuer, "Matter and Intrinsic Form." The invitation to this lecture featured a photograph of the abbey church's banner and northern façade.

64 Church Committee minutes, October 18, 1956, SJA, box 5, folder 6.

65 Ibid. Breuer and his associates tested out the role of sun reflection by setting up lamps and models in their office. Sittard, "Church for the Twentieth Century," 62.

66 Roloff, *Abbey and University Church of Saint John the Baptist, Collegeville, Minnesota.*

67 Abbot Baldwin Dworschak, Collegeville, to Marcel Breuer, New York City, August 18, 1958, SUL, box 105, folder 2.

68 Roloff, *Abbey and University Church of Saint John the Baptist,* n.p.

69 John Eidenschink, Collegeville, to Hamilton Smith, New York City, October 1, 1953, SUL, box 114, folder 4. The brethren requested that the confessionals be built into the walls of the building rather than freestanding, as was the case in the nineteenth-century church.

70 The church as completed grew in size from its original conception to hold 1,220 people: 900 collegians, 220 preparatory students, and 100 seminarians. The monks made this move based on projections of student growth at the university.

71 Breuer, *Marcel Breuer,* 64.

72 Crosbie, *Houses of God,* 8.

73 O'Connell, *Church Building and Furnishing,* 133.

74 Klauser, "Directives for the Building of a Church," 18.

75 Thimmesh, *Marcel Breuer and a Committee of Twelve Plan a Church,* 49.

76 An undated typescript in the AAA, reel 5257, mentions that the communion rail would be sixty-seven feet long (including the altar gate) and raised one step above the nave floor.

77 For more on the lack of decoration in the apse see chapter 4.

78 Hamilton Smith, roundtable discussion, Collegeville, June 20, 2002. Bethune corresponded directly with Breuer's office about this change, and she was referring to a lantern over the altar to allow light to emphasize its placement within the building.

79 "Comments by the Church Committee on Various Comments in Father Cloud's Report," October 15, 1956, SJA, box 5, folder 6.

80 Val Michelson memorandum, Collegeville, to Marcel Breuer, New York City, October 6, 1958, SUL, box 102, folder 1.

81 Murray S. Elmslie, New York City, to David Wolfe Fredman, Chicago, July 1, 1957, SUL Breuer archives online, image 01201–011 (accessed May 24, 2012). He also says in the letter that Mr. Maurice Barron of Farkas & Barron, their structural engineer, would be in Chicago the next week and would call him.

82 Modern construction methods necessary for the pouring in place of concrete meant that all four walls of this building had to be erected at the same time, a contradiction to the medieval tradition in which builders finished the apse end of the building first to get the altar secured, leaving many west ends still incomplete to this day.

83 For more on Nervi see Huxtable, *Pier Luigi Nervi;* "A Philosophy for Building 'Correctly'"; and *Pier Luigi Nervi.* A September 9, 1953, telegram from Breuer to Father Cloud Meinberg at Saint John's stated that Nervi's consultation fee for the preliminary church design would be $500 maximum but probably much less. SJA, box 2, folder 13.

84 Nervi, "The Influence of Reinforced Concrete and Technical and Scientific Progress on the Architecture of Today and Tomorrow," 16.

85 Each long beam of the east and west walls was cast in place as one piece. In a letter to Abbot Baldwin, Breuer conveyed an idea of the new church by including photographs of his designs for the UNESCO complex. He singled out UNESCO's conference hall and informed the abbot that the "wide spanned structure with the folded end walls and roof system would, I believe, be of interest to you for the expression they convey. The photos may also help you visualize your church project." Marcel Breuer, Paris, to Abbot Baldwin Dworschak, Collegeville, July 30, 1956, SJA, box 2, folder 23.

On UNESCO see Jones, *Marcel Breuer*, 78–97; Papachristou, *Marcel Breuer*, 225–28; and Salvadori, "Contrasts in Concrete."

86 Hoffmeyer used air-entrained concrete for the entire structure. He explained: "We introduced very minute air bubbles in the concrete. As a result it will stand alternate freezing and thawing much better than ordinary concrete because the resilience of air-entrained concrete withstands weather changes." See Sittard, "Church for the Twentieth Century," 65.

87 "St. John's Abbey—a Master Plan," 28.

88 Victoria Young, June 1, 2011, interview with Larry McGough, Roseville, Minnesota. A cold joint is a plane of weakness in concrete caused by an interruption or delay in pouring. It occurs when the first batch of concrete has begun to set before the next batch is added, thereby preventing the two batches from intermixing.

89 Larry McGough, roundtable discussion, Collegeville, October 24, 2002. Gajte confirms the sale, p. 112. At a June 1, 2011, interview with the author Larry McGough confirmed that a metal centering bid from a scaffolding company of $115,000 seemed very high, so they had in-house engineer Ed Sosnik design a structural steel false work for $34,000. After the roof and walls were completed, McGough's crew dismantled the frame over a two-week period without cutting up any of the steel members and sold it to Cold Spring Granite Company for a small profit due to post–World War II inflation.

90 Sittard, "Church for the Twentieth Century," 62.

91 This structure is technically modified because it has a roof plate. The walls are true folded construction.

92 Gunite is also known as shotcrete. See Hoffmeyer, "Wet-Mix Shotcrete Practice."

93 Slump is the measure of the consistency in fresh concrete. Zero-slump concrete is stiff or extremely dry in consistency.

94 Ted Hoffmeyer kept detailed photo documentation of the church's construction process, and these al-

bums can be found in the abbey's archives. See image in Hoffmeyer's first book of construction photos showing Pete McGough and a mock-up. Another photo in the same book shows them unloading the new True Gun-All Machine on May 12, 1959. A few pages later another image shows Max True's workmen gunning concrete on a sample folded plate roof form for Breuer's approval in June 1959; True was the owner of the Gun-All Company.

95 Gatje, *Marcel Breuer*, 112. Shear is the ability of a structural material to resist internal sliding of its own particles against one another.

96 Ibid.

97 Ibid., 113.

98 Larry McGough in a roundtable discussion at Saint John's Abbey, October 24, 2001. Steel had to be added because once concrete cracks, steel bears all the tensile weight and weakens.

99 J. Henry Schipke, "Report on the Structural Safety of Roof Trusses at St. John's Abbey Church, Collegeville, Minnesota," September 27, 1960, SUL, box 70, folder 11.

100 Breuer and Leon paid $120,000 for the repair. According to Larry McGough, Saint John's remained solvent because they had $100,000 in errors and omissions insurance. Victoria Young, June 1, 2011, interview with Larry McGough, Roseville, Minnesota.

101 Hamilton Smith, roundtable discussion, Collegeville, June 20, 2002.

102 Breuer, *Marcel Breuer*, 70.

103 Breuer, "Architectural Details," 126.

104 Onderdonk, *The Ferro-Concrete Style*, 178.

105 Father Cloud Meinberg, Collegeville, to Marcel Breuer, New York City, November 11, 1953, SUL, box 114, folder 4.

106 "St. John's Abbey—a Master Plan," 28.

107 *Sacrosanctum Concilium* (Constitution on the Sacred Liturgy), chapter 1, section 1, paragraph 13. See http://www.vatican.va/archive/hist_councils/ii_vatican_council.

108 For more on these personal devotions see "Devo-

tion to the Blessed Virgin Mary," "Visits to the Blessed Sacrament," and "Relics" in the New Advent online Catholic encyclopedia, http://www.newadvent.org (accessed August 1, 2013).

109 For more on Saint Peregrine and how his relics ended up at Saint John's see http://www.saintjohns abbey.org/your-visit/abbey-church/saint-peregrine-martyr (accessed July 31, 2013).

110 Roloff, *Abbey and University Church of Saint John the Baptist*, n.p. The full skeleton of Saint Peregrine lies at the base of the altar wrapped in gold- and silver-embroidered silk ornamented with jewels.

111 A crying room is a space adjacent to but separated from the nave that allows families with small children to see the Mass but not be disruptive during it.

112 Abbot Baldwin Dworshak, Collegeville, to Marcel Breuer, New York City, October 23, 1957, SUL, box 104, folder 1.

113 Breuer appreciated Le Corbusier's contributions to architecture, writing in an undated letter to Le Corbusier (likely late 1957), "This would make you the most productive and youngest mind, the most productive and youngest hands of these times—the happiest. This would bring us all, again and again, the greatest encouragement." AAA, reel 5714.

114 Marcel Breuer, Paris, to Abbot Baldwin Dworschak, Collegeville, July 30, 1956, SJA, box 2, folder 23.

115 The reliquaries hold relics from saints from antiquity to the twentieth century. They include relics from Saint Benedict and Saint John the Baptist, as well as fragments of the true cross on which Jesus died.

116 Onderdonk, *The Ferro-Concrete Style*, 177.

117 Lighting contractors on the church were Cold Spring Electric; the pews were made by the firm of Joseph Tuohy and Sons of Chatfield, Minnesota, for a bid of $162,000. SJA, box BA 7.

118 Concelebration of the Mass means to participate as a joint celebrant who recites the Canon in unison with other celebrants. See the conclusion for a discussion of the private chapels and concelebration.

119 Hughes, *The Monk's Tale*, 173.

120 Building Committee minutes, October 20, 1953, SJA, box 5, folder 4.

121 Cork is used as a ceiling material throughout the lower level of the building.

122 Church Committee minutes, April 28, 1960, SUL, box 116, folder 22.

123 Breuer completed designs for the chapels dedicated to Saints Michael the Archangel, Henry, Thomas Aquinas, Scholastica, Gregory the Great, Boniface, Vincent de Paul, Anselm, Augustine of Canterbury, Joseph, Francis Xavier, Basil, Francis of Assisi, Pius X, and Patrick. Kacmarcik's altars are located in chapels devoted to Saints Cyril and Methodius, Anthony the Great, Thomas More, Maur, Martin, Leo, Jerome, Joachim and Anne, Bernard, Lawrence, Our Lady of Guadalupe, Cloud, Peter and Paul, Louis, Francis of Rome, Gertrude, Isaac Jogues, Augustine of Hippo, and Ansgar. The order of the chapels as listed reflects their layout in the lower crypt and begins from the first chapel of Michael the Archangel in the northeast corner of the building. Breuer and Kacmarcik did not complete fifteen and nineteen original designs, respectively. Seven of Breuer's designs were fashioned twice with small changes, as were nine of Kacmarcik's. Each man fabricated an additional design to bring the total to thirty-four. See Church Committee minutes, January 30, 1961, SUL, box 115, folder 5.

124 Abbot Baldwin Dworschak, Collegeville, to Hamilton Smith, New York City, April 5, 1957, SUL, box 104, folder 1.

125 Father John Eidenschink, Collegeville, to Hamilton Smith, New York City, November 24, 1958, SUL, box 105, folder 2. The altar now rests away from the wall.

126 Father Cloud Meinberg, Collegeville, to Marcel Breuer, New York City, November 11, 1953, SUL, box 114, folder 4.

127 Breuer, *Marcel Breuer*, 80.

128 Father John Eidenschink, Collegeville, to Hamil-

ton Smith, New York City, February 9, 1957, SJA, box BA 6.

129 Father John Eidenschink, memo to the community, October 20, 1953, SUL, box 114, folder 4.

130 Benedict Avery, "Minutes for October 8–9 Meeting of Art Committee with Maurice Lavanoux," 3, SUL, box 116, folder 2.

131 Sittard, "Church for the Twentieth Century," 62.

132 Ibid.

4. A MINISTRY OF ART

1 For more on the role of the Benedictines as artists see Zarnecki, *The Monastic Achievement*, and Luxford, *The Art and English Benedictine Monasteries, 1300–1540*.

2 The tradition of hand writing manuscripts continues today. The Saint John's Bible, commissioned by the monks of the Welsh calligrapher Donald Jackson in 1998, is the first completely handwritten and illuminated Bible produced since the invention of the printing press. For more on the Bible see http://www.saintjohnsbible.org (accessed June 6, 2014).

3 Lercaro, "The Christian Church," 13.

4 Pope Pius XII, *On the Sacred Liturgy*, 156, in Seasoltz, *The New Liturgy*. In the twentieth century the Vatican took a great interest in new forms of sacred art. In 1932 Pope Pius XI founded a new Vatican art gallery with contemporary sacred art. In an address of October 27, 1932, he stated, "Open wide the portals and give the most cordial welcome to every good and progressive development of the approved and venerable traditions, which in so many centuries of Christian life . . . have given such proof of their inexhaustible capacity to inspire new and beautiful forms, whenever they have been called upon or studied and cultivated by the twofold light of genius of faith." Cited in Seasoltz, *The House of God*, 176.

5 Supreme Congregation of the Holy Office of the Vatican, "Instruction of the Church on Sacred Art," June 30, 1952. http://www.traditioninaction.org/HotTopics/c029_Instruction.htm (accessed July 30, 2013).

6 "Conversation with Mr. Breuer," June 10, 1958, SJA, box 1, folder 18.

7 Klauser, "Directives for Building a Church," 22.

8 For more on the society see White, *Art, Architecture, and Liturgical Reform*, 80. The society assisted parishes through the formation of a building and information service, as well as a craftsmen's service. For more on Lavanoux see White, "The Legacy of Maurice Lavanoux"; White, "Maurice Lavanoux, Tenacious Commentator"; White, "Maurice Lavanoux."

9 Other journals such as *Commonweal* and the *Catholic Art Quarterly* also included articles on art and architecture. See Van Allen, *The Commonweal and American Catholicism*, and Murphy, *The Search for Right Reason in an Unreasonable World*.

10 White, *Art, Architecture, and Liturgical Reform*, 197.

11 Herwegen, "The Nature of Religious Art."

12 White, *Art, Architecture, and Liturgical Reform*, 107.

13 White mentions that Lavanoux came under Couturier's influence in the 1940s, when Couturier was exiled in America. Ibid., 143.

14 O'Meara, "Modern Art and the Sacred," http://www.spiritualitytoday.org/spir2day/863814omeara.html#11 (accessed online July 15, 2012).

15 For more on Assy see Rubin, *Modern Sacred Art and the Church of Assy*; Dillenberger, "Artists and Church Commissions"; and Chew Orenduff, *The Transformation of Catholic Religious Art in the Twentieth Century*.

16 Other artists completing work at Assy include Jean Bazaine, Jean-Constant Demaison, Ladislas Kijno, Claude Mary, Carlo Sergio Signori, and Théodore Strawinsky.

17 For more on Matisse and Vence see Billot, *Henri Matisse*.

18 For more on the conflict with Richier's sculpture at Assy see Sarah Wilson, "Germaine Richier, Disquieting Matriarch."

19 For example, Lavanoux was present at the meetings of the Saint John's art committee on October 8–9, 1960. SUL, box 116, folder 2. A Liturgical Arts Society flyer for membership that included the society's goals and history is located in the Breuer office papers at SUL, box 114, folder 3.

20 Father Cloud Meinberg, Collegeville, to Marcel Breuer, New York City, November 11, 1953, SUL, box 114, folder 4.

21 Marcel Breuer, New York City, to Abbot Baldwin Dworschak, Collegeville, July 18, 1958, and Abbot Baldwin Dworschak to Marcel Breuer, July 22, 1958, SJA, box 2, folder 23. For further information about Frank Kacmarcik's career see North American Academy of Liturgy, "Frank Kacmarcik—Berakah Award for 1981"; Hovda, "The Amen Corner"; Philibert and Kacmarcik, Seeing and Believing"; Seasoltz, "Living Stones Built on Christ"; Seasoltz, "From the Bauhaus to the House of God's People"; Tuzik, "Frank Kacmarcik: Artist and Designer," in Turzik, How Firm a Foundation, and personal conversations with author. Further information may be found on the website of Arca Artium. a collection of books, prints, art objects, and music Kacmarcik donated to St. John's in 1995. http://www.hmml.org/our-collections.html (accessed June 6, 2014).

22 North American Academy of Liturgy, "Kacmarcik—Berakah Award for 1981," 361.

23 Tuzik, How Firm a Foundation, 328.

24 Frank Kacmarcik, conversation with author, Collegeville, June 21, 2002.

25 Tuzik, How Firm a Foundation, 327.

26 "The Various Interests Involved in Building a Church," 75.

27 North American Academy of Liturgy, "Kacmarcik—Berakah Award for 1981," 363.

28 Ibid., 364. Emphasis in the original.

29 Frank Kacmarcik, Collegeville, to Marcel Breuer, New York City, November 12, 1953, SUL, box 114, folder 4.

30 Frank Kacmarcik, St. Paul, to Marcel Breuer, New York City, June 2, 1957, SUL, box 104, folder 7. Kac-

marcik also included a prayer in this letter to Breuer in which he asked that "the Holy Spirit guide you [Breuer] in the forming of the proper architectural setting for his work."

31 Marcel Breuer, New York City, to Frank Kacmarcik, St. Paul, June 5, 1957, SUL, box 103, folder 7.

32 Frank Kacmarcik, "Living Forms for a House of God," 7, undated typescript, SJA, box 1, folder 18.

33 Frank Kacmarcik, St. Paul, to Marcel Breuer, New York City, January 24, 1960, SUL, box 104, folder 7.

34 Klauser for the Bishops of Germany, "Directives for the Building of a Church"; Anson, Churches; and O'Connell, Church Building and Furnishing.

35 Both of these documents are reprinted in Seasoltz, The New Liturgy.

36 O'Connell, Church Building and Furnishing, 133.

37 Klauser, "Directives for the Building of a Church," 18.

38 For more on James Rosati see http://jamesrosati.org (accessed June 9, 2014). The altar cross was later redone by Kacmarcik with a corpus on one side only. When various congregations use the space, the monks can turn the cross to face the worshippers as needed.

39 Abbot Baldwin Dworschak, Collegeville, to James Rosati, New York City, SUL, box 115, folder 5.

40 As the numbers of fathers grew in the twentieth century, in the old church the monks had to fashion makeshift private chapel walls out of plumbing parts and cloth.

41 For a detailed description of each saint's relevance to the Benedictine Order at Saint John's see Benedict Avery, "The Principal Patron Saints for the New Church," February 10, 1960, SJA, box 1, folder 1, Altars and Chapels 1958–61.

42 Ibid.

43 Benedict Avery, "The Crypt Furnishings of the Church," September 12, 1961, SUL, box 114, folder 4.

44 Ibid.

45 Abbot Baldwin Dworschak, Collegeville, to Mein-

rad Burch, Zurich, February 29, 1960, SJA, box 1, folder 8. Burch would complete a cross, candlesticks, and figure of Saint Lawrence in metal for the chapel.

46 The Watts quote is cited in Abbot Baldwin Dworschak, Collegeville, to Peter Watts, Bath, England, May 2, 1961, SUL, box 115, folder 5.

47 Abbot Baldwin Dworschak, Collegeville, to Mario De Luigi, Venice, March 6, 1961, SUL, box 115, folder 5.

48 Abbot Baldwin Dworschak, Collegeville, to Reverend Theodor Bogler, O.S.B., Maria Laach, March 11, 1960, SUL, box 104, folder 6.

49 Art Committee meeting with Maurice Lavanoux, October 8–9, 1960, SUL, box 116, folder 2.

50 Another example is Abbot Dworschak's letter to James Rosati of New York, requesting his completion of the high altar crucifix, candleholders, and tabernacle. Although the abbot's letter specifically described the liturgical importance of each item, a four-page essay on the importance of the crucifix in history and at the present time was included. The brethren also requested that the crucifix be fashioned differently on each side since Mass would be, at that time, celebrated from both sides of the altar. Rosati completed their wishes by placing a corpus on the choir side of the cross and an abstract jeweled pattern on the opposite side facing the laity. SUL, box 115, folder 5.

51 Jaffe, *The Sculpture of Leonard Baskin*.

52 Leonard Baskin, Northampton, Mass., to Abbot Baldwin Dworschak, Collegeville, July 2, 1960, SJA, box 1, folder 5.

53 Abbot Baldwin Dworschak, Collegeville, to Leonard Baskin, Stonington, Maine, August 18, 1960, SJA, box 1, folder 5.

54 Abbot Baldwin Dworschak, Collegeville, to Leonard Baskin, Stonington, Maine, August 18, 1960, SJA, box 1, folder 5. In this letter the abbot mentions that there is one change in the chapel design. The walls will now be painted white, a decision made by the architect to lighten up the space and provide a more contrasting backdrop for the gray granite altars.

55 Leonard Baskin, Northampton, Mass., to Abbot Baldwin Dworschak, Collegeville, December 7, 1960, SJA, box 1, folder 5.

56 Jean Lambert-Rucki, Paris, to Godfrey Diekmann, Collegeville, October 14, 1954, SJA, box 1, folder 34.

57 Godfrey Diekmann, Collegeville, to Jean Lambert-Rucki, Paris, February 24, 1955, SJA, box 1, folder 34.

58 Abbot Baldwin Dworschak, Collegeville, to Jean Lambert-Rucki, Paris, August 17, 1960, SJA, box 1, folder 34.

59 Jean Lambert-Rucki, Paris, to Abbot Baldwin Dworschak, Collegeville, November 4, 1960, SJA, box 1, folder 34. The monks paid the artist $500 for the crucifix of the "glorious Christ" and $900 for the Saint Cloud figure.

60 Abbot Baldwin Dworschak, Collegeville, to Jean Lambert-Rucki, Paris, September 30, 1960, SJA, box 1, folder 34.

61 Abbot Baldwin Dworschak, Collegeville, to Jean Lambert-Rucki, Paris, December 5, 1960, SJA, box 1, folder 34.

62 See SJA, box 1, folder 44, for more on Bonnette.

63 Ibid.

64 Durken, "The Crucifixes of Collegeville," 4.

65 For more on Caesar see Bush, *Doris Caesar,* and Whitney Museum of American Art, *Four American Expressionists.* Caesar also completed statues of Saint Anthony and Our Lady of the Annunciation, as well as a crucifix for the private chapels. The Benedictines paid Caesar $2,500 for Saint John the Baptist.

66 Abbot Baldwin Dworschak, Collegeville, to Doris Caesar, Connecticut, January 10, 1959, SUL, Doris Caesar Papers, box 1, folder 1. Abbot Dworschak's emphasis.

67 Frank Kacmarcik, St. Paul, to Doris Caesar, Connecticut, February 4, 1959, SUL, Doris Caesar Papers, box 1, folder 1, Kacmarcik.

68 Doris Caesar, Connecticut, to Abbot Baldwin

Dworschak, Collegeville, undated handwritten note, SUL, Doris Caesar Papers, box 1, folder 1. The Weyhe Gallery in New York paid for the cast of the saint in bronze. See Abbot Baldwin Dworschak to Mr. Weyhe, May 18, 1961, SJA, box 1, folder 16.

69 Ibid.

70 In 1952 Breuer designed a cottage in Lakeville, Connecticut, for Caesar.

71 For more on Albers see Albers, *Interaction of Color*; Boucher, *Josef Albers*; Weber, Licht, et al., *Josef Albers*; Weber, Licht, and Danilowitz, *Josef Albers*; and Weber and Kearney, *The Sacred Modernist*.

72 Marcel Breuer, New York City, to Abbot Baldwin Dworschak, Collegeville, March 11, 1955, SUL, box 114, folder 3. Albers charged the monastery $400 for completion of the window, including design and installation.

73 Ibid.

74 For more on his color theory and the fifty paintings produced in this manner see Albers, *Interaction of Color*.

75 The lack of color in the abbot's chapel window may also have been influenced by Albers's love of black-and-white photography. See Haas, *Josef Albers in Black and White*.

76 Weber and Kearney, *The Sacred Modernist*, 20.

77 The Albers quotation is taken from a promotional brochure and cited in Stoddard, *Adventure in Architecture*, 76.

78 Ibid., 77.

79 Memorandum, April 26, 1955, SUL, box 114, folder 3.

80 The wall measures 178 feet wide by 65 feet tall for an area of 11,570 square feet.

81 Hyman, *Marcel Breuer, Architect*, 278. See also "An Architecture for Day and Night."

82 Stoddard, *Adventure in Architecture*, 125.

83 Abbot Baldwin Dworschak, Collegeville, to Alfred Manessier, Paris, August 18, 1958, SUL, box 105, folder 2.

84 Michael, "The Resurrection Window," typescript, SUL, box 116, folder 22.

85 For more on Manessier as a stained glass artist see Foucart, "Le XXe siècle des cathédrales"; Hodin, *Manessier*; and Weis, review of *Alfred Manessier*.

86 Abbot Baldwin Dworschak, Collegeville, to Alfred Manessier, Paris, August 18, 1958, SUL, box 105, folder 2.

87 Ibid.

88 Abbot Baldwin Dworschak, Collegeville, to Marcel Breuer, New York City, September 19, 1958, SUL, box 105, folder 2.

89 A select retrospective of Bak's work was held at Saint John's University Art Center October 13–November 30, 2001. A small flyer accompanied the exhibition and provides much of the background material for this discussion of Bak. See also "Bronislaw Bak, Glass."

90 Gomersall, "Architect vs. Artist," 107. Saint John's hired Bak to teach painting, printmaking, and two- and three-dimensional design.

91 Abbot Baldwin Dworschak, Collegeville, to Hamilton Smith, New York City, September 11, 1958, SUL, box 105, folder 2.

92 Ibid.

93 Hedahl, "Ambiguity in Glass," 34.

94 Marcel Breuer, New York City, to Abbot Baldwin Dworschak, Collegeville, November 24, 1958, SUL, box 105, folder 2.

95 Frank Kacmarcik, St. Paul, to Marcel Breuer, New York City, March 7, 1959, SUL, box 104, folder 7.

96 Ibid.

97 The monks agreed to this competition at a church committee meeting on August 4, 1959. SJA, box 5, folder 6.

98 Father John Eidenschink, Collegeville, to Marcel Breuer, New York City, September 4, 1959, SUL, box 105, folder 2. In early September 1959, Father Eidenschink mailed Albers a copy of Louis Bouyer's book *Paschal Mystery: Meditations on the Last Three Days of Holy Week* (1950) to aid him in formulating his design. SJA, box 1, folder 3.

99 Marcel Breuer, New York City, to Josef Albers, West Haven, Conn., August 19, 1959, SJA, box BA6.

100 Color symbolism traditionally in the Catholic Church is as follows: White signifies innocence, purity, joy, triumph, and glory, and is used on the feasts of Our Blessed Lord, of the Blessed Virgin, and of some saints. Red signifies God's love, martyrdom, and the Passion, and is used on the feasts of the Holy Spirit and of martyrs. Green signifies the Holy Spirit, eternal life, and hope, and is generally employed on Sundays from Epiphany to Pentecost. Violet signifies penance, humility, and melancholy, and is used in Lent and Advent. Black signifies sorrow, and is used on Good Friday and at Masses for the dead. Gold for joy is often used instead of white on great feasts.

101 Emil Frei, St. Louis, to Abbot Baldwin Dworschak, Collegeville, December 9, 1959, SJA, box 3, folder 17.

102 Marcel Breuer, New York City, to Abbot Baldwin Dworschak, Collegeville, December 9, 1959, SUL, box 105, folder 2.

103 Hamilton Smith, New York City, to Abbot Baldwin Dworschak, Collegeville, December 11, 1959, SUL, box 150, folder 2.

104 Ibid.

105 Frank Kacmarcik, St. Paul, to Marcel Breuer, New York City, December 2, 1959, SUL, box 104, folder 7.

106 Abbot Baldwin Dworschak, Collegeville, to Marcel Breuer, New York, December 15, 1959, SUL, box 105, folder 2.

107 Gatje, *Marcel Breuer*, 90.

108 The Rule of Saint Benedict, chapter 57, "The Artisans of the Monastery," and chapter 48, "The Daily Manual Labor."

109 Although Breuer went along with the decision, he refused to give Bak publicity for his design and kept his name out of many publications on the church. Years later Abbot Dworschak recalled a 1961 lecture by Breuer at the Walker Art Center in Minneapolis, where Breuer spent an hour talking about the abbey, not once mentioning Bak's name even though he was sitting in the audience next to the abbot.

Bak's name did not even find its way into the abbey's 1961 guidebook for the church. Abbot Baldwin Dworschak, "Spirituality and Architecture," lecture given in the series *The Arts and the Spiritual*, Saint John's Abbey, September 28–29, 1979. Cassette tape, SJA.

110 Sections of Church with Notations by Breuer, November 23, 1953, SUL. Pencil, colored pencil, and ink on paper. Breuer said that the handlebars of his bicycle inspired his work, particularly in determining the pipe diameter of the furniture. See Wilk, *Marcel Breuer Furniture and Interiors*, 37–41.

111 Hamilton Smith, New York City, to Father John Eidenschink, Collegeville, December 14, 1953, SJA, BA6.

112 Hamilton Smith, New York City, to Marcel Breuer, December 7, 1953, SUL, box 114, folder 4.

113 See *Sacred Art.*

114 Abbot Baldwin Dworschak, Collegeville, to Marcel Breuer, Paris, May 24, 1955, SJA, box 1, folder 34. The request for iconography occurs in a letter from Father Godfrey Diekmann to Lambert-Rucki, February 24, 1955.

115 On November 27, 1959, the church subcommittee on the apse screen held its first meeting with members Fathers Benedict Avery, Godfrey Diekmann, Michael Marx, Hilary Thimmesh, and Cloud Meinberg.

116 Benedict Avery, Collegeville, to Hamilton Smith, New York City, received May 11, 1961, SUL, box 115, folder 5.

117 Ibid.

118 A small number of artists would be paid invitees to the competition, but anyone could enter on a nonpaid basis.

119 Artists recommended by *L'Art Sacré*: Dom Robert de Chaunac (Abbey of En-Calcat); Paul Bony (Paris); Jacques Bony (Paris); Pauline Peugniez (Paris); Frères Debiève (Nord); Jacques Le Chevallier (Seine); Jean Lurçat (Paris contact); Gromaire (Paris contact); Jean Olin (Paris); Picart le Doux (Paris); Irène Zack (Seine); Robert Wogen-

sky (Paris); and Gino Severini (Paris). By *L'Art d'Église:* Théodore Strawinsky (Geneva); Jean Olin (Paris); Michel Martens (Bruges); and Dom Maur van Doorslaer, O.S.B. (Seine). By *Das Münster:* Max Faller (Munich); Elizabeth Hoffmann-Lacher (Munich); Prof. Karl Knappe (Munich); Prof. Franz Nagel (Munich); and Ludwig Baur (Westphalia). By *Liturgical Arts:* Elsa Schmid (New York); Mrs. Louisa Jenkins (California); and Virgil Cantini (Pittsburgh). Artists recommended by others: Ben Shahn (New York); Abraham Rattner (New York City); Manessier (Paris); Ewald Mataré (Cologne); Giacomo Manzu (Milan); Lambert-Rucki (Paris); Frank Kacmarcik (St. Paul); Gerald Bonnette and Jean Charlot (Hawaii). The original copy of this list can be found in the Church Committee notes, SJA, box 1, folder 45.

120 "Church sub-committee on program for apse-screen," November 27, 1959, SUL, box 115, folder 5.

121 Abbot Baldwin Dworschak, Collegeville, to editor of *Chiesa e Quartiere,* Bologna, December 3, 1959, SUL, box 105, folder 2.

122 Father Benedict, Collegeville, to Abbot Baldwin Dworschak, Collegeville, May 1, 1960, SUL, box 104, folder 7.

123 Hamilton Smith, New York City, to Father John Eidenschink, Collegeville, December 11, 1959, SJA, box BA6.

124 Abbot Baldwin Dworschak, Collegeville, to Maurice Lavanoux, New York City, December 3, 1959, SUL, box 115, folder 5.

125 Giuseppe Sav. Giacomini, Rome, to Marcel Breuer Associates, New York City, December 30, 1965, SUL, box 102, folder 5.

126 Abbot Baldwin Dworschak, Collegeville, to Giuseppe Sav. Giacomini, Rome, February 19, 1966, SUL, box 102 folder 5.

127 *Sacred Art at St. John's Abbey,* 4.

128 Frank Kacmarcik, conversation with author, Collegeville, November 13, 2001.

CONCLUSION

1 Father Cloud Meinberg, Collegeville, to Hamilton Smith, New York City, November 3, 1961, SUL, box 114, folder 4.

2 Hammond, *Liturgy and Architecture,* 9.

3 Articles on the church appeared in the following journals: *Architect and Building News, Architecture, Architecture Minnesota, L'Architecture d'Aujourd'hui, L'Architettura, Architectural Forum, Architectural Record, Architectural Review, Art in America, Art d'Église, Arts and Architecture, Arts Digest, Catholic Digest, Catholic Market, Church Property Administration, Der Monat, Deutsche Bauzeitung, Domus, Interiors, Jubilee, Liturgical Arts, Northwest Architect, Revista Espacios, Scriptorium, Time,* and *Worship.*

4 Diekmann received the Elbert Conover Memorial Award in 1976, a prize given by the Church Architecture Guild of America (later the American Institute of Architects Interfaith Forum on Religion, Art and Architecture) to nonarchitects in recognition of their contributions to religious architecture.

5 See Schmitt, *Die internationalen liturgischen Studientreffen 1951–1960.*

6 Vatican II was the twenty-first ecumenical council of the Catholic Church. For more on the council see Hollis, *The Achievements of Vatican II;* McCarthy, *The Catholic Tradition;* Rynne, *Vatican Council II;* and Yzermans, *American Participation in the Second Vatican Council.*

7 "The Constitution on the Sacred Liturgy" (December 4, 1963), in Seasoltz, *The New Liturgy,* 473–500. Pope John XXIII died on June 3, 1963, and the conclave elected Pope Paul VI on June 21, 1963.

8 Ibid., 499.

9 Father Alered, "Orientation of the High Altar," typescript, undated, SJA, box 1, folder 1.

10 Cited in Hughes, *The Monk's Tale,* 174.

11 "The Constitution on the Sacred Liturgy," 499.

12 Ibid., 473–500. Paragraphs 36, 54, 63, 101, and 113 of

the constitution deal with Latin and the vernacular ("the mother tongue").

13 Ibid., 487.

14 Sacred Congregation of Rites, "The Concelebration of the Mass and Communion under Both Kinds" (May 7, 1965), in Seasoltz, *The New Liturgy,* 544–73.

15 "New Look for St. John's," 87.

16 Edward Larrabee Barnes sent a letter to Margaret Firmage on May 24, 1954, to let Breuer know he had just received a questionnaire from the state of Minnesota regarding Breuer's license request; he returned it with the remark that "Mr. Breuer is a man of exceptional professional ability, both as a designer and administrator. His integrity and moral character are unquestionable. He is known as one of the leaders of modern architecture." Breuer's application was approved in June 1954. AAA, reel 5712, frame 244. Frame 245 is a copy of his Minnesota architect registration card as architect #4891.

17 *Abbey Banner* 1, 2 (Fall 1965).

18 For a list of all buildings at Saint John's see http://www.csbsju.edu/SJU-Archives/SJUHistory/SJUBuildings.htm (accessed December 6, 2013).

19 For more on the design of Annunciation see "Couvent de l'Annonciation à Bismarck"; "Couvent de l'Annonciation, Bismarck, North Dakota"; Hyman, *Marcel Breuer, Architect,* 223–25; "Breuer Designs a Convent"; Koyama and Burns, "A Convent Is Born"; "Le prieuré de l'Annonciation, Bismarck, North Dakota"; "North Dakota Community for the Benedictine Sisters"; "Of Materials That Age Gracefully"; "Priory of the Annunciation, Bismarck, North Dakota/USA"; and "Priory of the Annunciation, Bismarck, North Dakota."

20 Koyama and Burns, "A Convent Is Born," 362.

21 Breuer also completed buildings at the associated University of Mary.

22 "Breuer Designs a Convent," 185.

23 For more on the Muskegon church see "Bold Geometric Image for a Church"; Bruggink and Droppers, *When Faith Takes Form,* 44–61; "Église St-François de Sales, Muskegon, Michigan"; "Pfarrkirche in Michigan"; "Saint Francis de Sales Church, Muskegon, Michigan" (1962); "Saint Francis de Sales Church, Muskegon, Michigan" (1965); "St. Francis de Sales Church, Muskegon, Michigan, U.S.A."; "St. Francis de Sales Church, Muskegon, Michigan"; and "St. Francis de Sales Church, Muskegon, Michigan, 1967." Chicago contractor Mike Lombard poured the building in eight-foot sections.

24 Breuer, "The Contemporary Aspect of Pharaonic Architecture."

25 "Bold Geometric Image for a Church," 130.

26 See Hyman, *Marcel Breuer, Architect,* 218–29.

27 "History of the Building Plans," *The Record* 67 (21 May 1954, supplement): 4.

28 See Lavanoux, "The Reality of a Dream," 4–7; "Priory Chapel, St. Louis, Missouri, USA"; and "St. Louis Priory and Chapel, Missouri, USA."

29 Cited in Lavanoux, "The Reality of a Dream," 7.

30 Seasoltz, "From the Bauhaus to the House of God's People," 112.

31 Ibid.

32 Abbot John Klassen, "Homily for Fortieth Anniversary of the Dedication of the Abbey Church," http://www.saintjohnsabbey.org/abbot/011024.html (accessed July 10, 2002).

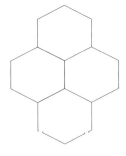

BIBLIOGRAPHY

ARCHIVES

AAA   Marcel Breuer papers, 1920–86. Archives of American Art, Smithsonian Institution

SJA   Office of the Abbot, New Church and Monastery Building Records, 1952–81 (bulk 1953–62), Saint John's Abbey (Collegeville, Minnesota)

SUL   Marcel Breuer Archives at Syracuse University Library

"Abbaye de St. John, Minnesota." *L'Architecture d'Aujourd'hui* 25 (July 1954): 85–87.

"Abbaye St. John, Monastère Bénédictin, Collegeville, États-Unis." *L'Architecture d'Aujourd'hui* 33 (February 1962): 40–47.

Albers, Josef. *Interaction of Color.* New Haven, Conn.: Yale University Press, 1975.

"Altar Canopy, Abbey Church of St. John's, Collegeville, Minnesota." *Architect and Building News* 221, no. 24 (June 13, 1962): 686–87.

"Ancient Religious Ideals." *Northwest Architect* 18 (September/October 1954): 34–38.

Andreas, Alfred Theodor. *The Encyclopedia of Chicago.* Chicago: Lakeside Press, 1886.

Anson, Peter F. *Churches: Their Plan and Furnishing.* Milwaukee: Bruce, 1948.

Arca Artium: Collections of the Visionary and Liturgical Designer in the Monastic Tradition; Frank Kacmarcik. Collegeville, Minn.: Saint John's, 1997.

"An Architecture for Day and Night: De Bijenkorf Department Store." *Architectural Record* 122, no. 5 (November 1957): 167–75.

"Architettura religiosa contemporanea in Austria." *Fede e Arte* 8 (July–September 1960): 316–54.

"Art for Today's Religious Buildings." *Architectural Record* 118, no. 6 (December 1955): 38–42.

"Award of Merit: St. John's Abbey Church, St. John's Abbey." *AIA Journal* 37 (May 1962): 54–55.

Baglione, Chiara. "Il mondo sulla soglia: L'architettura sacra di Rudolf Schwarz." *Casabella* 640–41, no. 12/1 (December 1996/January 1997): 34–54.

Bailey, James. "Marcel Breuer at St. John's." *Architectural Forum* 128 (May 1968): 40–57.

Barry, Colman J. *Worship and Work: Saint John's Abbey and University, 1856–1980.* Collegeville, Minn.: Liturgical Press, 1980.

Bayer, Herbert, Ise Gropius, and Walter Gropius. *Bauhaus: 1919–1928.* New York: Museum of Modern Art, 1938.

Beales, Derek. "Joseph II and the Monasteries of Austria and Hungary." In *Enlightenment and Reform in Eighteenth-Century Europe*, 227–55 (London: Tauris, 2005).

———. *Prosperity and Plunder: European Catholic Monasteries in the Age of Revolution, 1650–1815.* Cambridge: Cambridge University Press, 2003.

Beauduin, Lambert. *Liturgy: The Life of the Church.* Translated by Virgil Michel. Collegeville, Minn.: Liturgical Press, 1926.

Belluschi, Pietro. "Architecture To-day: A Symposium." *Liturgical Arts* 19 (November 1950): 21.

———. "The Churches Go Modern." *Saturday Evening Post*, October 4, 1958, 36–39.

———. "The Modern Church—or Traditional?" *New York Times Magazine*, March 14, 1954, 14–15, 60.

"A Benedictine Monastery: Preview of the Designs for St. John's Abbey in Minnesota." *Architectural Forum* 101, no. 1 (July 1954): 148–56.

Benevolo, Leonardo. *History of Modern Architecture.* 2 vols. Cambridge, Mass.: MIT Press, 1971.

Bénézit, Emmanuel. *Dictionnaire des peintres, sculpteurs, dessinateurs, et graveurs.* 14 vols. Paris: Librairie Grund, 1999.

Bergdoll, Barry. "For Great Buildings, Get a Great Client," *New York Times*, July 21, 2002.

———, and Leah Dickerman, eds. *Bauhaus 1919–1933: Workshops for Modernity.* New York: Museum of Modern Art, 2009.

Bernhardt, Eisele, Koob Harms, and Walter Schoeller. *Bauhaus.* Darmstadt: Edition Braus, 1994.

Biedrzynski, Richard. *Kirchen unserer Zeit.* Munich: Hirmer Verlag, 1958.

Biéler, André. *Architecture in Worship.* Philadelphia: Westminster Press, 1965.

Billot, Marcel, ed. *Henri Matisse: The Vence Chapel; Archive of a Creation by M. A. Courturier, L. B. Rayssiguier, H. Matisse.* Translated by Michael Taylor. Houston: Menil Foundation, 1999.

Blake, Peter, ed. *An American Synagogue for Today and Tomorrow.* New York: Union of American Hebrew Congregations, 1954.

———. "The House in the Museum Garden, Marcel Breuer, Architect." *Museum of Modern Art Bulletin* 16, no. 1 (1949): 3–12.

———. *Marcel Breuer: Architect and Designer.* New York: Architectural Record and the Museum of Modern Art, 1949.

———. "The Selective Eye of Marcel Breuer." *House Beautiful*, March 1967, 153–58.

"Bold Geometric Image for a Church: St. Francis de Sales Church in Muskegon, Michigan." *Architectural Record* 142 (November 1967): 130–37.

Borchardt, Susan. *Religious Architecture in America.* Washington, D.C.: St. John's Church, 1976.

Bosslet, Albert. *Vom Zeichnen und Bauen: Albert Bosslet 1880–1940.* Munich: Schnell, 1940.

Boucher, François. *Josef Albers: Despite Straight Lines; An Analysis of His Graphic Constructions.* 2nd ed., rev. Cambridge, Mass.: MIT Press, 1977.

Bouyer, Louis. *Dom Lambert Beauduin: Un homme d'Église.* Paris: Casterman, 1964.

———. *Life and Liturgy.* London: Sheed and Ward, 1956.

Brannach, Frank. *Church Architecture: Building for a Living Faith.* Milwaukee: Bruce, 1932.

Braunfels, Wolfgang. *Monasteries of Western Europe: The Architecture of the Orders.* New York: Thames and Hudson, 1982.

Breuer, Marcel. "Architectural Details." *Architectural Record*, February 1964, 121–36.

———. "The Contemporary Aspect of Pharaonic Architecture." Preface to *Living Architecture: Egyptian*, by Jean Louis de Ceneval, 3–5. New York: Grosset and Dunlap, 1964.

———. "The Faceted, Molded Facade: Depth, Sun, and Shadow." *Architectural Record* 139, 4 (April 1966): 171–86.

———. *Marcel Breuer: Sun and Shadow.* New York: Dodd, Mead, 1955.

——. "Matter and Intrinsic Form." Second Annual Reed and Barton Design Lecture, presented at the University of Michigan, March 6, 1963. Taunton, Mass.: Reed and Barton, 1963.

——. "Sun and Shadow: A Design Philosophy." *Architecture* 49 (April 1968): 65–71.

——. "Tell Me, What Is Modern Architecture?" *House and Garden*, April 1940, 71.

——. "What Is Happening to Modern Architecture?" Statement made during the Museum of Modern Art Symposium, excerpt. *Arts and Architecture* 65 (May 1948): 31.

——. "Where Do We Stand? Modern Movement." *Architectural Review* 77 (April 1935): 133–36.

"Breuer Designs a Convent." *Architectural Record* 119, 4 (April 1956): 183–86.

"Breuer for 1961." *Architectural Review* 129 (January 1961): 1.

Britton, Karla, ed. *Constructing the Ineffable: Contemporary Sacred Architecture*. New Haven, Conn.: Yale University Press, 2011.

Bruggink, Donald J., and Karl H. Droppers. *When Faith Takes Form: Contemporary Churches of Architectural Integrity in America*. Grand Rapids, Mich.: Eerdmans, 1971.

Brülls, Holger. "Albert Bosslet (1880–1957): Die Romantik im Schaffen eines konservativen Architekten der expressionistischen Generation." In *Neue Dome*, 70–138. Munich: Verlag für Bauwesen Berlin, 1994.

——. "Deutsche Gotteshäuser: Kirchenbau im Nationalsozialismus; Ein unterschlagenes Kapitel der deutschen Architekturgeschicte." *Kritische Berichte* 1, no. 23 (January 1995): 57–68.

Brütsch, H. A., A. Hofmann, C. Humbel, et al. *Hermann Baur 1894–1980: Architektur und Planung in Zeiten des Umbruchs. Eine Ausstellung im Architekturmuseum Basel vom 27. August bis 30. Oktober 1994*. Basel: Architekturmuseum Basel, 1994. Exhibition catalog.

Burchard, John Ely. "A Pilgrimage: Ronchamp, Raincy, Vézelay." *Architectural Record* 123, no. 3 (March 1958): 178.

Busard, Paul. "A Plan for a New Church." *Catholic Digest* 19 (November 1954): 70–73.

Bush, Martin H. *Doris Caesar*. Ithaca, N.Y.: Cornell University Press, 1970.

Butler, Edward Cuthbert. *Benedictine Monachism: Studies in Benedictine Life and Rule*. London: Longmans, Green, 1924.

Byrne, Barry. "A Philosophy of Design for Concrete." *Liturgical Arts* 2, no. 2 (1933): 54–55.

——. "Plan for a Church." *Liturgical Arts* 10, no. 3 (May 1942): 58–60.

Campbell, Louise. *Coventry Cathedral: Art and Architecture in Post-War Britain*. Oxford: Clarendon Press, 1996.

Carroll, Laura Burns. "Reconciling Modernism and Tradition: Seven Pacific Northwest Churches of Pietro Belluschi, 1939–1955." PhD diss., University of Washington, 1992.

Cary-Elwes, Columba, O.S.B. "The Theology of the Church and the Architect." *Liturgical Arts* 31 (November 1962): 9, 28.

Casel, Odo. *The Mystery of Christian Worship and Other Writings*. Translated by I. T. Hale. Westminster, Md.: Newman Press, 1962.

Catholic Church. *Ordo for the Liturgy of the Hours and Mass in the Churches and Oratories of the American-Cassinese Federation*. Collegeville, Minn.: Saint John's Abbey, 1975–.

Chappell, Sally Kitt, and Ann Van Zanten. *Barry Byrne and John Lloyd Wright: Architecture and Design*. Chicago: Chicago Historical Society, 1982.

Chew Orenduff, Lai-Kent. *The Transformation of Catholic Religious Art in the Twentieth Century: Father Marie-Alain Couturier and the Church at Assy, France*. Lewiston, N.Y.: Edwin Mellen Press, 2008.

Chiat, Marilyn J. *America's Religious Architecture: Sacred Places for Every Community*. New York: John Wiley & Sons, 1997.

"Chiesa della pace a Vienna (Quellenstrasse): Arch. R. Kramreiter." *L'Architettura Italiana* 31 (1936): 276–77.

"Christ Church." *Architectural Forum* 93 (July 1950): 80–85.

"Christ in Concrete: Marcel Breuer's Church of St. John the Baptist for the Benedictine Abbey of St. John at Collegeville, Minnesota." *Interiors* 121 (February 1962): 10.

Christ-Janer, Albert. *Eliel Saarinen.* Chicago: University of Chicago Press, 1948.

Christ-Janer, Albert, and Mary Mix Foley. *Modern Church Architecture: A Guide to the Form and Spirit of 20th Century Religious Buildings.* New York: McGraw-Hill, 1962.

"Church for a Monastic Community, St. John's Abbey, Collegeville, Minnesota." *Arts and Architecture* 71, no. 6 (June 1954): 14–15.

"Churches Designed by A. Bosslet." *London Studio* 11 (April 1936): 198–204.

"Churches: Must the Church Build in Gothic or Can Contemporary Architecture Meet the Needs of Today's Church?" *Architectural Forum* 91, no. 6 (December 1949): 57–73.

Clausen, Meredith. *Pietro Belluschi: Modern American Architect.* Cambridge, Mass.: MIT Press, 1994.

———. *Spiritual Space: The Religious Architecture of Pietro Belluschi.* Seattle: University of Washington Press, 1992.

Collins, Peter. *Concrete: The Vision of a New Architecture; A Study of August Perret and His Precursors.* New York: Horizon Press, 1959.

———. "The Doctrine of Auguste Perret." *Architectural Review* 114 (August 1953): 90–98.

Conant, Kenneth John. *Benedictine Contributions to Church Architecture.* Latrobe, Pa.: Archabbey Press, 1949.

"Conference Building and Offices, UNESCO House, place de Fontenay, Paris." *Architects' Journal* 128 (December 11, 1958): 859–70.

"Contrasts in Concrete: UNESCO Headquarters, Paris." *Architectural Record* 123, no. 2 (February 1958): 165–69.

Couturier, Marie-Alain. "Religious Art and the Modern Artist." *Magazine of Art* 45, no. 7 (November 1951): 268–72.

———. *Sacred Art.* Austin: University of Texas Press, 1989.

"Couvent de l'Annonciation à Bismarck." *L'Architecture d'Aujourd'hui* 35 (September 1966): 74–75.

"Couvent de l'Annonciation, Bismarck, North Dakota." *L'Architecture d'Aujourd'hui* 32 (June 1961): 80–82.

Cram, Ralph Adams. *American Church Building of Today.* New York: Architectural Book Publishing, 1929.

———. *American Churches.* New York: American Architect, 1915.

———. *The Catholic Church and Art.* New York: Macmillan, 1930.

———. *Church Building.* Boston: Marshall Jones, 1924.

———. *The Gothic Quest.* New York: Baker and Taylor, 1907.

———. *My Life in Architecture.* Boston: Little, Brown, 1936.

Cret, Paul. "Reinforced Concrete and Ecclesiastical Architecture." *Liturgical Arts* 2, no. 2 (1933): 51–53.

Crichton, James Dunlop. *Lights in Darkness: Forerunners of the Liturgical Movement.* Collegeville, Minn.: Liturgical Press, 1996.

Crosbie, Michael. *Houses of God: Religious Architecture for a New Millennium.* Mulgrave, Vic., Australia: Images Publishing, 2006.

Crosby, S. M., and P. Z. Blum. *The Royal Abbey of Saint-Denis from Its Beginnings to the Death of Suger, 475–1151.* New Haven, Conn.: Yale University Press, 1987

Curran, Kathleen. "Friedrich von Gärtner's Farb- und Ornamentaufassung und sein Einfluss auf England und Amerika." In *Friedrich von Gärtner: Ein Architektenleben, 1791–1847; Mit den Briefen an Johann Martin von Wagner*, edited by Winfried Nerdinger, 184–217. Munich: Klinkhardt und Biermann, 1992.

———. "The German Rundbogenstil and Reflections on the American Round-Arched Style." *Journal of the Society of Architectural Historians* 47, 4 (December 1988): 351–73.

———. *The Romanesque Revival· Religion, Politics, and Transnational Exchange*. University Park: Pennsylvania State University, 2003.

Curtis, William J. R. *Modern Architecture since 1900*. New York: Prentice-Hall, 1997.

Dahinden, Justus. *New Trends in Church Architecture*. New York: Universe Books, 1967.

Daly, Lowrie J. *Benedictine Monasticism: Its Formation and Development through the 12th Century*. New York: Sheed and Ward, 1965.

Debuyst, Frédéric. *Modern Architecture and Christian Celebration*. Richmond, Va.: John Knox Press, 1968.

DeSanctis, Michael E. *Building from Belief: Advance, Retreat, and Compromise in the Remaking of Catholic Church Architecture*. Collegeville, Minn.: Liturgical Press, 2002.

———. *Renewing the City of God: The Reform of Catholic Architecture in the United States*. Chicago: Archdiocese of Chicago, 1993.

"A Different Gem in a Homely Setting." *Architecture Minnesota* 7, no. 6 (December/January 1981–82): 28–31.

Dillenberger, John. "Artists and Church Commissions: Rubin's *The Church at Assy* Revisited." *Art Criticism* 1, no. 1 (Spring 1979): 72–82

Dimier, Anselme. *Stones Laid before the Lord: A History of Monastic Architecture*. Kalamazoo, Mich.: Cistercian Publications, 1999.

Documents for Sacred Architecture. Collegeville, Minn.: Liturgical Press, 1957.

Douaire, James. "Pilgrimage to Assy—an Appraisal." *Liturgical Arts*, November 1950, 28–30, 35–39.

Draper, Joan. "The Ecole des Beaux-Arts and the Architectural Profession in the United States:
The Case of John Galen Howard." In Kostof, *The Architect*, 209–37.

Drexler, Arthur, ed. *The Architecture of the Ecole des Beaux-Arts*. Cambridge, Mass.: MIT Press, 1977.

Dunn, Marilyn. *The Emergence of Monasticism: From the Desert Fathers to the Early Middle Ages*. Oxford: Blackwell, 2000.

Durken, Daniel. "The Crucifixes of Collegeville." *Abbey Banner* 2, no. 1 (Spring 2002): 4–5

Dworschak, Abbot Baldwin. "Marcel Breuer: In Grateful Memory." *Saint John's* 21, no. 1 (Fall 1981): 1–4.

———. "Observations on the Silver Anniversary of the Church." *St. John's Abbey Quarterly* 4 (October 4, 1986): 6–7, 11.

———. "Spirituality and Architecture." Lecture given in the series *The Arts and the Spiritual*. St. John's Abbey, September 28–29, 1979. Cassette tape.

Egbert, Donald Drew. "Religious Expressionism in American Architecture." In *Modern Perspectives in Western Art History*, edited by W. E. Kleinbauer, 312–38. New York: Holt, Rinehart and Winston, 1971.

"Eglise St-François de Sales, Muskegon, Michigan." *L'Architecture d'Aujourd'hui* 34 (June 1963): 16–18.

Eliade, Mircea. *The Sacred and the Profane: The Nature of Religion*. New York: Harcourt, Brace, 1959.

Esherick, Joseph. "Architectural Education in the Thirties and Seventies: A Personal View." In Kostof, *The Architect*, 238–89.

Evans, Iltud, O. P. "St. John's Abbey Church: An Appraisal." *Worship* 35, no. 8 (August–September 1961): 515–21.

Eversole, Finley, ed. *Christian Faith and the Contemporary Arts*. New York: Abingdon Press, 1962.

Filthaut, Theodor. *Church Architecture and Liturgical Reform*. Translated by Gregory Roettger. Baltimore and Dublin: Helicon, 1968.

Fitch, James Marston. *Walter Gropius*. New York: George Braziller, 1960.

Forgács, Éva. *The Bauhaus Idea and Bauhaus Politics.* Budapest: Central European University Press, 1995.

Forty, Adrian. *Concrete and Culture: A Material History.* London: Reaktion Books, 2012.

Foucart, Bruno. "Le XXe siècle des cathédrales." *Connaissance des Arts,* no. 585 (July–August 2001): 74–81.

Frampton, Kenneth. *Modern Architecture: A Critical History.* New York: Thames and Hudson, 1980.

Franciscono, Marcel. *Walter Gropius and the Creation of the Bauhaus in Weimar: The Ideals and Artistic Theories of Its Founding Years.* Champaign: University of Illinois Press, 1971.

Franklin, R. W. *Virgil Michel: American Catholic.* Collegeville, Minn.: Liturgical Press, 1988.

Fry, Timothy, ed. *The Rule of St. Benedict in English.* Collegeville, Minn.: Liturgical Press, 1982.

Gärtner, Friedrich von. *Sammlung der Entwürfe ausgeführter Gebäude.* Munich: Cotta, 1844.

Gatje, Robert. *Marcel Breuer: A Memoir.* New York: Monacelli Press, 2000.

Gerdts, William H. *Art across America: Two Centuries of Regional Painting.* New York: Abbeville Press, 1990.

Getlein, Frank, and Dorothy Getlein. *Christianity in Modern Art.* Milwaukee: Bruce, 1961.

Geva, Anat. *Frank Lloyd Wright's Sacred Architecture: Faith, Form, and Building Technology.* London and New York: Routledge, 2012.

Giedion, Sigfried. *Walter Gropius.* 1954. Reprint, New York: Dover, 1992.

Gieselmann, Reinhard. *New Churches.* New York: Architectural Book Publishing, 1972.

———, and Werner Aebli. *Kirchenbau.* Zurich: Verlag Girsberger, 1960.

Goldhagen, Sarah. "Something to Talk About: Modernism, Discourse, Style." *Journal of the Society of Architectural Historians* 64, 2 (June 2005): 144–67.

Gomersall, Amica. "Architect vs. Artist: A Neglected Window at the Abbey Church of St. John, Collegeville, Minnesota." *Stained Glass Quarterly* 83 (Summer 1988): 102–8.

Guardini, Romano. *The Spirit of the Liturgy.* Translated by Ada Lane. London: Sheed and Ward, 1937.

Guéranger, Prosper. *L'année liturgique.* Paris: Oudin, 1841–1901.

Haas, Karen E. *Josef Albers in Black and White.* Boston: Boston University Art Gallery, 2000. Exhibition catalog.

Hammond, Peter. "A Liturgical Brief." *Architectural Review* 123 (April 1958): 240–55.

———. *Liturgy and Architecture.* London: Barrie and Rockcliff, 1960.

———, ed. *Towards a Church Architecture.* London: Architectural Press, 1962.

Hampton, Roy A., III. "The Church Architecture of Adolphus Druiding: A Study of the Ecclesiastical Work of a Late Nineteenth Century German Catholic Immigrant." Master's thesis, University of Louisville, 1994.

———. "German Gothic in the Midwest: The Parish Churches of Franz Georg Himpler and Adolphus Druiding." *Catholic Historian* 15, no. 1 (Winter 1997): 51–74.

Haquin, André. *Dom Lambert Beauduin et le renouveau liturgique.* Gembloux, Belgium: Duculot, 1976.

Harwood, Elain. "Liturgy and Architecture: The Development of the Centralised Eucharistic Space." *Journal of the Twentieth Century Society,* no. 3 (1998): 51–74.

Hasler, Thomas. *Architektur als Ausdruck: Rudolf Schwarz.* Berlin: Mann, 2000.

Hauser, Nathanael, Patrick McDarby, Peregrine Berres, and Hugh Witzmann. *Sacred Art: Beuronese Art at Saint John's.* Collegeville, Minn.: Saint John's Abbey, 1998. Exhibition catalog.

Hawley, David. "Russian Architect Val Michelson's Life 'Was like a Novel." *McClatchy-Tribune Business News,* August 5, 2006, 1.

Hayes, Bartlett H. *Tradition Becomes Innovation.* New York: Pilgrim, 1983.

Heathcote, Edwin, and Iona Spens. *Church Builders.* Chichester, UK: John Wiley and Sons, 1997.

Hedahl, Susan Karen. "Ambiguity in Glass: A History of the North Wall Window at the Abbey Church of St. John the Baptist, Collegeville, Minnesota." Master's thesis, St. John's University, 1983.

Hederer, Oswald. *Friedrich von Gärtner, 1792–1847: Leben, Werk, Schüler.* Munich: Prestel, 1976.

Heller, Ena Giurescu. *Reluctant Partners: Art and Religion in Dialogue.* New York: Museum of Biblical Art, 2004.

Henze, Anton, and Theodor Filthaut. *Contemporary Church Art.* New York: Sheed and Ward, 1956.

Hermann Baur. Basel: Architekturmuseum Basel, 1994.

"Hermann Baur: Architektur und plannung in Zeiten des Umbruchs." *Domus* 767, no. 1 (January 1995): 99–100.

Herwegen, Ildefons. "The Nature of Religious Art." *Liturgical Arts* 1, no. 1 (Fall 1931): 4.

Himes, Kenneth R. "Eucharist and Justice: Assessing the Legacy of Virgil Michel." *Worship* 62, no. 3 (1988): 224.

Hines, Thomas S. *Richard Neutra and the Search for a Modern Architecture: A Biography and History.* 2nd ed. Berkeley: University of California Press, 1982.

"History of the Building Plans." *Record* 67 (May 21, 1954, supplement): 4.

Hitchcock, Henry-Russell. *Architecture of the Nineteenth and Twentieth Centuries.* 4th ed. New Haven, Conn.: Yale University Press, 1992.

———. *Latin American Architecture since 1945.* New York: Museum of Modern Art, 1955.

———, and Arthur Drexler, eds. *Built in USA: Post-war Architecture.* New York: Museum of Modern Art, 1952.

———, and Philip Johnson. *The International Style: Architecture since 1922.* New York: W. W. Norton, 1932.

Hochman, Elaine. *Bauhaus: Crucible of Modernism.* New York: Fromm International, 1997.

Hodin, Josef Paul. *Manessier.* New York: Praeger, 1972.

Hoffman, Kurt. "Portrait of Father Guardini." *Commonweal* 60 (September 17, 1954): 576.

Hoffmann, Richard, and Dr. Ing. Steinlein. *Albert Bosslet: Querschnitt durch sein Schaffen.* Munich: Süddeutsche Verlagsanstalt, 1934.

Hoffmeyer, T. A. "Wet-Mix Shotcrete Practice." *Shotcreting,* SP-14, 59–74. Detroit: American Concrete Institute, 1966.

Hollis, Christopher. *The Achievements of Vatican II.* New York: Hawthorn, 1967.

Horn, Walter, and Ernest Born. *The Plan of St. Gall: A Study of the Architecture and Economy of, and Life in, a Paradigmatic Carolingian Monastery.* Berkeley: University of California Press, 1979.

Hovda, Robert. "The Amen Corner: Frank Kacmarcik—Art as Skill in Making." *Worship* 61 (1987): 358–64.

Howarth, Shirley Reiff. *Marcel Breuer: Concrete and the Cross.* Muskegon, Mich.: Hackley Art Museum, 1978. Exhibition catalog.

———. "Marcel Breuer: On Religious Architecture." *Art Journal* 38, no. 4 (Summer 1979): 257–60.

Hughes, Kathleen. *How Firm a Foundation.* Vol. 1, *Voices of the Early Liturgical Movement.* Chicago: Liturgy Training Publications, 1990.

———. *The Monk's Tale: A Biography of Godfrey Diekmann, O.S.B.* Collegeville, Minn.: Liturgical Press, 1991.

Hull, Judith. Review of *Houses of God: Region, Religion, and Architecture in the United States,* by Peter W. Williams (Urbana: University of Illinois Press, 1997), and *America's Religious Architecture: Sacred Places for Every Community,* by Marilyn J. Chiat (New York: J. Wiley and Sons, 1997), in *Journal of the Society of Architectural Historians* 58, no. 2 (June 1999): 249–50.

Huxtable, Ada Louise. *Pier Luigi Nervi.* London: Braziller, 1960.

Hyman, Isabelle. *Marcel Breuer, Architect: The Career and the Buildings.* New York: Abrams, 2001.

"Hyperbolic Paraboloids—but Very Much a Church!" *Architect and Building News* 1, no. 1 (September 11, 1968): 62–67.

Illinois State Museum. "Bronislaw Bak, Glass." *Craftsmen in Illinois.* Springfield: Illinois Art Education Association, 1965. Exhibition catalog.

Isaacs, Reginald. *Gropius: An Illustrated Biography of the Creator of the Bauhaus.* Boston: Little, Brown, 1983.

Jaffe, Irma B. *The Sculpture of Leonard Baskin.* New York: Viking Studio, 1980.

James-Chakraborty, Kathleen. "From Isolationism to Internationalism." In *Bauhaus Culture: From Weimar to the Cold War,* edited by Kathleen James-Chakraborty, 153–70. Minneapolis: University of Minnesota Press, 2006.

———. *German Architecture for a Mass Audience.* New York: Routledge, 2000a.

———. *In the Spirit of Our Age: Eric Mendelsohn's B'nai Amoona Synagogue.* St. Louis: Missouri Historical Society Press, 2000b.

———. "Spirituality in Concrete and Steel: Churches by Bartning and Böhm." In *Architects and the Reinterpretation of Tradition,* edited by James Steele, 103–25. Berkeley: Center for Environmental Design Research, University of California, 1994.

Jencks, Charles. *Modern Movements in Architecture.* New York: Doubleday Anchor, 1973.

Jöckle, Clemens. "Albert Bosslet (1880–1957): Ein Kirchenbaumeister zwischen Historismus und Moderne." *Jarhrbuch des Vereins für Christliche Kunst in München* (Munich: Verein für Christliche Kunst, 1974), 544–617.

Johnson, Brian. "McGough Construction—Still Prospering after Five Generations." *Finance and Commerce,* April 17, 2001.

Johnson, Cuthbert. *Prosper Guéranger (1805–1875): A Liturgical Theologian.* Rome: Pontifico Ateneo Sant'Anselmo, 1984.

Jones, Cranston. *Marcel Breuer: Buildings and Projects, 1921–1961.* New York: Praeger, 1962.

Jordy, William H. "The Aftermath of the Bauhaus in America: Gropius, Mies, and Breuer." *Perspectives in American History* 2 (1968): 485–543.

Jungmann, Josef A. "Church Art." *Worship* 29, no. 2 (1955): 68–82.

Kahle, Barbara. *Deutsche Kirchenbaukunst des 20. Jahrhunderts* (Darmstadt: Wissenschaftliche Buchgesellschaft, 1990).

Kardon, Terrence. *The Benedictines.* Wilmington, Del.: Glazier, 1988.

Kennedy, Roger. *American Churches.* New York: Stewart, Taboria and Chang, 1982.

Kervick, Francis W. *Architects in America of Catholic Tradition.* Rutland, Vt.: Charles E. Tuttle, 1962.

Kery, August C. "Monte Cassino, Metten, and Minnesota." *Minnesota History* 8 (1927): 217–31.

Kidson, Peter. "Panofsky, Suger, and St. Denis." *Journal of the Warburg and Courtauld Institutes* 50 (1987): 1–17.

Kieckhefer, Richard. *Theology in Stone: Church Architecture from Byzantium to Berkeley.* New York: Oxford University Press, 2004.

Kirchenbauten von Hermann Baur und Fritz Metzger: Sakrale Kunst; Herausgegeben von der Schweizer St. Lukasgesellschaft. Vol. 2. Zurich: NZN Buchverlag, 1956.

Klauser, Theodor, for the Bishops of Germany. "Directives for the Building of a Church." In *Documents for Sacred Architecture,* 15–23.

———. *A Short History of the Western Liturgy.* Oxford: Oxford University Press, 1979.

Klenze, Leo von. *Anweisung zur Architektur des christlichen Cultus.* 1822. Reprint, Nördlingen: Uhl, 1990.

Knowles, David. *The Benedictines.* London: Sheed & Ward, 1929.

Koenker, Ernest B. *The Liturgical Renaissance in the Roman Catholic Church.* Chicago: University of Chicago Press, 1954.

Kostof, Spiro, ed. *The Architect: Chapters in the History of the Profession. New York: Oxford University Press, 1977.

Koyama, Shin, and Anne Burns, O.S.B., "A Convent Is Born." American Benedictine Review 12, no. 3 (1961): 361–68

Kramreiter, Robert. Die Schottengruft in Wien. Vienna: Self-published, 1962.

Krieg, Robert Anthony. Romano Guardini: A Precursor of Vatican II. Notre Dame, Ind.: University of Notre Dame Press, 1997.

Lamprecht, Barbara Mac. Richard Neutra: Complete Works. Cologne and New York: Taschen, 2000.

Lavanoux, Maurice. "Collegeville Revisited." Liturgical Arts 22, no. 2 (February 1954): 44–47, 53–55.

———. Editorial. Liturgical Arts 1, no. 1 (Fall 1931): 2.

———. "The Reality of a Dream: Saint John's Abbey Church, Collegeville, Minnesota. Saint Mary and Saint Louis Priory Chapel, Saint Louis, Missouri." Liturgical Arts 31, no. 1 (November 1962): 4–20.

———. "Recent Trends in Catholic Church Design in America." Architectural Record 85 (1939): 76–83.

———. "Saint Patrick's Church, Racine, Wisconsin." Liturgical Arts 4, no. 2 (Spring 1935): 91–100.

Lawrence, C. H. Medieval Monasticism: Forms of Religious Life in Western Europe in the Middle Ages. London: Longman, 1989.

Le Corbusier. The Chapel at Ronchamp. New York: Praeger, 1957.

Leake, Kenneth Martin, ed. Egyptian Architecture. New York: Grosset and Dunlap, 1964.

Lehrman, J. B. "Religious Expression in Contemporary Architecture." AA Files 69, no 775 (September–October 1953): 72–78.

Leonard, William J. "The Liturgical Movement in the United States." In The Liturgy of Vatican II: A Symposium in Two Volumes, edited by William Baraúna, 293–331. Chicago: Franciscan Herald Press, 1966.

Lercaro, James. "The Christian Church." In Documents for Sacred Architecture, 5–14.

Lindblad, Owen. "Full of Fair Hope: The Beginnings of a Benedictine Mission in Minnesota." American Benedictine Review 51, no. 2 (2000): 198–212.

Lockett, William, ed. The Modern Architectural Setting of the Liturgy. London: S.P.C.K., 1964.

Lord, Joseph. "Neu-Deutschland and German Catholic Youth." Orate Fratres 5, no. 7 (1930–31): 303–8.

Luxford, Julian M. The Art and Architecture of English Benedictine Monasteries, 1300–1540: A Patronage History. Woodbridge, UK: Boydell Press, 2005.

Lypgens, Walter. "Romano Guardini, a German Priest." Dublin Review 222 (Spring 1949): 80–92.

Mack, Linda. "From Russia, with Visions of Modernism." Minneapolis Star Tribune, October 22, 2000, F5.

Maeder, Fr. Tobias. "St. John's First Abbey Church (II)." Scriptorium 20, no. 1 (1961): 31–76.

Maguire, Robert, and Keith Murray. Modern Churches of the World. London: Studio Vista, 1965.

Mainberger, Gonsalve, trans. Kirchenbauten von Hermann Baur und Fritz Metzger. Würzburg: Echter-Verlag, 1956.

Major, Mate. "Marcel Breuer and Hungary." New Hungarian Quarterly 23, no. 85 (1982): 179–83.

"Marcel Breuer." Process: Architecture 32 (September 1982): 70–73.

"Marcel Breuer: The Buildings of St. John's Abbey, Collegeville, Minnesota." Walker Art Center Design Quarterly 53 (1961): 1–31.

"Marcel Breuer Designs a Monastery." Arts Digest 29, no. 2 (October 15, 1954): 12–13.

"Marcel Breuer Monastery in Minnesota." Art in America 45, no. 3 (Fall 1957): 26–28.

"Marcel Breuer, Teacher and Architect." House and Home 1, no. 5 (May 1952): 102–15.

Marx, Paul B. Virgil Michel and the Liturgical Movement. Collegeville, Minn.: Liturgical Press, 1957.

Masello, David. Architecture without Rules: The Houses of Marcel Breuer and Herbert Beckhard. New York: W. W. Norton, 1993.

Masiero, Roberto. "Rudolf Schwarz: L'altra modernità." Casabella 640–641, no. 12/1 (December 1996/January 1997): 28–33.

"Maurice Lavanoux, Tenacious Commentator." *Liturgy* 80 (1988): 5.

McCarthy, Timothy G. *The Catholic Tradition: Before and after Vatican II, 1878–1993.* Chicago: Loyola University Press, 1994.

McCoy, Esther. *Richard Neutra.* New York: George Braziller, 1960.

McDannell, Colleen. *Material Christianity: Religion and Popular Culture in America.* New Haven, Conn.: Yale University Press, 1998.

McGurn, William. "Holy Terror: From Bauhaus to God's House." *Wall Street Journal,* April 21, 2000, W15.

McNamara, Denis Robert. *Heavenly City: The Architectural Tradition of Chicago.* Chicago: Liturgy Training Publications, 2005.

———. "Modern and Medieval: Church Design in the United States, 1920–1945." PhD diss., University of Virginia, 2000.

Meier, Richard. *Recent American Synagogue Architecture.* New York: Jewish Museum, 1963.

Merrill, Peter C. *German Immigrant Artists in America.* Lanham, Md.: Scarecrow Press, 1997.

Metropolitan Museum of Art. *Marcel Breuer at the Metropolitan Museum of Art.* New York: Metropolitan Museum of Art, 1973.

Michael, Vincent. *The Architecture of Barry Byrne: Taking the Prairie School to Europe.* Champaign: University of Illinois Press, 2013.

———. "Express the Modern: Barry Byrne in 1920s Europe." *Journal of the Society of Architectural Historians* 69, no. 4 (December 2010): 534–555.

Michel, Virgil. "Architecture and the Liturgy." *Liturgical Arts* 5, no. 1 (1936): 13–18.

———. "The Liturgy in the Vernacular." *Orate Fratres* 12 (October 1938): 566–67.

Millete, Brian, O.S.B. "St. John's New Abbey Church: A Chronicle of Construction." *Scriptorium* 20, no. 1 (1961): 76–103.

Mills, Edward D. *The Modern Church.* New York: Praeger, 1956.

Milner, John D. "Church of the Assumption (Roman Catholic), Historic American Buildings Survey." Minnesota State Historic Preservation Office, June 1964.

Mitchell, William Bell. *History of Stearns County Minnesota.* Vol. 1. Chicago: H. C. Cooper, Jr., 1915.

Mock, Elizabeth, ed. *Built in the USA since 1932: A Survey of Contemporary American Architecture.* New York: Museum of Modern Art, 1944.

"Modern Fortress for an Ancient Faith: Abbey of St. John's at Collegeville." *Architectural Forum* 115, no. 5 (November 1961): 130–37.

"Monastery for Portsmouth Priory." *Architectural Record* 116, no. 6 (December 1954): 140–41.

"Monastery in Minnesota." *Art in America* 45, no. 3 (Fall 1957): 26–27.

"Monastery in Modern Mood." *Architectural Forum* 105, no. 6 (December 1956): 107–9.

"Monastic Wing for Saint John's Abbey, Collegeville: Views and Plan." *Liturgical Arts* 24 (May 1956): 60–61.

Morgan, David, and Sally Promey, eds. *The Visual Culture of American Religions.* Berkeley: University of California Press, 2001.

Morper, Johann Joseph. "Der Neubau von Münsterschwarzach." *Die Kunst* 77 (April 1938): 217–19.

Mumford, Lewis. "A Modern Catholic Architect." *Commonweal,* March 2, 1927, 458–59.

Murphy, Maureen T. *The Search for Right Reason in an Unreasonable World: A History of the Catholic Art Association, 1937–1970.* Notre Dame, Ind.: University of Notre Dame Press, 1975.

Nerdinger, Winfried. *Walter Gropius: The Architect Walter Gropius, Drawings, Prints, Photographs, Complete Project Catalogue. Catalogue of the exhibition at the Busch-Reisinger Museum, Harvard University, Cambridge, and at the Bauhaus Archiv, Berlin.* Berlin: Mann Verlag, 1985.

Nervi, Pier Luigi. *Aesthetics and Technology in Building.* Cambridge, Mass.: Harvard University Press, 1965.

———. "The Influence of Reinforced Concrete and

Technical and Scientific Progress on the Architecture of Today and Tomorrow." *Arts and Architecture* 78 (December 1961): 16–17, 28–30.

———. *Pier Luigi Nervi: Buildings, Projects, Structures, 1953–1963.* New York: Praeger, 1963.

Neutra, Richard Joseph. *Life and Shape.* New York: Appleton-Century-Crofts, 1962.

———. *Nature Near: The Late Essays of Richard Neutra.* Santa Barbara, Calif.: Capra Press, 1989.

———. *Richard Neutra, Promise and Fulfillment, 1919–1932: Selections from the Letters and Diaries of Richard and Dione Neutra.* Carbondale: Southern Illinois University Press, 1986.

"A New Abbey for St. John's." *Jubilee* 2 (July 1954): 36–39.

"New Architecture for the Changing Church?" *Architectural Record* 142, no. 5 (November 1967): 129–43.

"New Departure with an Anchor in Tradition: St. Ann's Church, St. Louis; Joseph Denis Murphy Architect." *Architectural Record*, September 1947, 102–3.

"New Look for St. John's." *Time*, April 26, 1954, 87.

"New Projects: Marcel Breuer." *Architectural Record* 131, no. 3 (March 1962): 121–36.

Niebling, Howard Vincent. "Modern Benedictine Churches: Monastic Churches Erected by American Benedictines since World War II." PhD diss., Columbia University, 1973.

———. "Monastic Churches Erected by American Benedictines since World War II." Pts. 1 and 2. *American Benedictine Review* 26, no. 2 (June 1975): 180–226; 26, no. 3 (September 1975): 298–340.

"The 1962 AIA Honor Awards." *AIA Journal* 37, no. 5 (May 1962): 49–55.

Norman, Edward. *The House of God: Church Architecture, Style, and History.* London: Thames and Hudson, 1990.

North American Academy of Liturgy. "Frank Kacmarcik—Berakah Award for 1981." *Worship* 55 (1981): 359–80.

"North Dakota Community for the Benedictine Sisters." *Architectural Record* 134, no. 6 (December 1963): 95–102.

"Obituary Albert Bosslet." *Baumeister* 55, no. 1 (January 1958): 52.

O'Connell, John B. *Church Building and Furnishing: The Church's Way.* London: Burns and Oates, 1955.

Oetgen, Jerome. *An American Abbot: Boniface Wimmer, O.S.B., 1809–1887.* Washington, D.C.: Catholic University of America Press, 1997.

———. *A History of Saint Vincent Archabbey, the First Benedictine Monastery in the United States.* Washington, D.C.: Catholic University of America Press, 2000.

"Of Materials That Age Gracefully: Priory of the Annunciation, Bismarck, North Dakota." *Architectural Record* 129, no. 1 (January 1961): 103–9.

Olivarez, Jennifer Komar. "Churches and Chapels." In *Eero Saarinen: Shaping the Future*, edited by Eeva-Liisa Pelkonen and Donald Albrecht, 266–75. New Haven, Conn.: Yale University Press, 2006.

Olszewski, Gabriel Gerardo. "Form Follows Liturgy: Marcel Breuer's Abbey Church of St. John the Baptist, Collegeville, Minnesota." Master's thesis, University of Texas, 1996.

O'Meara, Thomas F. "Modern Art and the Sacred: The Prophetic Ministry of Alain Couturier, O.P." *Spirituality Today* 38, no. 1 (Spring 1986): 31–40.

Onderdonk, Francis S. *The Ferro-Concrete Style.* New York: Architectural Book Publishing Company, 1928.

"One Great Architect's Legacy to Minnesota." *Architecture Minnesota* 7, no. 6 (December 1981–January 1982): 24–27.

The One-Hundredth Anniversary of the Building and Dedication of St. Francis Xavier Cathedral, Green Bay, Wisconsin, 1881–1891. Green Bay: The Cathedral, 1981.

O'Neill, Daniel P. "The Development of a German-American Priesthood: The Benedictines and the St. Paul Diocesan Clergy, 1851–1930." In *A Heritage Fulfilled: German Americans*, edited by Clarence

Glasrud, 145–55. Moorhead, Minn.: Concordia College, 1984.

Osman, Mary E. "The 1977 AIA Honor Awards." *AIA Journal* 66, no. 6 (May 1977): 28–49.

Panofsky, Erwin. *Abbot Suger on the Abbey Church of St.-Denis and Its Art Treasures.* 2nd ed. Princeton, N.J.: Princeton University Press, 1979.

Papachristou, Tician, ed. *Marcel Breuer: New Buildings and Projects 1960–1970.* New York: Praeger, 1970.

Parker, Timothy Kent. "The Modern Church in Rome: On the Interpretation of Architectural and Theological Identities, 1950–1980." PhD diss., University of Texas, Austin, 2010.

Parsch, Pius. *The Liturgy of the Mass.* 3rd ed. Trans. H. E. Winstone. With an introduction by Clifford Howell. London and St. Louis: B. Herder, 1957.

———, and Robert Kramreiter. *Neue Kirchenkunst im Geist der Liturgie.* Vienna-Klosterneuburg: Volksliturgisher Verlag, 1939

Pauly, Danièle. "The Chapel of Ronchamp as an Example of Le Corbusier's Creative Process." In *Le Corbusier*, edited by H. Allen Brooks, 127–42. Princeton, N.J.: Princeton University Press, 1987.

———. *Le Corbusier: La Chapelle de Ronchamp / The Chapel at Ronchamp.* Paris: Fondation Le Corbusier, and Boston: Birkhauser Verlag, 1997.

Pecklers, Keith F. *The Unread Vision: The Liturgical Movement of the United States, 1926–1955.* Collegeville, Minn.: Liturgical Press, 1998.

Pehnt, Wolfgang, and Hilde Strohl. *Rudolf Schwarz 1897–1961.* Milan: Electa, 1997, 2000.

Pendlebury, John. "The Urbanism of Thomas Sharp." *Planning Perspectives* 24, no. 1 (January 2009): 3–27.

"Pfarrkirche in Michigan." *Deutsche Bauzeitung* 102 (December 1968): 948–51.

Philibert, Paul, O.P., and Frank Kacmarcik. *Seeing and Believing: Images of Christian Faith.* Foreword by Gerard S. Sloyan. Collegeville, Minn.: Liturgical Press, 1995.

"A Philosophy for Building 'Correctly': Nervi." *Architectural Record* 119, no. 4 (April 1956): 257–63.

Pichard, Joseph. *L'art sacré moderne.* Paris: Arthaud, 1953.

———. *Modern Church Architecture.* Translated by Ellen Callman. New York: Orion Press, 1960.

"The Planning of St. John's Abbey." *Church Property Administration* 19 (January/February 1955): 44–47, 144–48.

Ponti, Gio. "Per una Abbazia Benedettina nel Minnesota." *Domus* 391 (June 1962): 1–6.

Price, Lorna. *The Plan of St. Gall in Brief.* Berkeley: University of California Press, 1982.

"Le prieuré de l'Annonciation, Bismarck, North Dakota." *Art d'Église* 29, no. 117 (October-December 1961): 108–11.

"Priory Chapel, St. Louis, Missouri, USA." *Architecture and Urbanism*, no. 12 (December 1990): 22–27, 227.

"Priory of the Annunciation, Bismarck, North Dakota." *Kenchiku Bunka* [Architectural culture] 19 (March 1964): 77–83.

"Priory of the Annunciation, Bismarck, North Dakota/ USA." *Deutsche Bauzeitung* 3 (March 1966): 188.

Proceedings: 1940 National Liturgical Week. Newark, N.J.: Benedictine Liturgical Conference, 1941.

Proctor, Robert. *Building the Modern Church: Roman Catholic Church Architecture in Britain, 1955 to 1975.* Surrey, England: Ashgate, 2014.

"Proposed Abbey Church, Monastery Wing and Chapter House: Saint John's Abbey, Collegeville, Minnesota; Views and Plans." *Liturgical Arts* 22 (February 1954): 53.

Quitslund, Sonya. *Beauduin: A Prophet Vindicated.* New York: Newman, 1973.

Rapp, Urban. "Modern Church Architecture." *Furrow* 13, no. 11 (November 1962): 653–65.

"Reality of a Dream: Saint John's Abbey Church, Collegeville, Minn.; Saint Mary and Saint Louis Priory Chapel, Saint Louis, Mo." *Liturgical Arts* 31 (November 1962): 12–25.

"Recent Work of Marcel Breuer." *Architectural Record*, January 1960, 125–38.

Regamey, Pie R. "Christianity or Paganism in Modern

Architecture?" *Journal of Arts and Letters*, Spring 1950. Typescript at SJA Archives.

Reid, Alcuin. *The Organic Development of the Liturgy: The Principles of Liturgical Reform and Their Relation to the Twentieth-Century Liturgical Movement prior to the Second Vatican Council.* 2nd ed. San Francisco: Ignatius Press, 2005.

"A Reinforced Concrete Church." *Builder* 133 (September 23, 1927): 460–61.

Reinhold, Hans Ansgar. *Speaking of Liturgical Architecture.* Notre Dame, Ind.: Liturgical Programs, University of Notre Dame, 1952.

"Religious Art." *Art in America* 45, no. 3 (Fall 1957): 12–13.

"Religious Arts in America Today." *Art in America* 45, 3 (Fall 1957): 14–17, 69.

Religious Buildings. Reprinted from *Architectural Record,* December 1955. New York: F. W. Dodge, 1955.

"Resurrection Church, St. Louis, Mo." *Architectural Record* 110 (August 1951): 132–35.

Richards, J. M. "Marcel Breuer 1902–1981," obituary. *Architectural Review* 170, 1014 (1981): 69–70.

Riley, Terence. *The International Style: Exhibition 15 and the Museum of Modern Art.* New York: Rizzoli, 1992.

Rippinger, Joel. *The Benedictine Order in the United States: An Interpretive History.* Collegeville, Minn.: Liturgical Press, 1990.

Roemer, Theodore. *The Ludwig-Missionsverein and the Church in the United States (1838–1918).* New York: Joseph F. Wagner, 1933.

Roloff, Ronald. *Abbey and University Church of Saint John the Baptist, Collegeville, Minnesota.* Collegeville, Minn.: St. John's Abbey, 1965.

Roman, Antonio. *Eero Saarinen.* New York: Princeton Architectural Press, 2002.

"Roman Catholic Church in Dornach, Switzerland." *Progressive Architecture* 26, no. 12 (December 1945): 60–63.

Ronchamp and Vence. Paris: Cerf, 1955.

Ross, Marion Dean. "The 'Attainment and Restraint' of Pietro Belluschi." *AIA Journal* 63, no. 1 (1972): 17–25.

Rothan, Emmet H. "The German Catholic Immigrant in the United States (1830–1860)." PhD diss., Catholic University of America, 1946.

Rouet, Albert. *Liturgy and the Arts.* Translated by Paul Philibert. Collegeville, Minn.: Liturgical Press, 1997.

Roulin, E. *Modern Church Architecture.* St. Louis: Herder, 1947.

Rubin, William S. *Modern Sacred Art and the Church of Assy.* New York: Columbia University Press, 1961.

Ruff, Anthony. *Sacred Music and Liturgical Reform: Treasures and Transformations.* Chicago: Liturgy Training Publications, 2007.

"Russian Architect Val Michelson's Life 'Was like a Novel.'" *Saint Paul Pioneer Press,* August 5, 2006.

Rykwert, Joseph. *Church Building.* New York: Hawthorn Books, 1966.

Rynne, Xavier. *Vatican Council II.* New York: Farrar, Straus and Giroux, 1968.

Saarinen, Eero. "The Changing Philosophy of an Architect." *Architectural Record* 116, no. 2 (August 1954): 182.

———. *Eero Saarinen.* With introduction and notes by Rupert Spade. New York: Simon and Schuster, 1971.

———. *Eero Saarinen on His Work: A Selection of Buildings dating from 1947 to 1964 with Statements by the Architect.* New Haven, Conn.: Yale University Press, 1962.

Saarinen, Eliel. *The Search for Form.* New York: Rheinhold, 1948.

Sack, Manfred. *Richard Neutra.* Zurich: Artemis, 1994.

Sacred Art at St. John's Abbey. Collegeville, Minn.: Order of Saint Benedict, 1980.

Saint, Andrew. "The Battle of the Bauhaus." In *The Image of the Architect,* 115–37. New Haven, Conn.: Yale University Press, 1983.

"Saint Francis de Sales Church, Muskegon, Michigan." *Liturgical Arts* 33 (February 1965): 52–57.

"Saint Francis de Sales Church, Muskegon, Michigan." *Liturgical Arts* 30 (May 1962): 110–11.

"Saint John's Abbey by Breuer." *Architectural Record* 130, no. 5 (November 1961): 131–42.

"Saint Joseph's Church, Le Havre, France: Auguste Perret." *Progressive Architecture* 44 (November 1963): 144–47.

Salvadori, Mario. "Contrasts in Concrete: UNESCO Headquarters, Paris." *Architectural Record* 123, no. 2 (February 1958): 165–69.

Sanderson, Warren. "The Plan of St. Gall Reconsidered." *Speculum* 60 (July 1985): 615–32.

Schabert, Joseph A. "The Ludwig Missionsverein." *Catholic Historical Review* 8, no. 1 (April 1922): 23–41.

Schloeder, Steven J. *Architecture in Communion: Implementing the Second Vatican Council through Liturgy and Architecture.* San Francisco: Ignatius Press, 1998.

Schmitt, Siegfried. *Die internationalen liturgischen Studientreffen 1951–1960.* Trier: Paulinus Verlag, 1992

Schnell, Hugo. *Twentieth Century Church Architecture in Germany.* Munich: Schnell und Steiner, 1974.

Schnitzler, T. "Parsch, Pius." *New Catholic Encyclopedia.* 2nd ed. Vol. 10. Detroit: Gale, 2003.

Schwarz, Rudolf. *The Church Incarnate: The Sacred Function of Christian Architecture.* Translated by Cynthia Harris. Chicago: Henry Regnery, 1958.

——. *Kirchenbau: Welt vor der Schwelle.* Heidelberg: F. H. Kerle, 1960.

Schweitz, Greg. "Saint John's Abbey Church: A Modern, Lasting Expression of Concrete Faith and Form." *L&M Concrete News* 3, no. 1 (Spring 2002): 8–9.

Seasoltz, R. Kevin. "Contemporary Monastic Architecture and Life in America." In *Monasticism and the Arts,* edited by Timothy G. Verdon and John Dally, 313–44. Syracuse, N.Y.: Syracuse University Press, 1984.

——. "From the Bauhaus to the House of God's People: Frank Kacmarcik's Contribution to Church Art and Architecture." *U.S. Catholic Historian* 15, no. 1 (Winter 1997): 105–22.

——. *The House of God: Sacred Art and Church Architecture.* New York: Herder and Herder, 1963.

——. "Living Stones Built on Christ." *Worship* 57 (1983): 115.

——, ed. *The New Liturgy: A Documentation, 1903–1965.* New York: Herder and Herder, 1966.

——. *Sense of the Sacred: Theological Foundations of Christian Architecture and Art.* New York: Continuum, 2005.

"The Seven Archetypes of Rudolf Schwarz." *Architectural Record,* June 1948, 116–19.

Sharp, Dennis. *Modern Architecture and Expressionism.* New York: George Braziller, 1966.

Sharp, Thomas. *The Anatomy of a Village.* Harmondsworth, UK: Penguin, 1946.

——. *English Panorama.* 1936. Reprint, London: Architectural Press, 1950.

——. *Exeter Phoenix: A Plan for Rebuilding.* London: Architectural Press, 1946.

——. *Town Planning.* 1940. Reprint, Harmondsworth, UK: Penguin Books, 1945.

Shear, John Knox, ed. *Religious Buildings for Today.* New York: F. W. Dodge, 1957.

Shepherd, Massey H. *The Liturgical Renewal of the Church.* New York: Oxford University Press, 1960.

Short, Ernest, ed. *Post War Church Building.* London: Hollis and Carter, 1947.

Shuster, George N. "Catholic Culture in America." *Today* 8 (March 1953): 12–13

Silliem, Dom Aelred. "The Monastic Ideal." *Life of the Spirit* 7 (1953): 298–99.

Siry, Joseph. *Beth Shalom Synagogue: Frank Lloyd Wright and Modern Religious Architecture.* Chicago: University of Chicago Press, 2011.

——. *Unity Temple: Frank Lloyd Wright and Architecture for Liberal Religion.* Cambridge: Cambridge University Press, 1996.

Sittard, Herm. "Church for the Twentieth Century." *Catholic Market* 1, no. 1 (October 1962): 20–25.

Smith, G. E. Kidder. *The New Churches of Europe.* New York: Holt, Rinehart and Winston, 1964.

Solomon, Susan. *Louis I. Kahn's Jewish Architecture.* Lebanon, N.H.: University Press of New England, 2009.

Sovik, E. A. *Architecture for Worship.* Minneapolis: Augsburg, 1973.

Spade, Rupert. *Oscar Niemeyer.* New York: Simon and Schuster, 1971.

Spaeth, Otto. "Worship and the Arts." *Architectural Record* 118, no. 6 (December 1955): 162–95.

Spence, Sir Basil. *Phoenix at Coventry: Building of a Cathedral.* New York: Harper and Row, 1962.

Springer, Annemarie. "Nineteenth Century German-American Church Artists." PhD diss., Indiana University, 2001.

"St. Francis de Sales Church, Muskegon, Michigan." *AIA Journal* 59, 5 (May 1973): 32–33.

"St. Francis de Sales Church, Muskegon, Michigan, 1967; Architects: Marcel Breuer and Associates." *Process: Architecture* 32 (September 1982): 94–99.

"St. Francis de Sales Church, Muskegon, Michigan, U.S.A." *A+U: Architecture and Urbanism* 6, no. 333 (June 1998): 34–43.

"St. John's Abbey—a Master Plan." *Arts and Architecture* 79, no. 2 (February 1962): 18–20, 28–29.

"St. John's Abbey, Collegeville: Hanson and Michelson, Associates, Architects." *Architectural Forum* 119 (December 1963): 108–13.

"St. Louis Priory and Chapel, Missouri, USA," *Architect and Building News* 222 (November 1962): 754.

"St. Luke's Episcopal Church, Rochester, N.Y., M. Breuer, Arch." *Architectural Record* 139 (April 1966): 178–79.

Stansfield, Kathryn. "The Poetry of Planning: A Study of the Life and Work of Dr. Thomas Sharp and His Contribution to the Planning Movement." Master's thesis, University of Manchester, 1974.

Steiner, Rudolf. *Architecture as a Synthesis of the Arts: Lectures by Rudolf Steiner.* Translated by Johanna Collis et al. London: Rudolf Steiner Press, 1999.

Stirling, James. "Ronchamp: Le Corbusier's Chapel and the Crisis of Rationalism." *Architectural Review* 119, no. 711 (December 1992): 62–68.

Stoddard, Whitney S. *Adventure in Architecture: Building the New St. John's.* New York: Longmans, Green, 1958.

Stoller, Ezra. *The Chapel at Ronchamp.* New York: Princeton Architectural Press, 1999.

"Strength or Banality? A New Reformation Challenges Church Design." *Architectural Forum* 119, no. 6 (December 1963): 69–83.

Stroik, Christopher V. *Path, Portal, Path: Architecture for the Rites.* Meeting House Essay no. 10. Chicago: Liturgy Training Publications, 2007.

Stubblebine, Jo, ed. *The Northwest Architecture of Pietro Belluschi.* New York: F. W. Dodge, 1953.

"Successful Beehive: Department Store in Rotterdam." *Time*, June 3, 1957, 74.

"Sun and Shadow: A Design Philosophy." *AIA Journal* 49 (April 1968): 65–71.

Sweeney, James Johnson. "Barry Byrne and New Forms in Church Construction." *Creative Art*, Summer 1932, 61–65.

Tegeder, Vincent. "The Benedictines in Frontier Minnesota." *Minnesota History* 32 (1951): 34–43.

———. "Collegeville, Minnesota." In *Encyclopedia of Monasticism: M–Z*, edited by William M. Johnston, 317–19. London: Taylor & Francis, 2000.

Tenoever, Donald A. "Edward J. Schulte and American Church Architecture of the Twentieth Century." Master's thesis, University of Cincinnati, 1974.

Thimmesh, Hilary. *Marcel Breuer and a Committee of Twelve Plan a Church: A Monastic Memoir.* Collegeville, Minn.: Saint John's University Press, 2011.

———, ed. *Saint John's at 150: A Portrait of This Place Called Collegeville, 1856–2006.* Collegeville, Minn.: Liturgical Press, 2006.

Thiry, Paul, Richard M. Bennett, and Henry L. Kamphoefner. *Churches and Temples.* New York: Reinhold, 1953.

"Thomas Sharp." *Architects' Journal* 97 (April 29, 1943): 278.

Thompson, E. K. "Pietro Belluschi, the 1972 Gold Medallist." *Architectural Record* 151 (April 1972): 119–26.

Tingerthal, Fr. Rhaban. "St. John's First Abbey Church." *Scriptorium* 19, no. 1 (1961): 1–40.

Torevell, David. *Losing the Sacred: Ritual, Modernity, and Liturgical Reform.* Edinburgh: T&T Clark, 2000.

"Trinity Church, Presbyterian, Natick, Mass." *Architectural Record* 114, no. 6 (December 1953): 130–32.

Turner, Harold W. *From Temple to Meeting House: The Phenomenology and Theology of Places of Worship.* The Hague: Mouton, 1979.

Tuzik, Robert L. *How Firm a Foundation.* Vol. 2, *Leaders of the Liturgical Movement.* Chicago: Liturgy Training Publications, 1990.

Two Hundred Years of American Synagogue Architecture. Waltham, Mass., Brandeis University: Rose Art Museum, 1976. Exhibition catalog.

Tyldesley, Michael. *No Heavenly Delusion? A Comparative Study of Three Communal Movements.* Liverpool: Liverpool University Press, 2003.

Uldrich, John. "Architect and Psychologist: Breuer Interviewed during Visit." *Record,* November 27, 1959, 2.

Upton, Julia A. *Worship in Spirit and Truth: The Life and Legacy of H.A. Reinhold.* Collegeville, Minn.: Liturgical Press, 2009.

Van Allen, Rodger. *The Commonweal and American Catholicism: The Magazine, the Movement, the Meaning.* Philadelphia: Fortress Press, 1974.

Van Zeller, Dom Hubert. *The Benedictine Idea.* London: Burns & Oates, 1959.

"The Various Interests Involved in Building a Church." In *Church Architecture: The Shape of Reform,* 69–85. Washington, D.C.: Liturgical Conference, 1965.

Vidler, Anthony. *Histories of the Immediate Present: Inventing Architectural Modernism.* Cambridge, Mass.: MIT Press, 2008.

Viollet-le-Duc, Eugène-Emmanuel. *Lectures on Architecture.* 2 vols. New York: Dover, 1987.

Voelker, Evelyn Carole. "Charles Borromeo's *Instructiones Fabricae et Supellectilis Ecclesiaticae,* 1577." PhD diss., Syracuse University, 1977.

Vogt, Von Ogden. *Art and Religion.* Boston: Beacon Press, 1960.

Ward, Fiona. "Merseyside Churches in a Modern Idiom: Francis Xavier Verlade and Bernard Miller." *Journal of the Twentieth Century Society,* no. 3 (1998): 95–102.

Watkin, David. "The Transformation of Munich into a Royal Capital by Maximilian I Joseph and Ludwig I." *Court Historian* 11, no. 1 (July 2006): 1–14.

Watkin, William Ward. *Planning and Building the Modern Church.* New York: F. W. Dodge, 1951.

Weber, Nicholas Fox, and Fiona Kearney, eds. *The Sacred Modernist: Josef Albers as a Catholic Artist.* Cork: Glucksman, 2012.

——, Fred Licht, and Brenda Danilowitz. *Josef Albers: Glass, Color, and Light.* New York: Guggenheim Museum, 1994. Exhibition catalog.

——, Fred Licht, et al. *Josef Albers: A Retrospective.* New York: Guggenheim Museum, 1988. Exhibition catalog.

Weis, Helene. Review of *Alfred Manessier: Retrospective of His Stained Glass Work, 1948 to 1993* (exhibition catalog). *Stained Glass* 88 (Spring 1993): 45–47.

White, James F. "Current Trends in American Church Building." *Studia Liturgica* 4, no. 2 (Summer 1965): 94–113.

White, Susan J. *Art, Architecture, and Liturgical Reform: The Liturgical Arts Society (1928–1972).* New York: Pueblo, 1990.

——. "The Legacy of Maurice Lavanoux." *Faith and Form* 20 (1987): 20–24.

——. "Maurice Lavanoux." In Tuzik, *How Firm a Foundation,* 207–12.

———. "Maurice Lavanoux, Tenacious Commentator." *Liturgy* 80 (1988): 5–7.

Whitney Museum of American Art. *Four American Expressionists: Doris Caesar, Chaim Gross, Karl Knaths, Abraham Rattner.* New York: Praeger, 1959. Exhibition catalog.

Wilk, Christopher. *Marcel Breuer: Furniture and Interiors.* New York: Museum of Modern Art, 1981. Exhibition catalog.

Williams, Peter. *Houses of God: Region, Religion, and Architecture in the United States.* Urbana: University of Illinois Press, 1997.

———. "Interpreting America's Religious Landscape and Architecture." *Chronicle of Higher Education* 43, no. 46 (July 25, 1997): B8–B9.

Wilson, Sarah. "Germaine Richier, Disquieting Matriarch." *Sculpture Journal*, December 2006, 51–70.

Young, Victoria. "The Design and Construction of Saint John's Abbey Church." In Thimmesh, *Saint John's at 150*, 117–28.

———. "Modernism and Monasticism: Marcel Breuer's Designs for St. John's Abbey in Collegeville, MN." *Casabella* 67 (October 2003): 28–39.

Yzermans, Vincent A., ed. *American Participation in the Second Vatican Council.* New York: Sheed and Ward, 1967.

Zalot, Charlotte Anne. "Revisioning Liturgical Space and Furnishings in American Roman Catholic Churches, 1947–2002: The Pioneering Role of Frank Kacmarcik, Artist–Designer and Consultant in the Sacred Arts." PhD diss., Drew University, 2004.

Zarnecki, George. *The Monastic Achievement.* New York: McGraw-Hill, 1972.

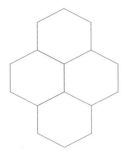

ILLUSTRATION CREDITS

Saint John's Abbey Archives: Figures I.1, I.2, I.3, I.4, I.5; 1.10, 1.12, 1.13, 1.15, 1.16; 2.1, 2.2, 2.3; 3.1, 3.2, 3.5, 3.6, 3.8, 3.10, 3.11, 3.13, 3.14, 3.15, 3.16, 3.17, 3.18, 3.19, 3.20; 4.1, 4.2, 4.3, 4.4, 4.5, 4.6, 4.7, 4.8, 4.9, 4.10, 4.11, 4.12, 4.13; C.2, C.3; Plates 1, 3, 8, 9, 10, 12, 13, 14, 15, and 17.

Andrea Jemolo / SCALA / Art Resource, New York: Figure 1.1.

Foto Marburg / Art Resource, New York: Figures 1.2, 1.7, 2.5, and 2.6.

Minnesota Historical Society: Figures 1.3, 1.4, 1.5, 1.9, and 1.11.

Diocese of Green Bay Archives: Figures 1.6 and 1.8.

Vanni / Art Resource, New York: Figure 1.14.

Manuel Cohen / The Art Archive at Art Resource, New York: Figure 2.4.

Felicity Rich: Figures 2.7 and 2.19.

Liturgical Arts Magazine: Figure 2.8.

University Archives Photograph Collection, Special Collections Research Center, North Carolina State University Libraries (item no. 0006517): Figure 2.9.

Library of Congress, Prints and Photographs Division,

Balthazar Korab Archive (LC-DIG-krb-00020): Figure 2.10.

Los Angeles Public Library Photo Collection: Figure 2.11.

Royal Institute of British Architects, RIBA Library Photographs Collection: Figure 2.12.

Mary Reid Brunstrom: Figure 2.13.

Marcel Breuer Papers, Special Collections Research Center, Syracuse University Libraries: Figures 2.14, 2.17, 3.3, 3.4, 3.7, 3.9, and 3.12.

The Museum of Modern Art / Licensed by SCALA / Art Resource, New York: Figure 2.15 (digital image copyright held by the Museum of Modern Art).

Olga Ivanova: Figure 2.16; Plates 2, 4, 5, 6, 7, 11, and 16.

Barry Byrne Family: Figure 2.18.

Chicago History Museum, photograph by William C. Hedrich for Hedrich–Blessing (HB-30953-V): Figure C.1.

Benedictine Sisters of Annunciation Monastery: Figures C.4 and C.5.

Steve Vorderman: Figure C.6.

Catherine R. Osborne: Figure C.7

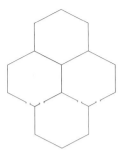

INDEX

Beaux-Arts methods, 52

Bec Abbey (1042–63, Normandy, France), 2

bell banner: Annunciation Monastery, 149–50; Saint Francis de Sales church, 150, 152

bell banner, St. John's Abbey Church of 1961, *xiv*, 117, 129, 130, 148, *Plate 13*, *Plate 16*; baptistery's relationship to, 81, 84; as beginning of spiritual axis, 78–83, 79, 109; Breuer's fascination with, xvi, 153, 172n51; construction of, 83; cross in, xvi, 80, 81, 82, 96; plans for, 82

Belli, Edo J. and Anthony J., 65; Marmion Abbey, 64

Belluschi, Pietro, 49; as candidate for St. John's Abbey Church of 1961 architect, xviii, 45, 48–49, 64; First Presbyterian Church in Oregon, 49; Portsmouth Abbey in Rhode Island, 49

Benedictines: architectural traditions of, xv, xx, 1–4, 20, 27, 54, 58, 133, 154; artistic traditions of, 20, 27, 109–10, 123, 133; establishment of St. John's Abbey and University, 4–17, 5, 6, 7; leadership of liturgical movement, xiv–xvi, xvii, 32, 33–34, 77, 141, 149; mission work of, 4–5, 7, 17, 159n18. *See also* collaboration: Benedictines–Breuer; monasticism, Benedictine; *and individual abbots and priests*

Benedict of Nursia, Saint, 1–2; painting of, 14; relics of, 175n115. *See also* Rule of Saint Benedict

Benet Hall, St. John's Abbey and University, 18

Bethune, Ade, 90, 173n78

Bible: increasing knowledge of, 22. *See also* Saint John's Bible

Blessed Sacrament Chapel, St. John's Abbey Church of 1961, 99, 104, 105

Böhm, Dominikus: architecture by, 40, 41, 130; Church of Saint Engelbert, 36–37, 37; Kramreiter as assistant to, 47, 166n67

Bonnard, Pierre, xx

Bonnette, Gerald, 116; apse screen mosaic design, 98, 136, 137, *Plate 12*; northern stained glass window design, 129, 129; Saint Francis Assisi Chapel art, 125

Bosslet, Albert: as candidate for St. John's Abbey Church of 1961 architect, xviii, 45, 46–47, 64

Boston Avenue Methodist Episcopal Church (1929, Tulsa, Oklahoma), 64–65

Braque, Georges, xx

Braunfels, Wolfgang: *Monasteries of Western Europe*, xv

Breuer, Marcel, *xviii*, *xix*, 53, 55, 78, 91; age of, 62–63; Annunciation Monastery, 148–50, 149 151, 153; on Bonnette's work, 125; concrete use in buildings by, xiii, xxi, 74–76, 145, 147, 155, 167n102; De Bijenkorf department store, 91, 129; domestic designs by, 84–85, 139, 147, 148, 167n101, 179n70; emigration to America, 163n8; exhibition house at MOMA, 55, 56; Franciscan convent, 153; Garden City of the Future, 73, 74; Gropius's work with, 53; innovation as hallmark of, xvii; interest in sculpture, 57, 81, 82, 86, 167n102; on Le Corbusier, 175n113; modernism in designs of, xvii, 58, 75–76, 77, 107, 182n16; religious affiliation of, 62, 168n120; sacred spaces designed by, xiii, 27, 72–76, 89–90, 116, 148–50, 153, 155; Saint Francis de Sales church, 150, 152, 153; Starkey House, 75; UNESCO complex, xiii, 58, 59, 73, 75, 80, 92, 129, 173n85; at University of Mary, 182n21; visit to Maria Laach Abbey, 71–72, 102, 104

Breuer, Marcel, and St. John's Abbey Church of 1961: altars designed by, 104, 117–19, 175n123; and apse screen mosaic, 136, 137; as candidate for project architect, xviii, 45, 48, 51, 55, 57–59, 60, 62–63, 65, 153; as career triumph, 148; at consecration ceremony, xi, 157n1; and decoration of, xxi, 98, 111, 116–17, 154–55; education in monasticism and church design, 70–72, 116, 171n23, 171n25; fees charged by, 169n2; hexagon design used by, 91, 91–92, 98, 127, 129; and northern stained glass window controversy, 91–92, 126–27, 129–31, 133–35, 180n109; repair of shear cracks, 95–96, 174n88, 174n95, 174n98, 174n100; on roof construction, 95; shadow-building technique, 169n1; skill level of, 62. *See also* collaboration: Benedictines–Breuer; concrete, in St. John's Abbey Church of 1961; one-hundred-year master plan, St. John's Abbey and University; trapezoid, St. John's Abbey Church of 1961 in shape of

brick: in Annunciation Monastery, 150; Murphy's work in, 54; Saarinen's use of, 50; St. John's Abbey

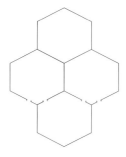

VICTORIA M. YOUNG is professor of modern
architectural history at the University of
St. Thomas in St. Paul, Minnesota, and chair
of the Department of Art History. Her work is
featured in *Nineteenth-Century Art Worldwide*,
Casabella, and *Saint John's at 150: A Portrait of
This Place Called Collegeville*. She is curator
of the permanent exhibition installed in Frank
Gehry's Winton Guest House, owned by the
University of St. Thomas.